"Inspiring, comprehensive and profoundly relevant, *Choosing Change* is an excellent and empowering read. With inspirational leadership stories, a simple yet comprehensive format and the congruent perspectives of Susan and Walter, this is recommended reading for all change-focused leaders, organizations and individuals alike."

—Danny McCarthy, General Manager Mining for Australian Mining, Thiess Pty Ltd.

"Each year, the field of change management is flooded with books. Many are worth the read and, if we are lucky, a few actually offer content worth serious consideration. I rarely see a manuscript that is pivotal in its nature, but *Choosing Change* is just such a seminal work. This is no rehash of familiar ground in an effort to mimic thought leadership—this is the real deal. It is a formative writing in two respects: it offers new information, fresh perspectives, and deft insights for both change practitioners and the leaders they serve, and it is a call to action for the whole of the change facilitation profession to practice our craft at a higher altitude. The depth of understanding this book offers and its easy-to-absorb writing style combine to make it an indispensable resource for anyone facing the realities of transformative change in organizational settings."

—Daryl Conner, Chairman Conner Partners, bestselling author and internationally-recognized leader of organizational change

"McFarland and Goldsworthy have written a classic! Combining wonderful stories from 60 successful global executives with cutting-edge neuroscience and leadership theories, the authors show the reader how to effectively change individuals, groups and organizations. *Choosing Change* is truly insightful, interesting and inspiring."

—Mike Marquardt, Professor, George Washington University and President of the World Institute for Action Learning

"Sometimes the most obvious is not only the most powerful and desperately needed—but also the most absent. This book is such an example. Joining up the individual and organizational aspects of change is a hugely significant contribution. No real world leader is able to separate the two and yet most literature does just that. This book closes that gap. Combined with leading edge organizational, psychological and neurobiological research it is a must-read for the executive who truly wants to be effective at leading change."

—Duncan Coombe, coauthor, award-winning *Care to Dare*, Associate Faculty, Ashridge Business School

"In a world where change is constant, transformational leadership all too rare and effective change leadership even more rare, what could be more important than a book that serves as a map for the VUCA world that lies ahead and, especially, for those who must navigate their companies safely through the rapids and rip tides of change? Susan Goldsworthy and Walter McFarland share just such a map in this book and just in time!"

—Rebecca Ray, PhD, Senior Vice President, Human Capital, The Conference Board

"In this book an experienced consultant and a coach engage in what the late Donald Schön called 'reflective practice': They critically assess what they have learned through experience, contrast it with established and emerging scholarship, and share the lessons learnt with others. One hopes that their courage will spur other experienced readers to engage in such critical thinking themselves."
—**Dr. Rafael Ramírez, fellow in Strategy and Director, Oxford Scenarios Programme, Saïd Business School, University of Oxford**

"Goldsworthy and McFarland introduce a compelling framework that will help you harness the true power of choice, make sense of the complexities of change, and build your capability and capacity for achieving better results. Their insights and stories are like having your own highly effective personal coach and consultant supporting you throughout your change journey. Readers will benefit greatly from their extensive experience and wisdom."
—**Tim Tobin, Vice President, Global Learning and Leadership Development, Marriott International, Inc.**

"Many change initiatives fail to realize their potential benefits. In addressing this, each of us has a choice to make—am I part of the problem or part of the solution? Choosing the latter path may seem disconcerting, but McFarland and Goldsworthy (and the many change leaders they've interviewed) are there to guide you every step of the way. Read and apply the lessons within."
—**Stephen Jenner, author of** *Managing Benefits*™ **and coauthor of** *Management of Portfolios*®

"*Choosing Change* reminds us that leaders seeking to change organizations must first change themselves. Challenging oneself to change behavior is possible only if we are brave enough to move out of our comfort zones into areas that may prove to be uncomfortable or even threatening. Helpfully, *Choosing Change* provides a clear roadmap for translating our intellectual understanding into action. It provides us with the confidence to move from intellectual insight to personal and organizational change."
—**Robert M. Tobias, Director, Key Executive Programs, American University**

"This book is an important read for senior executives, business owners, entrepreneurs and anyone desiring to be successful and competitive in today's rapidly changing world. For those individuals and organizations that struggle to stay relevant there is a need to understand that without a "change-focused" perspective there can be no long-term success.

When a culture of change is embraced both individuals and organizations can rise to their full potential. How do you motivate people who will be content to live with the status quo? How do you inspire individuals and organizations to move out of their comfort zones and actually take risks, and eventually grow? Read this book and roll up your sleeves—it's time to make some changes!"
—**Gary Anzalone, CEO, CEO Clubs NYC**

"Successful organizations depend on the ability of their people to deliver sustainable high performance. The latter can be negatively influenced by rapidly changing environments and business requirements, which can create a lot of anxiety and concern. Susan Goldsworthy and Walter McFarland deliver important insights into what change is, how it should be viewed and how it can be managed. Their approach will help you and your people to successfully adapt to new requirements, while staying positive and continuing to trust that everyone can achieve great things in your organization."
—Klemen Cas, Joint CEO, cofounder, ecenta AG

"*Choosing Change* should be required reading for every leader and change practitioner. This is an integrative guide to leading through revolutionary, difference-making change. It is filled with rich experience, relevant research and applicable insights. The ideas are impactful and the stories are striking. Read and apply what you learn in order to unleash profound optimism, productive energy and new levels of performance as you improve your change effectiveness."
—Donna Brighton, CEO, Brighton Leadership Group, President and board member ACMP

"As one major raison d'être of a Corporate University is to support change and to aid transformations. *Choosing Change* is a book that all executives should read urgently! They will find a framework for the importance of a new mindset as the only approach to lifelong learning, growth, and improvement. Congratulations to Walt and Susan for this very useful book that combines theory and practice, testimonials and tools. I appreciate the strength of their vision and their smart guidance."
—Annick Renaud-Coulon, founder and chair, The Global Council of Corporate Universities (GCCU)

"This book takes us on a journey to create awareness of the holistic concept of the Five Ds so that leaders of organizations can better manage and leverage disruptive change in the workplace. What I like most is the sharing of personal insights by chief executive officers who had been there, seen it and done it. As change is a constant in our daily lives and disruptive change a norm in today's workplace, this book is a must-read for leaders who believe in riding the wind of change."
—Robert Yeo, Executive Director and CEO, Singapore Training and Development Association (STADA)

"The insightful testimonies and analysis exposed by Susan and Walt made me think: I want to be part of it; part of those leaders who succeed in changing their organization because they look beyond the technical or academic sides of change. These leaders' change journeys are to be read as a soul-searching experience, which the authors decoded and presented in an accessible model. This book is a must-read for change practitioners who seek to impact the future of their organization."
—Cécile Demailly, cochair, the Change Leaders (global alumni of HEC/Oxford University MSc, Coaching and Consulting Change)

"Susan and Walter have put together a valuable book focused on two important areas for business success: leadership and organizational change. Making sure leaders take on exploring and improving their own change capabilities before expecting that they'll be able to adroitly lead broader organizational change is logical but the two are rarely if ever addressed together and in the right order. Take the opportunity to expand and change your own thinking; read this book, it is well done!"
—Karen Kochner, Chief Learning Officer, Cigna Corp.

"If you think everything has already been written about embracing change, think again. These authors deliver a practical guide full of real world examples for employing today's change bombardment as a catalyst for sustainable growth, both personal and corporate. Never before has the ability to choose change, and use it for our benefit, been more significant. I took the journey with Walt and Susan to sharpen my ability, and I came away with change as a new ally."
—Beth Jackson, President, Fluor University

"In a faster developing economy such as China, business leaders are encountering challenges on many fronts every day, and changes are 'inevitable.' We've seen many management theories and many books are flowing around, but rarely is there one that approaches the subject of change management in such granularity, addressing it from the layers of the individual and the organization, and pointing in the direction of establishing 'Change Leadership.' Walter's and Susan's rich experience and in-depth research as practitioners greatly contributes to why I give *Choosing Change* my thumbs-up. I strongly recommend it to my fellow Chinese business executives and entrepreneurs as a 'must–have' playbook."
—Wayne Wang, Chairman and CEO, CDP Group, Ltd.

"Change management is the Achilles' heel of management practice—despite great ideas and concepts most change projects fail. It is therefore essential to keep asking ourselves how we can reverse this situation and increase the odds of success in particular with regard to an increasingly complex and unpredictable environment. We have no choice but to build change capabilities into the organizational DNA and to help individuals to understand their own barriers to change. *Choosing Change* provides valuable insights and practical clues on how to move towards a new understanding of building change and learning as fundamental individual and organizational capabilities into organizations where change is not just something that they do but something that they are."
—Richard Straub, President, Peter Drucker Society Europe

CHOOSING CHANGE

How Leaders and Organizations Drive Results One Person at a Time

Walter McFarland, Susan Goldsworthy

New York   Chicago   San Francisco   Athens   London
Madrid   Mexico City   Milan   New Delhi
Singapore   Sydney   Toronto

1 2 3 4 5 6 7 8 9 0   DOC/DOC   1 0 9 8 7 6 5 4 3

ISBN   978-0-07-181624-3
MHID   0-07-181624-0

e-ISBN 978-0-07-181625-0
e-MHID   0-07-181625-9

From Susan: *For my children, Jack and Sydney, and their cousins, Carly, Kareena, and Max—carpe diem.*

From Walter: *For my children, Tobi and Burton. You inspire me.*

Contents

Foreword   vii

Acknowledgments   ix

Introduction   The Choice of Choosing Change   1

PART I   THE CHANGE-FOCUSED LEADER   17

Chapter 1   **Disruption:** What Conscious Choice
                    Will You Make?   19

Chapter 2   **Desire:** What Do You Really Want to Change?   37

Chapter 3   **Discipline:** What Are Your Small Steps
                    to Big Success?   57

Chapter 4   **Determination:** How Can You Embrace
                    the Setbacks?   75

Chapter 5   **Development:** How Will You Keep Growing
                    and Who Will Help You?   95

Bridge   **Moving from a Change-Focused Leader
                    to a Change-Focused Organization**   117

PART II   THE CHANGE-FOCUSED ORGANIZATION   119

Chapter 6   **Disruption:** Balancing Challenge and
                    Opportunity   121

Chapter 7   **Desire:** Building Motivation to Change   141

Chapter 8   **Discipline:** Coordinating Energy, Focus,
                    and Effort   159

Chapter 9   **Determination:** Coping with Setbacks   177

Chapter 10   **Development:** Learning Continuously
                    About Change   195

Final Thoughts   **Focusing on the Future of Change**   209

Notes   211

Index   229

Foreword

At ASTD (American Society for Training and Development), we think about learning in the workplace in all of its forms and at every level—that is, the individual, the team, and the organization. And learning is the key driver for change. Think about any change you've made—in your life or in your work—and you'll realize that to make the change effectively, you probably had to learn something.

In today's global business environment, influenced by ever-advancing technology, the constant for every leader and every organization is change. Change is opportunity, which means that managing change well is an imperative for success.

I believe that learning is at the heart of any successful change initiative. No other functional area affects engagement and performance, elevates a brand, or creates a sustainable competitive advantage more. Learning is essential to human and organizational performance. Learning transforms.

Transformative learning in organizations has the ability to produce better leaders at every level. This idea of leaders who learn is vital in a business environment that demands change faster than ever before.

In *Choosing Change*, Susan and Walt focus on an important type of leader: one who is focused on leading real change within him- or herself and within organizations. By embracing change as an opportunity to grow personally, to collaborate better, and to find new and creative ways to improve performance, these learning and change-focused leaders affect others through their personal example.

In this book, Susan and Walt share their Five Ds framework—a powerful tool to walk the individual and the organization through change. They provide practical techniques that every leader can use. When you finish reading *Choosing Change*, you will see change in a new light: as a rare opportunity that combines pressure and uncertainty and creates a vehicle for accelerated personal development.

Embracing the opportunity that change provides means having an infrastructure in place that supports what is at the heart of well-managed change: learning. A culture of learning is a key driver for delivering meaningful results. Organizations and leaders that embrace the development of their people know this.

Choosing change will not be an option for the new generation of emerging leaders; change will be their reality. But choosing to manage change well *will* be an option. Ensuring that every organization and every person is equipped to adapt continuously means providing an environment of continuous learning.

In *Choosing Change*, Susan and Walt provide the framework to make certain that we are more than prepared to manage change effectively. And, learning this will be of benefit to us individually, to our teams, and to our organizations.

Tony Bingham
President and CEO, ASTD

Acknowledgments

This book was made possible through the time, creativity, and insight of wonderful friends. We received help and encouragement at every step of the process, and we are profoundly grateful for all of it. One of our first advisors was Elaine Biech, whose vast experience in publishing helped us refine our thinking. The insight and advice of two accomplished authors, Ron Kaufman and David Rock, were also invaluable. We will mention them again in a moment. We would like to thank Knox Huston at McGraw-Hill, who believed in this book from the very start. Also, we thank Daina Penikas, editing supervisor at McGraw-Hill, and Alice Manning, copyeditor, for their excellent work. Our patient editor, Herb Schaffner, applied his experience and insight to help us refine and shape the final product, while Marianne Wallace contributed much appreciated talent, support, and attention to detail in the copyediting and proofing phase.

We also received the active support of several organizations. First among them is the American Society for Training and Development (ASTD). The president and CEO, Tony Bingham (an accomplished author himself), was a supporter and friend whose insight was invaluable. We promised Tony that we would say these words whenever possible: *learning makes everything better*. It truly does. Thank you, Tony.

We are also grateful to Ron Kaufman, CEO of UP! Your Service, for his contributions in Chapter 5 and Chapter 7 and his great insight into both personal- and national-level change.

David Rock and the NeuroLeadership Institute he founded have both been central to our learning and our insights on neuroscience in both parts of this book. David, you're making a difference—thank you.

We are both members of the Change Leaders, a group for graduates of the HEC/Oxford University MSc in Coaching and Consulting for Change. We are grateful to our colleagues in this group, with special mention to Cecile Demailly (TCL board cochair), Joanne Flinn, Rick Torseth, Dan Ballbach, Charles Bark, and Mike Staresinic.

We are both grateful to thought leaders Marshall Goldsmith, Michael Watkins, Patrick Sweeney, Daryl Conner, Jean-François Manzoni, Dan Denison, and Richard Olivier for their support.

We also want to extend a special thanks to our interviewees—the 60 executives who contributed their time and insight to this book. These impressive men and women come from four continents, more than a dozen global Fortune 500 organizations, and other great companies in every industry. Their insight is what this book is about. Thanks, everyone; you taught us a lot.

Special Acknowledgments from Susan

Thank you, Walt. It has been such a pleasure, learning process, and joy to coauthor this book with you, and I have grown as part of this journey. You are a star, partner.

Special mention must go to Dr. Jean-François Manzoni, Shell Chaired Professor of Human Resources and Organisational Development and Professor of Management Practice, INSEAD. Your passion for change is positively infectious, and it is a privilege and a pleasure to work with you. Your sheer brilliance and influence are deeply embedded throughout Part I.

Deep gratitude goes to Nick Shreiber, a secure base, for his support, guidance, and significant contributions, as well as for sharing his insights for the Introduction. I am also grateful to everyone interviewed for the book, with special mentions to those people who feature in the lead stories of Part I: Sara Mathew, chairman and CEO of Dun & Bradstreet; Marc Herremans, wheelchair triathlete, author, and motivational speaker; Pierre Deplanck, COO of Rustan's Supercenters Inc., Philippines; Alan Murray, CEO of NextFoods; and Tom Miller, CEO of Symbolist—thank you for your generosity and inspiration.

Thanks, also, to Professors George Kohlrieser, Duncan Coombe, Michael Watkins, Ginka Toegel, Jack Wood, Ben Bryant, Winter Nie, Anand Narasimhan, Dan Denison, Martha Maznevski, Francisco Szekely, and Roy Gillett, as well as Josh Davis, Dr. Sven Hansen, and violinist Miha Pogacnik, all of whom I have the pleasure of knowing and who have inspired me in writing this book with their thinking, insight, and approach.

Words cannot properly express my gratitude to Annie Tobias, Robyn Renaud, Pamela Slater, Nigel Goldsworthy, Stephen Jenner, Ethel Chalopin, and Katherine Armstrong, all of whom read the whole or sections of Part I and whose belief, comments, and suggestions for improvement were enormously helpful.

Thanks, also, to Terry Small, Peter Meyers, Henry Nwume, Michael Kenyon, Pepe Gonzaléz, Alastair Robertson, Robin Elfving, Jorgen Haglind, Jonathan Lachowitz, Klemen Cas, Andreas Wortmann, Danny McCarthy, Hossam Fares, Jim Pulcrano, Allan Lam, Aidan Lynam, Glen Pearce, Henrik Schurmann, Rachel Bamber, Nina Schwalbe, Gail Small, Jack Seymour, and Kristy Fraijo for your contributions and support. And to fellow coaches Jean-Pierre Heiniger, Kai Foong Tan, Ayin Jambulingam, Suzanne Weeks, Joyce Crouch, Sharon Busse, Andreas Neumann, Alejandro Altieri, and, of course, Robyn Renaud for your energy, wisdom, and friendship.

Eternal gratitude, as always, to my family, who encouraged me throughout this process. I am truly blessed to have you in my life. Also, thank you to Jack Queen, former Olympic coach, for your influence and inspiration throughout the years and to Al Richards for "caring and daring" me to sporting success.

Finally, I am grateful to all the people who shared their stories with me for this book and all the executives I have the privilege of coaching—I learn from and am inspired by you all.

Special Acknowledgments from Walter

First, I want to thank Susan for having the original idea for this book and for sharing her experience and generosity in helping me at every step. Susan, you are a wonderful partner.

Kimo Kippen, a former ASTD board chair and chief learning officer for Hilton Worldwide, contributed his great insight to Chapter 6. Martha Soehren, ASTD's 2013 chair-elect and chief learning officer of Comcast, contributed her great insight to Chapter 8, while Mary Slaughter, chief learning officer of SunTrust Banks, provided her great insight in Chapter 9. Thanks also to Professor Victoria Marsick of Teachers College, Columbia University, for her contribution to Chapter 10 and her ongoing support.

I have also been influenced by the work of Michael Tushman at Harvard University; by the insight of Michael Marquardt of George Washington University and founder of the World Institute for Action Learning; and by research from the Center for Creative Leadership, particularly that of Jeffery Yip, Chris Ernest, and Michael Campbell on the topic of boundary-spanning leadership. Thanks everyone—your thinking is making a difference.

I drew heavily on our friends in what I will call "the global community of practice for organizational change"—specifically: Maria Darby and Donna Brighton from the board of directors of the Association for Change Management Professionals; Cecile Demailly, board cochair of the Change

Leaders group affiliated with HEC Management School in Paris and Oxford University, England; Rebecca Ray and Amy Abel of the Conference Board; and Josh Davis from the NeuroLeadership Institute. Grateful thanks.

Next, I want to thank Richard Olivier, poet William Ayot, Yvette Forbes, and other friends associated with Olivier Mythodrama in London for their unique insight into individual and organizational change. Richard's training program for change leaders based on Shakespeare's play *The Tempest* is a must-see for aspiring change leaders, and William Ayot's poem "The Mystery of Kindness" is a must-read. Thank you all.

Finally, I want to thank several colleagues for special contributions: Tim Tobin, Beth Jackson, Steven Pal, Saira Stahl, Karen Kocher, Jose Fay, Jennifer Pope Moore, Libia Vania, Dan Radecki, and Joao Steinle. Thanks, friends.

Introduction

The Choice of Choosing Change

The world as we have created it is a process of our thinking. It cannot be changed without changing our thinking.

—Albert Einstein

As the title says, this book is all about choosing change. We believe that a key factor in carrying out change better is leading it better. Furthermore, we think that leading change better, both in yourself and in your organization, begins with a conscious choice. We are passionate about helping others improve their ability to change. This book is about equipping you to be more successful in leading change, both in yourself and in your organization.

You have probably noticed that the topics of leading change in yourself and leading it in organizations are usually discussed separately—as if people and organizations are not connected. People and organizations are deeply connected—and are becoming more so. Organizations consist of people and depend upon the excellence of those people for competitive advantage. Likewise, people often need organizations to achieve their personal potential. We are social beings, and we are at our best when we are focused on achieving an important common goal.

So why is change so hard for people and organizations? We have a world of knowledge about what works and what doesn't work. Yet, when we try to apply a change process to ourselves or our organizations, we often have difficulty turning that knowledge into behavior.

Imagine going to your bank manager or a venture capitalist and asking to borrow a substantial amount of money to start a business that involves telling people how to accomplish something when everyone already knows exactly what to do. Well, that's exactly what the diet industry does. Estimated to be worth more than $60 billion globally[1] today and predicted to be worth more than $200 billion by 2015,[2] the diet industry succeeds even though practically everyone on the planet knows exactly which two things he or she has to do to lose weight: (1) exercise more and (2) eat better. And yet people spend a substantial amount of money to purchase items that promise them a quick fix or miracle result. Individual change is difficult—look at all those failed New Year's resolutions and unused gym memberships.

Organizations also struggle. Organizational change efforts "often underperform, fail, or make things worse."[3] As with people, this occurs even when the organization's "life" is at stake. Once-mighty companies like Kodak, Digital Equipment, Compaq, and Woolworths, to name but a few, are either shadows of their former selves or no longer exist because of their inability to adapt and embrace a changing world. Despite all the knowledge and research, it is estimated that up to 75 percent of organizational change initiatives either fail entirely or do not achieve the promised results.[4]

So what's happening here? Why does change cause so much anxiety, stress, and negative emotion? As real-life practitioners, we believe the reason for these damning statistics lies in the fundamental approach to change taken by both individuals and organizations.

The change we're discussing in this book is triggered by the leadership of oneself *and* an organization; it leads to putting new approaches and processes in place to achieve a goal, or growth of some sort, that has consequences and implications for everyone involved.

Change is a natural part of life. Evolutionary change is happening every second, every minute, and every hour of every day. Revolutionary change happens on occasion, often brought about by some external event. One problem we see in today's business world is that change readiness occurs only at the moment of revolutionary change, when the threat is great and the fear is building. We propose a different model—one that sees change as part of daily practice. And it starts with you. Why? If you want to lead others to change, you need to first be open to change yourself. And while that process can be painful, the growth achieved makes it all worthwhile. Think about Olympic athletes who train for four years or more for one event. When they enter the stadium at the opening ceremony, wearing their national uniforms and greeted by the cheers of hundreds of thousands of spectators, all of their sacrifices fade into insignificance.

Just as we know that change starts within oneself, organizational change must also start from within. It appears that most organizations operate under the "change when you have to" model, waiting for a crisis or urgency to unfold. Blaming external events or circumstances for one's situation is the perfect way of remaining in a victim state and staying in the comfort of the discomfort. We believe that it is time for organizations to make peace with change and embrace it as the natural order of the universe, rather than considering it an isolated activity to be managed when needs must. Indeed, we suggest that companies embrace change proactively as an opportunity to gain a competitive advantage.

For this book, we interviewed or had dialogues with more than 60 executives in numerous organizations, including a dozen Fortune Global 500 firms, on the subject of individual and organizational change. As demonstrated by the examples used throughout the chapters, effective change leaders start with themselves. Once they have worked through their own issues, they are far better equipped to empower everyone in the organization to take a healthier approach to managing change in their daily working lives. As the book's subtitle suggests, change leaders and organizations drive results by managing change one individual at a time. This means that every individual in the company has an important role and responsibility in managing change—choosing to be active rather than passive. Organizations that employ a change-focused workforce will generate the best results and establish clear competitive advantage.

Aligning Individual and Organizational Change

This book is divided into two parts relating to individual and organizational change. You will hear two very different voices used because the parts were written separately by Susan and Walter, two authors who have different experiences and who bring different perspectives. Part I was written in a "coaching" voice while Part II was written in a "consulting" voice. This explains why the Part I chapter titles were written as coaching questions and the Part II chapter titles were written as recommendations. This unique combination gives you the benefits of both approaches to learning how to choose change.

Part I, The Change-Focused Leader, builds upon Susan's experiences as an Olympic athlete, a business executive, and an executive coach. By exploring ways to make the personal changes needed in order to perform better, it will help you become what we call a "change-focused leader" who is equipped to continuously change, adapt, and grow. In our view, leadership is, after all, a lifelong journey of discovery. This part combines proven techniques from the coaching profession with new thinking from neuroscience to help you become more effective at leading change in yourself. We suggest that this is a worthy goal for any person.

Part II, The Change-Focused Organization, builds upon Walter's extensive experience and success in leading large-scale organizational change and addresses how you lead change in your organization by building the ability to change continuously into the organization's DNA. It does this by guiding you through a complex, large-scale organizational change effort that we refer to as *revolutionary change*. Like Part I, it introduces new thinking from several fields, including neuroscience, adult learning theory, and management, and applies them to organizational change. This part also advises you on how to lead a successful organizational change effort today while simultaneously building enhanced change capability for tomorrow. To put it another way, it is written to help you transform your organization into a "change-focused" one.

If you are seeking to become more effective in leading change in your organization, we believe that it is essential for you to read Part I because the first step in leading change better within your organization is learning to lead change in yourself. The concept of "being the change," as recommended by Gandhi, Mandela, Obama, and others, is a foundational competency for every organizational change leader.

The Five Ds: A Framework for Individual and Organizational Change

Examining individual and organizational change together is a complex undertaking but it can enhance our understanding of each area. To examine both areas, we've found it useful to have a structure to guide us through what is needed to effect change. Therefore, throughout the book we use a framework called the Five Ds—disruption, desire, discipline, determination, and development—to compare the key elements to be aware of during both individual and organizational change. Following her successful international swimming career, Susan first used a version of the Five Ds when she gave motivational talks to young swimmers. With the five Olympic rings in mind, each D represented one of the things required to achieve success in any aspect of life. Working together with Walter, she has since expanded the Five Ds to provide a way of thinking about important elements in both individual and organizational change.

The Five Ds are a way for us to share with you a framework for the importance of a new mindset as the approach to lifelong learning, growth, and improvement.

The Five Ds

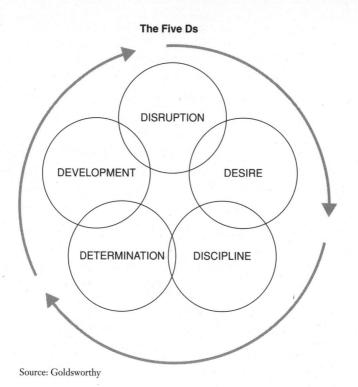

Source: Goldsworthy

We are confident that when you reflect upon any successful change you have made, at either an individual or an organizational level, you will find the elements of the Five Ds.

To introduce you to the Five Ds, we share insights from Nick Shreiber, a former CEO with more than 30 years of senior leadership experience. Nick was a partner at McKinsey & Company and later group president and CEO of the Tetra Pak Group, a $13 billion world-leading global food processing and packaging solutions company. Currently, he serves on the boards of the Campbell Soup Company, a $9 billion international food corporation, and North Highland, a privately held, midsize management consulting firm. He also mentors senior executives in association with Merryck & Company. Throughout his career, Nick has dealt extensively with the challenges of leading change, both within himself and within organizations. During his interview, Nick was clear that he views the role of a CEO as somewhat transitory, similar to that of a runner in a relay race; he took over programs initiated by previous CEOs and initiated programs that were continued by his successor. His comments are made in this spirit of continuity.

Disruption

The first D is for Disruption. This relates to an event or experience that triggers a conscious choice to change. The disruption creates an awareness of something that might require attention and creates a case for change.

When asked about disruption, Nick shared his experience of championing changes at Tetra Pak, a company that he led between 2001 and 2005. Like many successful companies, Tetra Pak ran the risk of becoming complacent, making it difficult to achieve lasting change. The business landscape was changing in ways that would affect the company down the road. For example, most other players in the value chain—from suppliers to customers and retailers—were consolidating rapidly, thus shifting the "balance of influence" away from Tetra Pak. Competition was becoming increasingly intense as a result of new packaging formats such as plastics and innovation from other competitors in carton packaging. As Nick put it,

> These trends were not reflected immediately in the company's strong business results, so the trick was to find a real platform that would convince the organization of the need for dramatic change in order to remain competitive in the years ahead. The main lever came from an unexpected angle: We prided ourselves on being a customer-centric company, but initial results from customer satisfaction surveys revealed that our customers did not always share that same positive view of the relationship. The results of the first three trials undertaken in the Americas were weak enough to raise alarm.

For Nick and Tetra Pak, this high level of customer dissatisfaction was the disruptive event. "At the beginning, other parts of the world claimed that their customers' situations were different. However, following a further half-dozen pilot programs in Asia and Europe, we became convinced that we had serious customer concerns worldwide. What's more, we discovered that the same three or four business issues were the source of most complaints, regardless of geographic area or customer size." Under the banner of "Know Me, Hear Me, Grow Me," the company launched a global customer satisfaction initiative (CSI), placing it firmly on the group's balanced scorecard. CSI became the disruptive event that Tetra Pak needed; it drove the company to make significant improvements in the way it operated, especially in the way it related to its customers around the world.

In the lead story of Chapter 1, we share a powerful example of individual disruption from Sara Mathew, chairman and CEO of Dun & Bradstreet while in Chapter 6, you will hear about significant organizational disruption from Kimo Kippen, the chief learning officer of Hilton Worldwide.

Once a disruption has occurred and been registered, the individual or organization then has to have the desire to make change happen—to choose to change.

Desire

The second D is for Desire. What exactly does the person or organization want to achieve, does it believe in the possibility, and how serious is it about making the change happen?

Referring to a collective desire, Nick shared how Tetra Pak decided to work on a new vision statement for the company. "What was impressive about the vision process was that it came from a desire within the company," said Nick. As CEO, he attempted to create an environment in which everyone throughout the organization felt that he or she could ask questions and raise ideas. By choosing to invest the time to run Q&A sessions with groups from around the company, he was able to notice patterns or trends in the questions employees asked.

> One such trend, repeated at several of these sessions, was the questioning of Tetra Pak's existing vision statement. It was seen as a comment on the business we were in, not an inspirational statement; moreover, because of innovation, the previous statement no longer represented the company's entire range of product offerings. Based on this expressed desire of the organization, we decided to work on a new vision statement.

A small internal project team undertook external benchmarking and carried out extensive internal interviews. A commitment was made that Tetra Pak's vision statement would be short, memorable, and inspiring, and that, along with the company's core values, it would be the corporate "glue" that united the company. Within six months of its launch in 2002, an employee survey showed that unaided 98 percent of the company could remember and repeat the company's new vision statement. The new vision appealed as much to the younger generation as to the more tenured employees. It has stood the test of time and is still in place more than a decade later.

In the lead story of Chapter 2, we share an inspiring example of individual desire from wheelchair triathlete and author Marc Herremans, while in Chapter 7, you can read an impressive story of organizational desire to improve service at the national level in Singapore from bestselling author and expert on service Ron Kaufman.

With the disruption and the desire firmly in place, it then takes discipline to see it through.

Discipline

The third D is for Discipline: applying those small, consistent, and frequent steps required to build the momentum that delivers sustainable change. Discipline is essential in order to manage the many demands of life and to keep pressure on the processes of change.

Nick brought an added dimension to discipline through his quest to achieve an acceptable work-life balance for himself and for the members of his management team. As CEO of Tetra Pak, he stressed the importance of executives having a hobby or some meaningful form of leisure activity. "Striving for work-life balance has helped me throughout my career. Recent neuroscience research underscores the importance of giving your brain some calm time away from work routines, allowing the 'noise' to subside and parallel neural connections to take place." Nick had played the piano for most of his life.

> After six months in the top spot, I realized with some shock that I had virtually stopped playing the piano—and had stopped pretty much every other activity outside of work. After a moment of panic, the obvious answer to how to restore balance was to set myself specific goals. For the piano, I set myself the ambitious target of recording a CD! An amateur one, of course, but one that would require the discipline of practice and dedication for months.

Less than a year later Nick produced his first CD.

> Apart from the joy of leaving something to my grandchildren, it was symbolic in that it proved to me what I could achieve when I focused and applied the necessary discipline toward a goal, alongside my "normal" business challenges. When I am immersed in playing the piano, I often feel a sense of "flow" and my unconscious churns away. Not only do I find that I am refreshed and reenergized after practicing, but equally important, new ideas often pop into my conscious mind as I play. I strongly believe that developing a leisure activity really does improve the quality, effectiveness, and efficiency of our work lives.

In the lead story of Chapter 3, French executive Pierre Deplanck shares how discipline is helping him with his leadership and his life. He is now chief operating officer of a joint venture between Dairy Farm and Rustan's Supercenters Inc. (RSCI) in the Philippines. In Chapter 8, Martha Soehren, senior vice president and chief learning officer (CLO) of Comcast, shares the discipline needed to lead a major enterprisewide transformation of the learning and development function.

While discipline, in the form of practice or processes, is an essential part of achieving any goal, there will inevitably be times when setbacks occur. At those times, determination is vital.

Determination

The fourth D is for Determination: having the resilience to focus and deliver even when faced with setbacks. Determination is a necessary requirement for achieving success at any level, because any major program of change will create resistance and will have setbacks.

Nick shared his perspective on determination. "It is only natural to get pushback when implementing worldwide change initiatives. The 'not invented here' syndrome is a normal defensive response to global programs such as the customer satisfaction initiative mentioned earlier. People do not appreciate going through a major change process unless they thoroughly understand the reason for it and can see some way in which they might benefit—so it is important to involve them as much as possible."

Originally trained as an engineer, Nick is an introvert by nature. However, the CEO role demanded that he push himself out of his comfort zone and "into the limelight." "I quickly became aware that, as CEO, almost everything I said or did was 'interpreted' by others in the organization who were looking for ulterior meanings, whether I intended them or not. The symbolic impact of my actions and statements became magnified. Aware of the power of symbolism that can be wielded by the CEO, I determined to use it wisely and harnessed it to help overcome resistance to change."

Like many other leaders, Nick found that continuous, articulate, and honest communication was a critical tool in a CEO's determination to lead change. When up-front, visible, and continuous leadership is lacking, key messages simply do not take hold. "I heard a story about an acclaimed change management consultant who took a complaint from a CEO client who said: 'Look, you and I worked out the change message, I've delivered it 20 times to the organization, and I'm fed up with delivering it.' The consultant replied:

'Go back and give the speech 200 times. Once you have done that, you can come back and complain." Following intensive coaching and practice, Nick decided to introduce an important change in the live, closed-circuit television broadcasts that were made several times a year to company audiences all over the world. They had previously been filmed in a private studio with only the interviewer and the CEO present. Nick said, "I realized that we could have a greater impact if other company leaders joined me onstage and if we were interviewed in the presence of a live audience. This change was so successful in reaching out to our employees that we took the show on the road, broadcasting live from the factory floor in several locations around the world." While this arrangement certainly took Nick out of his comfort zone, the value of engaging people in a common determination to achieve the organization's goals was clear. And the feedback from the organization was resoundingly positive.

In the lead story of Chapter 4, Alan Murray, the CEO of NextFoods, shares the role that determination has played in shaping his personal leadership, while in Chapter 9, Mary Slaughter, chief learning officer of SunTrust Banks, reflects on the importance of determination in leading successful revolutionary change in an organization.

With the disruption, desire, discipline, and determination in place, success also requires learning, growth, and support through continuous development.

Development

The fifth and final D is for Development. It covers continuous improvement, feedback, and ongoing learning, both for the individual and for the organization.

Nick shared how Tetra Pak worked on the development of people through its own Tetra Pak Academy. "Enhancing an initiative of my predecessor, the head of HR and I worked closely together to introduce an Academy program called 'Inspiring Leaders.' This was used as a way to unite the company in the execution of our global strategy." Focused on the top 125 leaders from around the world, Inspiring Leaders brought groups of 25 of these leaders together every few months to spend three days with the CEO in an intimate dialogue at an off-site location. Apart from being motivating and stimulating meetings, these sessions highlighted capabilities that the company would need to develop in order to secure the implementation of its chosen strategy. They also led to the creation of six "Leadership Challenges"—areas in which leadership skills had to improve—that were then communicated throughout the company and incorporated into the corporate culture.

In addition, Nick said,

A mindset of continuous improvement also helped me when I retired from corporate life and wanted to "reinvent myself." Today, I serve on a couple of corporate boards, engage in numerous not-for-profit activities, mentor senior international executives, and give talks to corporations on leadership topics. Earlier, I even enjoyed a spell as executive in residence at IMD business school in Switzerland. On the family side, I have time for leisure travel with my wife, and I have stepped up my piano playing and sports activities. I feel privileged, both personally and professionally and I know that, whatever legacy I aspire to leave, lifelong learning will be an essential ingredient.

In the lead story of Chapter 5, Tom Miller, CEO of Symbolist, shares his journey of development in transforming both himself and his company. In Chapter 10, Victoria Marsick, professor of adult and organizational learning at Columbia University and codirector of the J. M. Huber Institute for Learning in Organizations, shares her perspectives on how change leaders can improve the learning abilities of their organization.

By peppering the book with examples of people who have chosen to change, we have attempted to make the Five Ds framework as practical as possible so that you can start applying the learning immediately. We believe that if you choose to focus on change at both the individual and the organizational levels, you can improve your chances of change success. And an important part of implementing change is understanding how your brain works.

How Neuroscience Is Informing Our Understanding of Change

Neuroscience is delivering exciting insights for business executives into what is happening during leadership, while at the same time validating and adding to the psychological theory. Breakthroughs in neuroscience imaging enable us to see what is happening inside the human brain in real time. Examples of these technologies include functional magnetic resonance imaging (fMRI), positron emission tomography (PET), and brain wave analysis technologies such as quantitative electroencephalography (QEEG).[5] These technologies, assisted by computer analysis, are enabling new research linking the brain (the physical organ) with the mind (the human consciousness that thinks, feels, acts, and perceives) and are producing "greater depth, resonance, and reliability in our understanding of human capability and behavior."[6]

Within the fields of social, cognitive, and affective neuroscience, research is starting to provide more insight into various aspects of the real world[7]—including the fields of individual and organizational change. The NeuroLeadership Institute, led by CEO David Rock, is at the forefront of this research.

Engaging Your Brain for Yourself and for Your Organization

Neuroscience research can inform efforts to engage the workforce by focusing on engaging our brains. Change often triggers responses in the brain similar to those triggered by physical pain, even when the people involved understand the reasons for the change.[8] Understanding why change efforts have this effect on people requires understanding several things about the brain.

First, the brain's number one job is to keep you alive, and therefore, it is focused on survival. According to neuroscientist Dean Mobbs of the Neuro-Leadership Institute, "Our brains evolved to detect biologically salient stimuli and to optimally pursue a course of action."[9] Furthermore, the brain has proved to be great at surviving. In fact, it is probably the most successful biological organ in history.

It's important to note that for most of human history, the brain saw survival as *physical* survival—life and death. Recent research indicates that in modern times, the brain also sees survival as *social* survival—it acts to protect our social status in much the same way that it acts to protect our life.[10]

Indeed, research indicates that social pain lights up the same part of the brain as physical pain, demonstrating that the pain of exclusion caused by change can be quite literal.[11]

Second, the external environment is of keen interest to the brain. From long experience, the brain has learned that even minor changes in the environment can mean the difference between life and death. For this reason, the brain views environmental changes with profound suspicion. For most of human history, the external environment meant the outdoors. As people moved into organizations, however, the external environment came to include the organizational environment.

Third, the brain has evolved specialized systems to quickly detect and react to changes in its environment. Key ones include working memory, long-term memory, error detection, and the fear response.

Fourth, each of these systems operates in each of us all the time. The initiation of change affects each of us through these systems in different and significant ways, as noted here. Therefore, change triggers common reactions in these systems that include stress, physical discomfort, and even pain. We discuss each system briefly, as each of them has implications for our ability to change.

Working Memory

Working memory, the brain's initial holding area for new perceptions and ideas, is associated with the brain's prefrontal cortex, a small, energy-intensive region behind the forehead. When we activate working memory, we are processing incoming stimuli. The challenge is that working memory is quite limited—we can't process very much information at any one time.[12]

Because change efforts require a greater use of working memory, they can overwhelm it, causing physical discomfort and reducing the brain's capacity for learning, creativity, and adaptability.

Long-Term Memory

Long-term memory is held in the brain's basal ganglia, a low-energy, high-capacity part of the brain, located deeper inside the brain, which doesn't tire like the prefrontal cortex. Activities done repeatedly are referred by the prefrontal cortex to the basal ganglia, thus freeing up processing power in the prefrontal cortex.[13] We use this region for physical habits and activities we can do without thinking.

Change requires the difficult work of changing old habits—something that the basal ganglia actively resist.

Error Detection

The brain's focus on survival causes it to continuously scan the environment (up to five times per second) for "errors"—unexpected changes in the environment. Error signals are generated by the brain's orbital frontal cortex, which is closely related to the brain's fear circuitry in the amygdala, an almond-shaped set of neurons deep in the brain that performs a primary role in the processing of memory and emotional reactions.[14]

Change efforts can generate error signals, which can, in turn, trigger a fear response.

Fear Response

As noted earlier, change efforts can trigger error circuits in the orbital frontal cortex that may trigger a fear response in the amygdala, sometimes called an amygdala hijack.[15] The fear response is the brain's fight, flight, or freeze reaction to perceived danger.

The fear response, once triggered, is the most extreme resistance to change possible. People tend to avoid the kind of environmental uncertainty that change efforts evoke.

In summary, change efforts can threaten multiple systems in the brain (many of which are not conscious), eliciting behaviors to avoid and/or actively resist the change effort. Major initiatives that touch on people's work environments, from their job responsibilities to where they work, will trigger neural systems that motivate people to practice avoidance, over-whelming their working memory, forcing them to engage in the difficult and painful process of changing long-term habits, and potentially trig-gering profound fear. This is why it is vital to apply knowledge of how our brains work in focusing on change at both the individual and organiza-tional levels.

The Power of Choosing a Change Focus for Yourself and Your Organization

By choosing a change focus, you can improve both individual and organiza-tional development and performance. People who are involved in personal or organizational change frequently tell us that the experience has accelerated their development in unexpected ways. Something in the focus and intensity of the change effort enabled deeper learning. This idea is consistent with ideas in adult learning theory linking deep learning with disruptive events, some-times called disorienting dilemmas.[16] Events such as organizational change can be so personally disorienting that they elicit the kind of deep reflection needed to reexamine long-held perspectives. When used to best advantage, organizational change efforts are "learning incubators" for the workforce.

To put it another way, the person or organization that is changed is not just better but *more*. Whether the change happens in a person, a team, an organization, or a nation, successful change may elevate engagement and per-formance beyond the original goal of the effort. If you've ever been part of a successful change effort, you know what we mean. Successful change—particularly when done as part of a high-performance team—can release profound optimism and productive energy. It can take individuals and organi-zations to a new level of performance.

Success builds confidence, expertise, and capacity and reduces fear. Each new success makes the organization and the workforce more "change ready." Each new success sharpens the organization's ability to change in better, faster, and smarter ways, and with fewer resources. Each new success builds competitive advantage that is difficult for competitors to replicate. This is how you can make change your friend and not your enemy.

At the center of all organizational change challenges is the unprecedented upheaval that is taking place in the competitive environment. Today's world is described as a VUCA one, that is, volatile, uncertain, complex, and ambiguous. The twenty-first century is forcing organizations everywhere to change more, faster, and in different ways than ever before. Change is simultaneously attacking myriad organizational processes in different ways. The sheer volume of new information and uncertainty is promoting high levels of anxiety in the workforce. Today's organizations have never needed great change leaders and great organizational change more than they do now.

The executives interviewed for this book consistently highlighted important characteristics that we can isolate as being particularly effective in molding change-focused leaders. These attributes wouldn't surprise the great management scholars who have documented key behaviors that are correlated with effective change. However, beyond some generalities, little is known about the specific things that great change leaders do. In our interviews and experience, people often mention these behaviors as ingredients in change leadership. Specifically, great change leaders build brain-friendly environments as they:

- *Focus on people before tasks.* They constantly explain, help, coach, stretch, and praise people as part of the change effort.
- *Provide context and perspective.* They explain why the change matters and what to focus on in performing it.
- *Build capabilities in the workforce.* They lead the change effort and develop people in multiple ways.
- *Involve others in owning the change.* They know it is less about cascading information from top to bottom and more about viewing change communication as a series of waves involving people across all organizational levels.
- *Stay positive.* They see the potential, the gain in the pain, and the possibilities, and they have fun.
- *Remain calm under pressure.* They shield the team from unnecessary pressure and distraction.
- *Focus on learning.* They do this for themselves, for the team, and for the organization.
- *Lead change in themselves.* They personally change and grow, admit errors, and lead by example.

In exhibiting these behaviors, leaders build higher levels of competence, engagement, and performance in the workforce. Unfortunately, few organizations invest in developing these leaders. Many of the executives we surveyed reported that their organizations did not recognize change leadership as a special competency, had little or no formal training for change leadership, and did not assess the performance of leaders during change efforts. Leaders of change efforts were often selected based on personal reputation or a perceived ability to navigate in the organization's culture, or simply chosen randomly.

The change-focused organization creates competitive advantage by building the capability to change faster, better, smarter, and with fewer resources into the organization's DNA. Rather than relying on external experts and multistep processes, this type of organization relies on the power of the system to continuously enhance its own abilities to change and adapt. Organizational change stops being something that the organization *does* and becomes something that it *is*.

The executives we interviewed agreed that such an approach could provide sustainable competitive advantage and that, because this approach becomes embedded in the culture, it may be difficult for competitors to replicate it with speed. And the more change-focused leaders are as individuals, the more equipped they are to lead the change-focused organization.

We firmly believe that by leveraging the Five Ds framework described in detail in Part I and Part II, you will be able to increase both your individual and organizational change effectiveness. We are passionate about helping individuals and organizations to become change-focused—that is, opening up to explore, be curious, and embrace the power of choosing change.

It is our deepest desire that you find this book helpful for yourself, for those around you, and for your organizations as well. It is time to make a choice. You can choose to change the way you approach change, or you can continue to struggle with the extraordinary waste of energy, resources, and money that results from poorly managed change. Choose to better manage your brain to ensure better results. Choose to be a change-focused leader in a change-focused organization. We urge you not to delay; choose to start your change today!

PART I

The Change-Focused Leader

CHAPTER ONE

Disruption

What Conscious Choice Will You Make?

Your living is determined not so much by what life brings to you as by the attitude you bring to life; not so much by what happens to you as by the way your mind looks at what happens.

—Khalil Gibran

T HE DEFINITION OF *disruption* is "a problem or action that interrupts something and prevents it from continuing."[1] Before we choose to initiate a change, our thinking needs to be disrupted in some way, usually by an external event. The essence of a disruption that enables change lies in asking yourself the question: can I afford to ignore this? Controlled change requires a conscious choice, triggered by an external event—an event that gains your attention; one that makes you reflect, stop, and think; one that disrupts your normal course of thinking or action. Think about Archimedes and his reputed cry of "eureka" when he discovered how to solve a complex problem he was facing by noticing the displacement of the water as he sat in his bath.

The circus ringmaster cracks a whip to gain the attention of both the animals and the audience. A disruption is the whip-cracking event that gets the attention of your working memory, your prefrontal cortex. At that moment, something that you see or hear or experience, either positive or negative, makes you stop and take notice. It is this disruption that paves the way for your change to occur. Equilibrium is about stability. Interestingly, equilibrium is a precursor to death; when a living system is in a state of equilibrium, it is less responsive to the changes that are occurring around it and therefore is at maximum risk.[2] There are countless historical examples of this including that of the dodo, which became extinct when sailors arrived in Mauritius. A flightless bird, its habit of nesting on open ground made it easy prey for humans and animals alike.

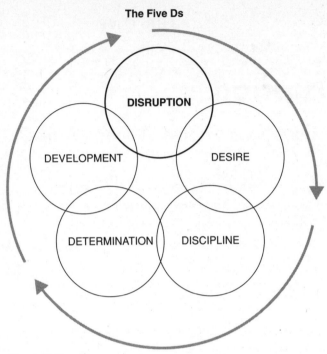

The Five Ds

Source: Goldsworthy

Disruption is often necessary in order to achieve growth and development. This chapter explores the importance of disruption for the change journey, highlighting the ways in which you can most effectively take advantage of a disruptive event to maximize your ability to choose change.

Leading and Living Change: Sara Mathew

Now chairman and CEO of Dun & Bradstreet, Sara Mathew was born and educated in India. After college, her marriage took her to the United States, and she realized that if she wanted some of the comforts of life, she had to work.

Interviewed for this book, Sara said,

> *My job search started in Cincinnati, and I quickly realized that to get a good job, you need an American degree, which I didn't have, so that dramatically limited my options. However, after months of rejection, Procter & Gamble hired me. I was ecstatic—until I got home.*
>
> *My husband looked at the weekly pay offer and asked me why I had accepted a job as a clerk! I was so naïve; I didn't understand the implications of starting out as a clerk.*

I quickly realized I had made a big mistake. P&G hires from the top business schools across America. If you start as a clerk you retire as a clerk. But with no American degree and no work experience, they were not willing to give me much more. Deep down, I thought I deserved more. I even dreamed about being a manager, but filled with self-doubt, hanging on to that dream was hard.

Displaying tenacity, Sara got an MBA in the evenings and managed to work her way into management. "Believe before you can see is a mantra I live by," she said. "As I step back and think of the crazy 18-hour days divided between a full-time job and full-time school, I never questioned my ability to do both and do them well.... There were many naysayers, but I refused to believe them."

Sara had set herself the goal of becoming the CFO of a publicly traded company by the time she was 45. After 18 years with P&G, at age 44, she received an offer to join Dun & Bradstreet as CFO and decided to go for it. Less than a year after she joined D&B, she came across old accounting errors going back a decade, errors that were significant enough to warrant a restatement of the books. When Sara informed the CEO, she shares,

I remember the alarm in his face....

"What are we going to do?" he asked.

I remember thinking, "Heck...I don't know. I've never done this before."

Then, instincts kicked in. I committed to get it done in six weeks. He asked if this was possible. To which I said anything is possible.

Looking back, I had no idea how long it would take or whether I was capable of the task at hand. I just made a commitment and now I had to deliver.

It was a grueling experience. D&B ultimately restated its books and communicated a sizable adjustment to investors without any loss of confidence. Sara said,

Restating D&B's books in six weeks put me on the map. I received accolades and monetary awards. I was on a proverbial "high"—that is, until our employee survey results came in. My results were close to last!

My organization was sending me a message about how I got the restatement done. The long hours and unyielding focus had taken its toll. I was now back in the CEO's office, and he was not happy. I remember the conversation—"You are not leading well, Sara." To which I responded, "You need to make a choice—what do you want, great results or happy people?" His response—"Great leaders do both."...

The CEO's words forced me to...pause and reflect on who I am, how I get things done, and the impact I can sometimes have in my urgency to deliver.

On reflection, what I did was great. How I did it was terrible. I decided to take action and get feedback from the people around me. In this process, I had to manage my own threat response and defensiveness. I realized that if I wanted to be effective, I had to change.

Two years later, Sara's employee survey scores were world-class. When she was offered the opportunity to become the next CEO, Sara thought seriously about whether she wanted the job. "What ultimately motivated me was the search for what was possible and the opportunity to continuously transform myself," Sara said. As of 2013, she is chairman and CEO of Dun & Bradstreet Corporation and a member of the board of directors of the Campbell Soup Company. "I believe leadership is a journey, one that never ends," Sara concluded in our interview. "It is an ongoing commitment to make every day count."[3]

The words of the then CEO telling Sara that she had to focus on the people as well as the results confronted her in her moment of denial. While she was initially resistant to the idea of changing, his words were strong enough to convince her to stop and reflect. Once she overcame her initial defensive reactions, she was able to consider her options, make a conscious decision to change, and choose her response.

Disruption Is an Opportunity to Choose

A disruptive event is an awakening, an unexpected jolt that gains the attention of your working memory and the right ventrolateral prefrontal cortex (RVLPFC), the brain region linked to self-control. You are confronted with a reality that you cannot ignore. It may be a comment from a boss or a business associate; it may be catching sight of yourself in a mirror or your reflection in a window; it may be feedback from a 360-degree evaluation process. Whatever the event, it sparks the beginning of a change.

On December 1, 1955, Rosa Parks, a 42-year-old African American seamstress, was riding on a bus in Montgomery, Alabama. The first rows of seats were reserved for whites; African Americans, who paid the same 10-cent fare as the whites, were required to find seats in the back. If all the seats were taken when a white passenger boarded the bus, then a row of African American passengers sitting in the middle of the bus would be required to give up their seats, even if it meant that they would have to stand. As Rosa boarded the bus, she was thinking about a workshop she was helping to organize; she was thus a bit distracted, and she took a seat in the row right behind the section reserved for whites. At the next stop, the Empire Theater, a group of whites boarded the bus. In the rows reserved for whites there were enough open seats for all but one of them. The bus driver said, "Let me have those front seats." Although only one white passenger needed a seat, all four African American passengers were required to stand up because a white person living in the segregated South at that time would not sit in the same row as an African American. Rosa Parks and the other three African Americans seated in her row didn't move. So the bus driver said, "Y'all better make it light on your-selves and let me have those seats." The man next to Rosa Parks stood up, and Parks let him pass by her. The two women in the bench seat across from her also got up. Rosa Parks remained seated. Despite the hostile looks from the bus driver and the other passengers, she refused to get up. The driver told Parks, "Well, I'm going to have you arrested." Parks responded, "You may do that." The driver called the police and they arrested Rosa Parks.

Rosa Parks was neither too old to get up nor too tired after a long day at work. Instead, she was just fed up with being mistreated. As she described in her autobiography, "The only tired I was, was tired of giving in." When Parks made the choice not to give up her seat, she was aware of the possible conse-quences, and yet, at that moment, she chose to disrupt a pattern imposed by society. What she could not have foreseen is that this single decision to refuse to move would reverberate throughout the United States and beyond as the catalyst that unleashed widespread change. In her mind, she was only looking to make a change within the realm of "self."

While she was on her way to jail, news of her arrest circulated around the city. That night, E. D. Nixon, a friend of Parks and the president of the local chapter of the NAACP (National Association for the Advancement of Colored People), asked her if she would be the plaintiff in a lawsuit against the bus company. She said yes. News of her arrest led to plans for a one-day boycott of the buses in Montgomery on Monday, December 5, 1955. Her trial on the same day lasted no more than 30 minutes, and she was found guilty. She was fined $10 and an additional $4 for court costs. The one-day boycott of the buses in Montgomery was so successful that it turned into a 381-day boycott, ending only when the Supreme Court ruled that the bus segregation laws in Alabama were unconstitutional. That disruptive moment when Rosa Parks had simply had enough and refused to leave her seat is considered to be the event that marked the beginning of the modern civil rights movement.[4]

Whatever the moment, once you confront it, you have to consider the event: you ask yourself how you feel about it, what it means, or how it matters to you. Is this something you need to do something about? You may even discuss it with a close friend or confidante and ask what that person thinks. The question is whether or not you are ready to listen to your own or the other person's response. At this stage, you then have to choose. You can dismiss the disruptive event and ignore it, or you can decide to act upon it, as Rosa Parks did, and make a conscious choice to change. The choice you make and the way you view the situation can then change the outcome.

Gail Small, the coexecutive director of Ometz, a not-for-profit social services agency in Canada, shares the following story about making a conscious choice and the power of managing oneself.

I was the CEO of several small organizations in the 1980s and 1990s. While I naturally assume leadership positions (and have done so since I was a child), I have always found the position of CEO to be stressful, extremely demanding, and at times lonely. My constant struggle, often unsuccessful, was to find a healthy balance between my work life and my personal life. In the late 1990s, I decided to take a senior management position in a much larger organization, acknowledging that I no longer wanted to be a CEO. When the CEO left several years later, I was asked to apply for the position, but I refused. I had observed how the former CEO managed in her position and felt that it seemed all-encompassing and all-consuming, leaving little time for anything else in her life. I also felt that the bar she had set for herself could never be my bar.

A new CEO was hired, but did not work out and was asked to leave within one year. During this time, I had the opportunity to reconsider my own ambitions and goals. I realized that I did not have to do the job in the same way as the previous CEO and concluded that I could set my own bar and do the job in my own way. I could in fact envision my own job and determine how I would do it. It is now 10 years later; I enjoy my job immensely, and I have achieved a nice balance between my work life and my personal life.

Gail Small was able to let go of her fears and demonstrate how her own needs and the needs of the company could be aligned for the benefit of both parties. When leaders can change themselves, they are more prepared for the complexities of guiding their teams and their companies through change.

Making a Conscious Choice

The late neurophysiologist Benjamin Libet was fascinated by the question of whether humans have free will. He led experiments to understand the mental timing involved when someone does a voluntary act. He chose a simple task: the lifting of a finger. His research showed that 0.5 seconds before the voluntary movement of the finger there is a brain signal related to the action that is about to occur; it's called an *action potential*. Your unconscious brain decides, "I will move this finger," 0.3 seconds before you are aware of it. At this point, there is a further 0.2 seconds during which you are aware that you are about to move your finger, and you can intervene in the process and stop the move.[5]

This is the exciting part. For every move you make, you have 0.2 seconds in which you can actively, consciously intervene in the process and choose a different response. Viktor Frankl, an Austrian psychiatrist and concentration camp survivor, was spot on when he wrote, "Between stimulus and response there is a space. In that space is our power to choose our response. In our response lies our growth and our freedom."[6] Now 0.2 seconds may not sound like much, but in brain terms, with billions of connections every second, it is a decent amount of time. Every time you make a decision, you have 0.2 seconds to choose a different response. Wow! Our right ventrolateral prefrontal cortex can step right in and intervene in the limbic process.

Our ability to control our thinking has been explored by many renowned academics and scientists. In recent years, new developments have deepened our understanding of how our brains work, thanks to technological advances in scanners that allow scientists to see and measure what is happening inside our brains. *Neuroscience* has become a word that laypeople are familiar with, and the news is full of the latest findings from brain research. However, what is fascinating is that many of the discoveries endorse the previous findings of psychologists and psychiatrists as to why we act the way we do.

Daniel Goleman led the way in helping the broader business community realize that emotional intelligence is at least as important as, if not more important than, intellectual intelligence,[7] while research by Duncan Coombe showed that the ability to stay calm, particularly when everyone else is not doing so, is a key leadership characteristic.[8] Therefore, practicing your ability to control your emotions under stress can certainly give you a competitive advantage. This means that instead of "losing it" when something happens that you don't like, you can control your emotions and respond in a more situation-appropriate way for the benefit of the business, yourself, and those around you.

So let us just take a moment and recap what is happening in your brain when you use your choice point (see Figure 1-1). A signal from the outside world comes into your brain via the sensory thalamus. This is a part of the

Figure 1-1   Using Your Choice Point

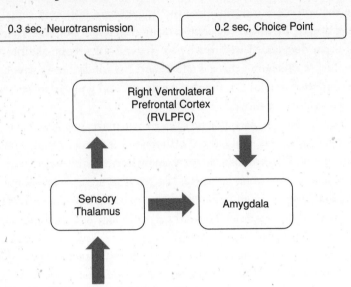

Source: Goldsworthy, 2011 based on Rock, Lieberman, Libet

brain that is responsible for receiving and transmitting signals (neurotransmission). The sensory thalamus then sends the signal to the amygdala, a group of nuclei in your brain that has been shown to have a primary role in the processing of memory and emotional reactions, be they negative or positive.

The amygdala then responds by releasing the appropriate chemicals into the body to elicit the appropriate response. For example, if there is a perceived threat, the amygdala releases a number of chemicals, including adrenaline and the stress hormone cortisol, to prepare your body for fight or flight. However, during the split second in which this is happening, your sensory thalamus also sends a signal to your right ventrolateral prefrontal cortex, and there is that 0.2 seconds in which you can "choose" to halt the ongoing response from the amygdala. Neuroscientist Matt Lieberman refers to this process involving the right ventrolateral prefrontal cortex as "the brain's braking system."[9] This concept was first presented in 2009 at the NeuroLeadership Institute Summit in Los Angeles.

Exercising Your Choice Point

So, if we can do this, why don't we do it all the time? Well, it takes considerable energy and attention to leverage that 0.2 second choice point. That's the bad news. The good news is that neuroscientists have discovered a relatively simple way for you to practice what we call your choice point on a daily basis.

Separate research by Matt Lieberman,[10] Elliot Berkman,[11] and Thomas Denson[12] has found that the neural pathway used for motor regulation is the same as that used for emotional regulation. That is, the brain uses the same neural pathway to carry out a physical activity and to carry out an emotional one. Therefore, for example, you can practice intervening by picking up your cup with your left hand instead of your right hand. This simple act requires a conscious intervention in your routine activity and is a way in which you can exercise your choice point. By practicing on a motor response, you can improve your ability to intervene in an emotional response. So exercising your choice point can actually help you avoid losing your temper. Just as Roger Federer practices on a basic tennis court every day and then performs at Wimbledon for only two weeks a year, you can also practice exercising your choice point with a simple task, like using your other hand to pick up a drink, open a door, or brush your teeth. Then, when the pressure is on, you will be more equipped to use this ability in an emotional situation.

If you do not have an awareness of your choice point, your habitual response will play out like a prerecorded program. This happens because our brain works to run our lives using as little energy as possible. For many activities that you engage in every day, this is helpful. It would be too exhausting for you to have to intervene and decide upon the course of action for every decision you made during any given day. Neuroscience shows that if you did so, the RVLPFC would literally run out of the oxygen and glucose that provide its fuel.[13] It would become paralyzing. If you had to think consciously and make choices every time you decided to brush your teeth in the morning, it would take you forever to get out the door! So, habitual responses are helpful, except when you want to change a behavior. Then, it becomes vital for you to catch yourself in the process of making a habitual response, so that you can exercise your choice point.

Catch the Cue

Habits have a three-step loop: cue, routine, and reward, according to Charles Duhigg.[14] The cue is the trigger that tells the brain to go into automatic mode and follow a particular habit. The routine can be physical, mental, or emotional. The reward then helps your brain work out whether the routine is worth remembering in the future. Habits can be ignored, changed, or replaced. However, when a habit develops, the brain stops participating actively in the decision-making process. So unless you deliberately fight a habit or replace it by finding new routines, the pattern will unfold automatically. This is why it is so important that you catch the cue.

Jean-François Manzoni, professor of leadership and organizational behavior at INSEAD, found a breakthrough insight in this pattern.

> I guess the piece of advice that has had the most profound impact on my life is "Catch the cue." This came up during my MBA, in a course called Skill Development. We had been exposed to Chris Argyris's work, and I had realized that I was more short-tempered than I wanted to be. The course instructor wrote in the margin of my term paper: "Catch the cue." I visited him at his home, and he explained to me, "Before you express your irritation or anger, is there a cue? Is there a sign that you're about to lose your temper?" I said, "Yes, I can feel my pulse racing and the adrenaline rush." "Well," he said, "that's the cue you need to catch in order to get hold of yourself and stop the expression of anger." This was an extremely important piece of advice because it helped me realize that I did not have to be on automatic pilot all the time, and I didn't have to be a slave to my "nature or my habits." I had a choice. At least as long as I'm mindful, I have a choice.

By becoming conscious of your own cues, you enable yourself to manage them better. To become conscious, you must become attuned to how you are feeling and how your body is responding. Catch your own cues—notice them and write them down. The more aware you can become, the more you know about yourself and about your triggers and your patterns, the more you are able to exercise your choice point at the opportune moment and the more you are then able to change your behavior.

Former CEO of Tetra Pak Nick Shreiber shared how he works to catch himself "in the moment."

> I ask myself quick questions such as, "Grain of truth?" (meaning is there a grain of truth in what that person just said?) or "Big deal?" (meaning is what somebody is saying important enough to fly off the handle?) or "Alternative interpretation?" (meaning might I have misinterpreted what I just heard; is there an alternative explanation to consider instead of losing my temper?). These quick mini-questions force me to pause before I respond and give my RVLPFC time to kick in. Though, of course, it is also a matter of practicing this until it becomes a habit.

Separating Personality from Patterns

Often people say things like, "I've tried changing, and I can't. It's just the way I am." The first part of that sentence is an excuse for the brain to remain in the cozy place where it often prefers to be—the world of the known, safe, and comfortable. The second part of the statement is actually inaccurate. It is the brain's way of maintaining the status quo: "It's just not me." "I want to be authentic, not fake." "Being like this has gotten me where I am today, so why change?" These comments, and others like them, are the brain's way of protecting itself. Protecting itself from what? you may ask. The brain is protecting itself from perceived threats and from expending the energy required to do the hard work of change or deal with facing fears, such as the fear of rejection or the fear of failure, linking to our need to belong and our need to achieve.[15] Karen Horney outlined three coping mechanism trends: moving toward people (compliance), moving against them (aggression), or moving away from them (withdrawal). These three trends stem from basic animal survival mechanisms: submission, fight, or flight. Much of our behavior can then be derived from the interplay and conflict between the three.[16]

When we are born, we have some basic personality traits. Psychologists believe that there are preferences that we are born with; for example, you may have a preference for using your right hand to write. You then spend your whole life practicing and perfecting that preference so that it becomes a habit and you can do it without thinking.

Pick up a pen, find a piece of paper, and sign your name—your normal signature. It's easy, right? Now put the pen in your other hand and sign your name once more. How did that feel? Unless you are ambidextrous or have practiced this exercise many times, signing your name with your "other" hand will have felt strange and a bit cumbersome. The result may also look a little like a child's writing. It no doubt looks far less flowing and proficient than your "normal" signature. This is why our preferences are so strong. We may be born with certain preferences, but we then practice them over and over and over for decades until we can use them almost without thinking.

We also learn through familiarity and by things being reinforced or modeled for us by the people around us. Positive reinforcement can strengthen an act that can become a negative habit over time. For example, in some cultures, love is expressed through the medium of cooking and food. This then creates a cycle in which the more you eat, the more you please the giver and the more food you are given. A child in such an environment may then grow up with a weight problem that is linked to the overconsumption of food as a representation of familial love.

So, those actions that we have repeated over and over and over throughout our childhood and adulthood can become patterns and habits that feel very much like part of us. This is where we can make mistakes. We can assume that a self-destructive behavior is inherent in our personality rather than being something that we have wired into our brains through years of responding the same way time after time. Most of us go through our lives repeating the same patterns over and over in the belief that this is "just the way I am." That's not necessarily so. It is the way we have learned to be. We can forget that we have choices about how we think, how we behave, and how we react. Through experience and self-reflection, we can become aware of some patterns that we may have developed. Then we have the power to choose what to do. Sometimes we choose to do nothing about these patterns, either because we have no interest in developing in that area or because we do not believe we have the ability to change them. Or, we can make a conscious choice to embark on a journey of exploration, stepping into the unknown to seek a change. Disruption usually takes us by surprise and gives us the opportunity to choose to change.

Awarded the Nobel Peace Prize in 1997, Jody Williams is an American political activist known for her work to ban land mines and support human rights, including those of women. Interviewed for *Time* magazine by Valerie Lapinski in March 2013, Jody was asked what had made her become an activist. She shared, "I was at university during the time of great social upheaval in the 1960s. But I floundered for another decade until I was given a leaflet that said, 'El Salvador: Another Vietnam?' It changed my life."

That disruptive moment led to a decade of work in Central America before Jody became involved in the movement to ban land mines. "I started thinking about land mines as a symbol of the long-term effects of war, and I got excited," said Jody. She recently published her memoirs, entitled, *My Name is Jody Williams*, and was asked why she had chosen to write something personal. She replied, "I think there's a mythology that if you want to change the world, you have to be sainted, like Mother Teresa or Nelson Mandela or Archbishop Desmond Tutu. Ordinary people with lives that go up and down and around in circles can still contribute to change."[17]

The ability to make a choice to pursue a path that is different from the one that is well trodden and well known is what makes the difference to each of us who wants to make a change in our daily life. In terms of your own development, you can choose to swim on the surface, enjoying the view. Or you can put your head down and snorkel, looking at what lies beneath from the surface of the water. Or you can choose to scuba dive, exploring the depths of your inner, as well as outer, life.

Charles, cofounder and owner of a successful IT consulting company, experienced the benefits of choosing a new path or approach. With a PhD in business IT, he is a strategic, logical, and fast thinker with a flair for business and for meeting customer needs. However, as the company has grown larger and become increasingly global, Charles has pursued knowledge on the subject of leadership. Intrigued by this less obviously measurable "soft science," he has stepped out of his comfort zone and embarked on a personal leadership journey and also sponsored a company-level leadership program. "For those of us trained as engineers, scientists, or mathematicians, it is like learning a new language," said Charles. "In terms of behavior, applying a primarily rational approach can result in a sometimes unexpectedly irrational response. Mastering the so-called soft skills of emotional intelligence and learning about what motivates people can produce tangibly hard results."

Identifying Patterns Exercise

We all have patterns that we repeat in our lives. What are the patterns that you are repeating over and over, and where do they come from? Identifying the roots of your behavior can help you to understand it and then work to change it. Try this life pictures exercise to help you become more aware of your behavior. Take a large piece of paper and divide it into four sections. In one section, draw a picture of your childhood; in the second section, draw a picture of your young adulthood; in the third section, draw a picture of your life today; and then in the fourth section, draw a picture of your life in the future (how you would like it to be in the years to come). For each section, add some key words that describe that period for you. For example, you might think about a defining phrase or word that illustrates that period of your life, like family, freedom, growth, learning, or routine—whatever comes to mind. Now share your "life pictures" with a close friend, colleague, or partner whom you trust. By discussing what you have drawn and the words you have written, you will gain greater insight into patterns that may be helpful in your life and also patterns that may be defense mechanisms that you have practiced over and over, but that, while possibly useful at some earlier stage of your life, may no longer be helpful to you today.

According to the late Randy Pausch, a professor of computer science, human computer interaction and design at Carnegie Mellon University, "We cannot change the cards we are dealt, just how we play the hand." When he was diagnosed with pancreatic cancer, Randy delivered his version of a popular academic tradition at many universities: he gave a last lecture. In this case, it was literally true—not the last lecture of a career, but of a life. The title of his lecture was "Really Achieving Your Childhood Dreams." The video of the lecture went viral, was featured in a *Wall Street Journal* column by Jeffrey Zaslow, and was turned into a bestselling book coauthored with Zaslow. In a television interview on *The Oprah Winfrey Show*, Randy commented that he saw life as being 10 percent white, 10 percent black, and 80 percent gray. "You can go through life and say, 'Gee, that 80 percent gray part, that's black, and life is a bad thing.' Or you can say that 80 percent gray part's part of the white, and it's the goodness and the light. I want to view life that way. It becomes a self-fulfilling prophecy. That 80 percent in the middle really can go either way, and if you decide you want to make it go good, not bad, you have a lot more power to make that happen than you might think."[18]

Looking at your life pictures is not about blaming your past, it is about being aware of your influences and where your patterns may have come from. It is about working with what you have and starting with where you are. If you're not running your own show, then who is? You decide where you spend your time and your mental energy. You decide about what you think, feel, and do.

When Gretchen, a highly successful editor who has worked on countless bestselling books with a number of authors, was considering a career change, a number of disruptive events helped with her decision. Gretchen explained,

> "The universe" or God or whatever force is out there sent me every possible signal that it was time to make a switch: a difficult client relationship, neck issues associated with sitting at my computer for protracted periods of time, eyestrain—all these made the editing work less attractive. On the other side, I saw the glimmer of a different opportunity. I had the financial safety net of a lucrative nonediting contract, and when I articulated to a longtime client that I sometimes daydreamed about being a permanent member of his team, he immediately initiated a dialogue about an exciting job offer. However, as much as I want to change what I do for a living, it does involve the hard work and conscious choice of saying "no" to work and to people who are important to me. I just had two more requests for editing proposals, and even though I declined, it would in many ways have been far simpler to just say "yes" and carry on.

When the disruption occurs, it takes courage to choose to change.

Choosing the Circles You Inhabit

In his highly acclaimed book *The Seven Habits of Highly Effective People*, Stephen Covey talked about two circles: the circle of influence and the circle of concern. Roy Gillett, a lecturer on change at Birkbeck College, University of London, has added a third circle: the circle of control (see Figure 1-2).

This simple diagram is extremely powerful in helping us to manage our own attitudes. Take a moment to look at the circles and think about yourself. In your day-to-day life, apart from your own attitude, what is actually fully within your control? The time you set your alarm for, the way you brush your teeth, the clothes you choose to wear on any particular day, the route you take to get to work. If you think about it, on a daily basis, when it comes to external events, there is not so much that is fully within your control.

Much of what happens around us on a day-to-day basis falls within our circle of concern. We may not like it, but there is absolutely nothing we can do about it. What are obvious examples of things that fall into our circle of concern? The weather. The result of a football match. The result of an election. Our plane being delayed at the airport. A merger or acquisition at a company where we work. These events may cause us some concern, but we have no power to change their outcomes. Take airplane travel, for example. You arrive at the airport and find out that your plane has been delayed by two

Figure 1-2   Circles and Choice

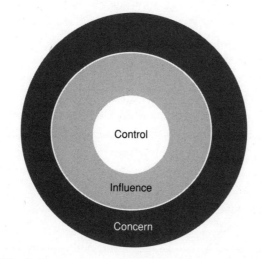

Source: Covey and Gillett, 2001

hours. You find this irritating, as your schedule and your plans are now disrupted. You will react negatively at first. (Your thinking may go something like: "@£!@—the darn plane is late again. Stupid airline!")

At that moment, you have a choice. You can stay in the pain of the delay and continue to focus on the negative. If you do this, you will spiral down into increased negativity, creating significant stress through the release of cortisol, adrenaline, and numerous other chemicals into your system. Or you can choose to focus on the gain—the benefit in the pain—and look at the opportunity.

Ask yourself, can I do anything about the delay? Can I influence it in any way? If I get upset, is the airline going to say, "Oh my, we've really upset Fred—why don't we bring the plane forward?" It's unlikely! So, this is clearly something that is outside your circles of control and influence. Therefore, you gain more by letting go of the frustration and thinking about what you can do with the two hours that you didn't plan to have at the airport. There are always options. You can read a book, work on your computer, make some phone calls, go shopping, have something to drink—there are many options from which to choose.

By focusing on the opportunities, you regain some element of autonomy and, as a result, feel better about the situation that you can't change anyway. Simple, right? You may be thinking, as our clients have many times, "Well, that's clear for the airport example, but how can I tell whether something at work is in my circle of influence or my circle of control?" Here, we advise you to follow the baseball rule: three strikes and you're out. If there is something you want to change and you are uncertain about whether it is within either your circle of influence or your circle of control, make an attempt to change it. If that fails, try again, but with a different approach. Do this three times in three different ways, and if you still fail, it is probably something that is within only your circle of concern. So, let it go. Many of us try repeatedly to change things using the same approach and are surprised when we continually fail.

Clearly, this technique does not hold when you are working on an innovation or an experiment. What we are talking about is your ability to influence others in an area where you may not have much impact. In these situations, the one thing that is fully under your control, but where most people abdicate responsibility, is your attitude. On any given day, at any given moment, your own attitude and mental state reflect a choice you make, even in the worst of situations. Viktor Frankl's words resonate once again in this reflection on his detainment in a concentration camp, "Everything can be taken from a man [or a woman] but one thing: the last of the human freedoms—to choose one's

attitude in any given set of circumstances, to choose one's own way."[19] For
inspiration related to our ability to control and choose our own thoughts and
attitudes, we highly recommend Frankl's short book *Man's Search for Meaning*.

Business executive Glen Pearce recalls the disrupting event that led to a
reprioritization of his life.

> I was taking a leadership course, and one of the tasks was to write
> a letter from your partner, 20 years in the future, saying what you
> would like that person to write about you. When it was my turn to
> share my letter, I just burst into tears. I realized the huge gap between
> what I would like her to say and the current situation. It became clear
> how selfish I had been with my partner, always putting my interests
> and my career first. I was doing well at work, but I had forgotten just
> how much she had sacrificed to support me. We had moved coun-
> tries, and she had walked away from her career, her family, her friends,
> her culture, and her language—all to support me in my professional
> growth. I made a decision then and there to be a more considerate
> partner and for us to work together to reprioritize what was important
> in our lives. My desire was to be seen as a good partner and a good
> father because of my actions, not just because of the financial contri-
> bution I was making. We have started to make life decisions putting
> the family first. I have now taken on the role of encouraging and sup-
> porting my wife's career and playing a more active part as a father.
> This change has given us a much more rewarding relationship and has
> also given my life true purpose. One discipline I apply daily is, when I
> get home from work, I ring the doorbell. One of the kids or my wife
> then comes to the door, and as soon as I step across the threshold, my
> attention is on them until they go to bed. If I need to work, I go back
> on the computer after they are asleep. This small change has made an
> enormous difference. Whereas previously I would let myself into the
> house and often be on the phone as I came in, now, as soon as I ring
> that doorbell, the family is my focus, and the reward is a huge smile
> or a hug.

Disruption is the first step in making change. Although it prompts initial
discomfort and even confusion, disruption is essential to growth and learning.
Disruptive events build on our self-awareness, which, according to a survey of
75 members of the Stanford Graduate School of Business Advisory Council, is
the most important capability for leaders to develop.[20] Once you have become
aware of a need for change and made a conscious choice to address it, then

the next step is to have the desire to achieve it, the belief in yourself that you can do it, and the focus to make it happen. In Chapter 2 we discuss *desire*, the second D in the Five Ds framework.

Key Points to Remember

- Disruption is a stimulus in the form of an event, an experience, a trigger, or a cue that prompts the need for change.
- You have the ability to make a conscious choice as to whether you act on that external stimulus.
- Your ability to notice when the external stimulus occurs and then reflect upon it increases your chances of changing.
- Catch the cue—notice the triggers that elicit a habitual response and then work to change them.
- Determine which events are within your circle of control or your circle of influence and manage your attitude accordingly.
- If external circumstances fall into your circle of concern, minimize the amount of time you spend there, as it is wasted energy.

CHAPTER TWO

Desire

What Do You Really Want to Change?

*To accomplish great things, we must not only act, but also dream; not only plan,
but also believe.*

—Anatole France, 1844–1924, French writer,
winner of 1921 Nobel Prize for Literature

D
ESIRE IS THE bridge between your dream and your reality.
After disruption has occurred—whether it is a crisis moment in your personal
life or your professional performance, changes in your team, new leadership
responsibilities, or the output from a 360-degree report or a performance
review—you may experience an awareness that perhaps you could do something differently. In this chapter, we'll discuss how you meet the challenge of
converting that disruption into a desire for change. There is an old expression,
"You can lead a horse to water, but you can't make it drink." And so it is with
change—the disruption shakes you, but you still have the ability to retreat
from the discomfort back into the safety of a comfort zone. This is why the
second step, desire, is so important. The essence of the desire for change lies
in asking yourself the question: do I really want to apply the focus necessary
to make a change or not? If the desire is not there, then any energy expended
is likely to be a waste of time.

The definition of desire is "a wish or longing."[1] In the context of change,
you may experience longings for stability, improved fortunes, or recognition,
but a desire that sticks and drives you into sustainable new behaviors is about
something more. It involves both a belief that change is possible and a conscious choice to be clear about what it is that you want to change. You must
choose to change. This chapter focuses on determining and understanding
your desire. It explains how to frame it, apply visualization, use symbols,

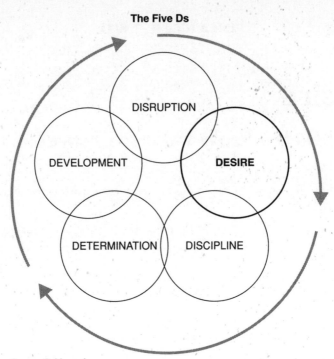

The Five Ds

Source: Goldsworthy

and take the steps required to channel your desire into an actionable and achievable goal.

In the midst of disruption, desire begins with questions such as, "What is it that I really want? Why do I want it? How serious am I about making it happen?" In our view, if your state of mind is merely a wish ("It would be nice if..." or "I wish that..."), then your chances of success are dramatically reduced. To adapt to and drive your role in making your desired change, you need to see the difference between a "wish," which indicates a certain lack of empowerment or engagement with the goal, and a "want," which is driven by a deep consciousness of your needs and goals. A want more closely aligns your head with the desires of your heart in a way that resonates with you. The desire then translates into a belief that its achievement is possible. In this chapter, we explain how you can anchor your desire in such a way that you maximize your chances of success. This process involves making a conscious choice, understanding your beliefs, and managing your focus and your inner critic. By visualizing your goals, using symbols to assist you, and articulating your goals clearly, you can empower yourself to achieve your goals.

Leading and Living Change: Marc Herremans

Marc Herremans, a Belgian athlete who started training for triathlons in 1998, displayed enormous potential. In 2001, Marc came in sixth in the Ironman triathlon in Hawaii. Encouraged by this positive performance, he began training intensely for the following year's race and believed that he could fulfill his dream of winning. However, on January 28, 2002, tragedy struck: a bicycle crash on Lanzarote left Marc paralyzed from the chest down. A mere two months after the accident, Marc revised his goal and started training to win the Ironman triathlon for wheelchair athletes. "It took me a few days to realize that a broken back doesn't mean you have a broken life," said Marc. "But I also realized that things were going to be a lot harder than before." Eight months later, he was on the starting line for the race. However, he had pushed himself too far too quickly, and he had to stop after the swimming leg. In 2002, the Belgian press voted Marc sports personality of the year. Keeping his goal foremost in his mind, he went back to training and finished third in the Hawaiian wheelchair athlete triathlon in 2003 and 2004. In 2005 he came in second. Finally, in 2006, four years after his accident, Marc Herremans won the Ironman triathlon for wheelchair athletes. In 2007, he became the first wheelchair athlete to finish the toughest mountain bike race in the world: the Crocodile Trophy in Australia, which involves a 1,400-km bike ride through rough terrain. For many years now, Marc has had a new goal. "I want to walk again. I firmly believe it can be done. I have started my own foundation that has that same name: To Walk Again. I have spoken with many people who are confined to wheelchairs, including the late Christopher Reeve. I believe that one day they will find a cure for paralysis. And when they do, I want to be prepared. I want my body to be ready."

Marc continues to inspire people with his energy, focus, and commitment. In 2010, he was featured in an advertising campaign with the tagline "When your reality changes, your dreams don't have to." Says Marc, "I have lost so many people in my life—some committed suicide and others had cancer or were in accidents—and those guys had no chance to fight back, but I did. I survived. They gave me the strength to carry on. They showed me that life can end or change in one second and every day that you complain and do not try to reach your goals is [a day] lost. You have to do it here and now; every day is a gift." In January 2013, Marc became the father of a daughter, Anne-Lou. He now trains young athletes, both able-bodied and disabled, across a number of sports, and also supports research into a cure for paralysis. "Stem cell research is making great progress. It is hoped stem cells could one day be widely used to repair damaged tissue caused by disease and following injury," says Marc. "I will never stop hoping. I believe that a cure is possible, and, if and when that day comes, I want to be prepared. So I'll stay as active as I possibly can."[2]

Aligning desire, meaning, and purpose strengthens your resolve and provides you with powerful positive energy to propel you forward toward your goal. Marc has found a meaning and purpose to his life in a way that benefits both himself and others. As well as coaching other athletes and disabled people and running his foundation, he is also a motivational speaker who inspires people from all walks of life with his story. "You can be perfectly at one with life and with yourself if you dare to look down as well and face reality. If I only looked up to people who can walk stairs, both literally and metaphorically, I would get depressed," said Marc. "Life is too short to be sorry; you have to move on." He also said, "Life's only limitations are the ones we make—it's all in the mind and nothing is impossible."

Marc has converted his belief about what is possible for him into an attitude that enables him to maintain a sense of hope and purpose while leading a rich and rewarding life. Your beliefs can either empower you or limit you in terms of what you want to achieve. By exploring your own beliefs and doing an inventory of them, you can become more aware, more conscious of your own situation, and thereby more able to achieve your goal.

Understanding Your Beliefs Exercise

Beliefs can be self-fulfilling. They can change how you view the world, and your biology can even adapt to meet the beliefs you hold.[3] According to psychologist Carol Dweck, "What people believe shapes what people achieve. Our self-theories can set the boundaries on what we are able to accomplish."[4] The strength of your belief that you can succeed can create a momentum that increases your chances of winning.[5] Adapting a quote from Henry Ford, "If you think you can, you might. If you think you can't, you're right."

John Seymour, vice president at National CORE, has translated his passion for sports into a passion for life. Says John, "At 50 years old, growing stronger each day and being a big wave surfer, snowboarder, and ocean swimmer requires a relentless belief in yourself to accomplish what others gasp at, fear, and cannot comprehend. My sports have taught me the fire, the determination, and the learned ability to visualize achieving clear goals and taught me to accomplish my desire through teamwork and self-discipline. This experience has translated into my family life, has given me a solid work ethic, and sustains me when dealing with the daily difficulties of business."

Your identification of your wants—the sustainable goals that will carry you through a major change initiative—can be strengthened by doing an inventory of the beliefs you have about yourself. We find that the "Beliefs House" exercise (see Figure 2-1) can increase your awareness of your own

Figure 2-1 Beliefs House: Building Your Success

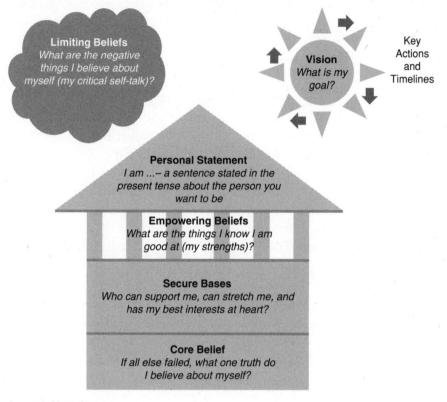

Source: Goldsworthy, 2009

beliefs and of how they may be helping or hindering the achievement of your desire. Complete each section as follows:

Core belief: If all else failed and you lost everything that is dear to you, what one truth do you believe to be true about yourself?

Secure bases: Who are the people who can both support and challenge you and who you believe have your best interests at heart? A secure base is defined as "a person...who provides a sense of protection, safety and caring and offers a source of inspiration and energy for daring, exploration, risk taking and seeking challenge."[6] How are you engaging your secure bases in pursuing your goal?

Empowering beliefs: What are your strengths—the things you know you are good at?

Limiting beliefs: What are the negative things you believe about yourself—the things that are embodied in your critical self-talk?

Personal statement: Write a sentence about the person you want to be when you've achieved your goal. It is important that you write it in the present tense because if you put it in the future tense, your brain does not have to do anything about it now.

Vision: What is your desire, your goal? And what are the key actions and timelines associated with it? (You may wish to return to this after reading about setting goals with STAMINA later in this chapter.)

Share your completed exercise with one of the secure bases that you have identified and decide what limiting beliefs you want to let go of.

People like Marc Herremans remind us that we are capable of much more than we often allow ourselves to believe. However, we have to be clear about what it is that we want. In *Alice's Adventures in Wonderland* by Lewis Carroll, Alice is walking along a path when she comes to a fork in the road. She looks up at the Cheshire Cat who is sitting in a tree. "Which road should I take?" Alice asks the Cheshire Cat. "That all depends on where you want to go," the Cheshire Cat replies. "I don't know where I want to go," says Alice. "Then it doesn't matter which road you take," responds the Cheshire Cat.[7]

A clear desire has had a big impact on the life of Hossam Fares. After working for a number of large, successful multinational companies in many different countries for 23 years and rising to the rank of managing director, he made the decision to return to his home country of Egypt. His return was based on two pillars: (1) family and (2) a sense of responsibility to his country with a focus on two areas: social responsibility through engaging in charity activities and politics through joining a political party in order to contribute to a revamped Egypt. Now working in his family business, Hossam says, "It is not without its struggles, but I am enjoying every second and have no regrets. My country is going through turbulent times, and it is important for me to be here and to try to contribute something back. Along with my family, this is what is most important in my life." Like Hossam, if you can be clear about your goal and your belief, and if your focused will is strong enough, you can achieve far more than you expected.

On December 17, 2012, a paralyzed woman named Jan Scheuermann made global headlines when she managed to feed herself chocolate using a robotic arm that she controlled via electrodes implanted in her brain. Fifty-two-year-old Jan, who had been diagnosed with a degenerative brain disorder in 1999, was inspired when she saw a film of a quadriplegic man using a similar device. Following this disruption, she said, "My first reaction was, 'Wow, it's so neat he can do that,' and my second reaction was, 'Wow, I wish I could do something like that.'" To achieve the task, Jan went through an intense training period, applying herself for four hours a day three days a week over ten months. The training focused on practicing a number of different skills, including gripping and moving small objects and stacking cones. Using the world's most advanced prosthetic arm and hand, Jan has been able to operate the technology using her mind with a level of fluidity, control, and expertise that has amazed experts.[8]

Take a moment to just think about what Jan has achieved. She has learned to move a robotic arm through the power of her mind. It's amazing. Her achievement sounds like something from a futuristic Hollywood film. Her brain controls a robotic arm, and through the intensity of her focus and repeated practice, she can make it move as she wishes. Doesn't this make you wonder about exactly what's possible?

On April 30, 2010, Philippa Plasited, a mother of two, underwent further surgery after a mastectomy at Lister Hospital, London. She trusted psychotherapist and hypnotherapist Charles Montagu to put her into a hypnotic state. After the surgical procedure, which was performed without the use of anesthetic, Philippa said, "The whole experience was tranquil. Although I was aware of what was going on, I had no fear or pain." Explained Montagu, "Pain has a purpose. It is there to tell us something needs attention. But sometimes it is not useful. What you can do with hypnosis is talk to the subconscious and explain pain is not required."[9]

These people are not superheroes; they are not more or less intelligent than most people; they do not claim to possess psychic capabilities—and yet they've been able to achieve feats that are normally reserved for fictional characters. Imagine for a moment what could be possible in terms of the power of your mind. Advances in science and neuroscience are revolutionizing our understanding of the power of what's possible in terms of our attention and focus.

Hypnosis was used to deal with pain during surgery long before anesthetics were available. Indeed, back in 1842, Dr. James Braid, a skilled and highly respected surgeon, was an important and influential pioneer of hypnotism and hypnotherapy.[10] Today, in many hospitals throughout the world, hypnosis is being used once more to manage pain. According to Dr. John Butler, another hypnotist, "Pain is a subjective thing. The body can still experience the signals of pain, but reinterpret them not as being painful but as pressure or touch. There is evidence that hypnosis can block the signals in the brain to the point where the pain is hardly noticeable."[11] The placebo effect is another example of the remarkable power of your brain. Numerous studies have shown that placebo effects can arise as a result of a conscious belief of some sort as well as from subconscious associations.

Eutimo Perez was a patient in a placebo group who underwent "fake" knee surgery for osteoarthritis and did not discover this until a couple of years later. "It's a mental thing," he said. "I think that if you believe in something, you can get well....I can dance, I can go away fishing, I can play basketball and it doesn't bother me one bit. Everything is wonderful."[12] Recent studies have shown that the placebo effect can work even when the people involved know that they are taking a placebo![13]

How can you harness the power of your own mind to help yourself succeed in achieving what you desire? How can you use your physiology and psychology in unison for your own benefit? And how can you use your own power of focus to help achieve your goal?

Strengthening Desire Through Pain, Gain, and Focus

William James wrote that whether we choose to believe or not to believe, or wait to believe, we choose our own peril, our own fate. The concept of choice is at the very heart of this book. We have the ability to choose where we put our focus. Is the universe basically hostile or basically friendly? Einstein believed that this is the most fundamental question you can ask yourself because it will determine how you view the world and therefore how you are in the world. Your brain will follow your attention (see Figure 2-2). If you give your attention to the perceived pain of the negative, the threats you notice in your environment, and the ways in which things can go wrong, you will put yourself into an anxious state that makes it harder for you to achieve your goal. If you focus on the gain, on the opportunity, and on the potential reward or benefit, then you put yourself into a more positive state and are more likely to help yourself achieve your goal. Similarly, when organizations undergo change, stress and fear can spread through the workforce as its members focus on the pain. The role of the leader is to manage his or her own anxiety and then help others to find the gain in the pain, as discussed further in Part II.

When Annie Tobias was heading up global learning and leadership development at Deloitte Touche Tohmatsu some years ago, she had a meeting with the firm's global CEO, Jim Quigley, to seek his endorsement for and active participation in a leadership program. Annie recalls,

> I remember walking into the large boardroom connected to Jim's office. There was an enormous board table occupying most of the room, and I placed myself midway down the table. Jim's chief of staff came in first and sat down beside me. "Jim will never go for this," he

Figure 2-2 Focus Your Brain

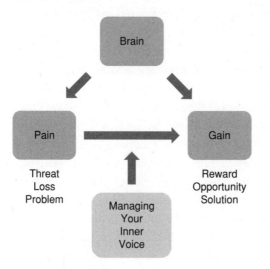

Source: Goldsworthy, 2011 adapted from Rock

commented, based on his familiarity with the requests funneling up to the CEO and based on Jim's time constraints.

It was a disruptive moment where, my mind racing, I mentally fought to avoid being derailed by the comment.

Jim Quigley came into the boardroom and placed himself directly opposite me on the other side of the table. I couldn't even reach across the span of that board table to shake his hand—that's how far away I was from the man I needed to engage. I remembered the words of my coach, Gifford, with whom I had dined the night before. He had told me, "Annie, remember to close the gap between you and the audience to create a connection, to make an impact." So, focusing on my goal, I stood up and walked around the table saying, "Jim, I hope you don't mind if I sit beside you. This table is too big." Not only did I physically close the gap, but I was now also able to engage with close eye contact. I ran him through my pitch, and at the end he said, "Wow, you are really passionate about this stuff. Count me in." He then looked across to his chief of staff sitting opposite us both and said, "Tom, this is a go." I looked at the chief of staff and he smiled at me, shaking his head in disbelief. I learned once more the power of staying focused on the goal and, in the moment, making a conscious choice to choose the gain over the pain.

Actors have a great deal to teach us about the ability to manage mental, physical, and emotional states. Peter Meyers, a director, author, and actor, has been training business people in communication, public speaking, and the practice of managing your state for more than a decade. According to Meyers, your state speaks louder than your words. Your state is critical to your performance. It is about the way you feel and your condition, psychologically, physically, and emotionally.[14] Your state is affected by your focus, your beliefs, and your mind/body connection. The quickest way to shift your state is to be aware of your physicality, your breathing, and your body position. If you hold your body in a confident, calm position, it sends signals of calm confidence to the brain. Holding your body in high power poses for as little as two minutes stimulates higher levels of testosterone and lower levels of cortisol (a stress hormone) according to a study by Amy J. C. Cuddy, a professor at Harvard Business School.[15]

Only 30 minutes before he was due to negotiate an important deal with a customer, Martin, a senior procurement executive with a large multinational company, received a text message from his wife saying that their purchase of his dream house had fallen through. Although he was upset by the news, he was able to manage his state and his emotions, taking a number of deep breaths, focusing his mind on the task at hand, and connecting with the customer in an engaged and professional manner. Later, upon his return home, he reconnected with his disappointment and feelings of loss.

When you focus on something, you are using the thinking part of your brain, the prefrontal cortex, and this action by itself can reduce arousal of the habitual part of your brain, the limbic system.[16] To achieve your desire, it is important that you place your focus as frequently as possible on what it is you want to attain, and that you limit the amount of time your mind acts as a critic and looks toward doubt and fear.

During the 2012 Summer Olympics in London, U.S. athlete Manteo Mitchell was running in the heats of the 4 × 400-meter relay when he felt a pop in his left leg, followed by searing pain. At that point in time, Mitchell had a conscious choice—a decision to make—he could stop right then and there, ruining the U.S. team's chances for a medal, or he could continue in enormous pain. To him, there was only one option. "I was doing my job," Mitchell said. "But probably at 201 meters, I heard it and I felt it. I pretty much figured it was broken, because every step I took, it got more painful," he said. "But I was out there already. I just wanted to finish and do what I was called in to do." A few days before the race, Mitchell had slipped on the stairs in the athletes' village, but he hadn't thought much about it. His training had gone well, and he felt fine when he lined up to start the race. "Even though track is an individual sport, you've got three guys depending on you, the whole world watching you," Mitchell said. "You don't want to let anyone down." Mitchell finished his heat in a more-than-respectable 46.1 seconds, and the United States tied the Bahamas in the second heat at 2 minutes, 58.87 seconds—the fastest time ever run in the first round of the relay at the Olympics. A few hours later, doctors confirmed what Mitchell had suspected: he had run the last half-lap with a broken left fibula.

Mitchell credited something more than simple adrenaline for enabling him to complete his leg of the race. He focused his mind on the benefit in the pain and repeated a mantra over and over in his mind. "Faith, focus, finish. Faith, focus, finish. That's the only thing I could say to myself," he said. Thanks to Mitchell's heroic efforts in the heats, the U.S. team made it to the finals of the men's 4 × 400-meter relay, where it won the silver medal.[17]

If Mitchell had spent any time at all focusing on the pain in his leg, it is unlikely that he would have been able to complete his race. By focusing on his goal, he found the strength to achieve the seemingly impossible.

Here's an exercise that we use with groups to demonstrate the power of focus and attention. We ask for a volunteer, then we instruct that person to look around the room and notice everything that is green. We count down 10 seconds and then ask the person to close his eyes. We then ask him to tell us everything in the room that is red. It is amazing how this immediately stumps people, even when there is a person right in front of them wearing a red sweater. Because the volunteer has been instructed to look for green, green is what he sees, to the exclusion of most other colors. Attention actually changes the brain. When you focus on something intently, you connect up several brain regions, creating a larger circuit in which different circuits fire together synchronously. This invokes Hebb's Law, which states: "Cells that fire together, wire together."[18] The circuitry of your brain can be changed by the way you focus over a relatively short period of time.[19] The way you focus your brain affects your physical, mental, and emotional states, which, in turn, demonstrably affect your results.

Robin Elfving was appointed managing director in Chile for a large packaging multinational. Upon his arrival, he discovered that one of the company's major customers was very unhappy with the relationship and had been for some time. Some changes needed to be made to the contract, and during the discussions, the customer was abrasive and very demanding.

The first few meetings between Robin and the customer did not go well. However, during a leadership workshop, the concept of managing your own focus was demonstrated so strongly that Robin decided to give it a try. Robin shared this:

> On my return to Chile, I consciously decided that the situation with the customer needed to be sorted out once and for all. I planned the next meeting meticulously, so as not to be caught out by any small details. I also made sure that any peripheral problems were under control so as to create some goodwill in advance. I then arranged a meeting with the customer. In my mind, I was determined to come out with an agreement. I mentally rehearsed how things might go. My account manager, who had been unable to reach a solution with the customer, told me, "You will not succeed. You have no chance." At the meeting, whenever I heard impossible arguments or emotional outbursts, or when I was about to lose my temper, I simply repeated, "Focus, focus" to myself. I managed the meeting with sheer determination. The ingredients were the same as before; what was new was that I stayed focused on my desire to solve the situation. Of course, there was give and take, and we had to make some concessions, but I was determined to make it work. The meeting was a breakthrough, and we managed to settle the contractual issue once and for all. I learned the importance of staying focused on the end goal to achieve your desire and to ensure that you are not derailed in the process.

The power of where you put your focus is demonstrated beautifully by a story relating to the Paris-to-Dakar car rally. In the desert, there was one tree. Drivers would regularly hit the tree, even though it was in the middle of nowhere. This is testament to the fact that what we focus on is what we achieve. When training to drive in icy conditions, you are taught to look away from the object you are skidding toward. If you look directly at it, you will hit it. The key is to look at where you want to go; then your body will follow your mind and you will steer away from the object. The voice in your head has more power than you may realize.

In his groundbreaking book *The Biology of Belief*, Dr. Bruce Lipton calls the brain "the source of the central voice." He writes about the subconscious mind and the conscious mind, with the subconscious part being a million times more powerful than the conscious part. The subconscious is "habitual"; it runs only the programs or patterns that have been loaded and repeated time after time. Lipton cites research indicating that 95 percent of our daily activities are controlled by the subconscious mind. In neuroscience terms, this is the work of the basal ganglia, that part of the brain that works primarily on autopilot. Our subconscious programs are a combination of those delivered to us through evolution (instincts), personality (traits), and patterns (learned through life experience). The conscious mind resides in our prefrontal cortex, which is termed our working memory. It can be creative, it watches and notices what the body is doing, and it has the ability to override the read-only subconscious programs and intervene in our thoughts, feelings, and actions.[20]

Sometimes referred to as your mind's eye, your focus relates to where you direct your attention and thus your energy. When you are able to talk to yourself with a positive, supportive voice, you increase your chances of success. This is a critical aspect of maintaining desire and motivation during periods of significant business change. When you talk to yourself with a negative voice, you can actually increase your chances of failure. If your brain focuses on stressful or negative thoughts, your body reacts as though it really is dealing with a stressful situation. Dr. Craig Hassed, the author of *Know Thyself: The Stress Release Programme*, writes, "Imagination, rumination, anticipation, exaggeration and dreaming—all can activate the fight/flight response."[21]

Taming Your Inner Critic

We all have an inner critic, a voice that tells us what may go wrong or what is not possible. If you are asking yourself, "What voice is that?," it is exactly that voice. To complete the process of defining and owning your desire for change, you'll need to confront your inner critic, that mental voice that raises doubts about your ability to achieve your goal by reminding you how you have failed in the past or how unlikely it is that you will succeed. The inner critic tends to speak in three distinct types of voices, as found by Otto Scharmer:

- The voice of judgment that limits your openness to possibilities and ideas (downloading instead of inquiring)
- The voice of cynicism that limits your ability to connect to others (disconnecting instead of relating)
- The voice of fear that limits your ability to move ahead (holding on to the past or the present instead of letting go)[22]

You can probably recall times when these voices came into your mind. In an interview for this book, Richard, a senior executive, shared his experience with his inner critic. After a new CEO was appointed from outside the company, a number of senior executives had been asked to leave. Even though he had received positive feedback, Richard had a limiting belief that he would not be credible with the new CEO, as he felt he was not good enough or quick enough in handling data. His inner voice of fear created unnecessary anxiety as he worried that his perceived shortcoming would be exposed in an important meeting. Stressed by these unhelpful feelings, he sought out a coach and worked on letting go of the negative script in his head and focusing instead on the positive inputs around him. Eighteen months later, he is still at the company and has been given increased responsibilities.

Marshall Rosenberg, a psychologist and the creator of the nonviolent communication process, talks about the concept of using the language of a jackal or a giraffe. A jackal crawls close to the ground; its voice comes from the head and is judgmental, dividing the world into black and white, right and wrong, good and bad. If the jackal's ears point outward, then you tend to judge others. If the jackal's ears point inward, then you are judging yourself. Instead of thinking and speaking from the place of the jackal, Rosenberg recommends that you think and speak from the place of the giraffe. With the largest heart in the animal kingdom, the giraffe is tall enough to look into the future, and it lives its life with gentility and strength. Likewise, the giraffe bids you to speak from the heart, to talk about what is going on without judging others or yourself. Giraffe is a language of requests; jackal is a language of demands. Stating a request in simple giraffe is a four-part process rooted in honesty: (1) describe your observation, (2) identify your feeling, (3) explain the reason for your feeling in terms of your needs, and (4) state your request.[23] This process is valuable whether you are speaking to yourself or speaking to others. According to Tim Gallwey, author of *The Inner Game of Golf*, your performance equals your potential minus your self-interference (P=p-i), so working on taming your inner critic is vital to your results.

Inner Critic Exercise

Identifying the voice of your inner critic, naming the emotion, and then separating and isolating the thought that comes from the critic is a way of managing negative thinking. By labeling your negative emotions in a few words, ideally using symbolic language, you can actually reduce the intensity of those emotions.[24]

In clarifying your goals and your wants, you can tame your inner critic by picking a character from fiction who represents or embodies evil for you.

Executives we have worked with have chosen characters such as Darth Vader, Cruella De Vil, and Shere Khan, to name but a few. Then, whenever that negative voice starts judging, being cynical, or speaking from a place of fear, you stop and imagine that it is the negative character speaking. This gives you the opportunity to distance yourself from the voice and to reflect, smile, and discard the negative thought rather than be distracted or demotivated by it. Practice this negative thought management technique for yourself and see how it can liberate you.

Linda, a manager in a large educational establishment, struggles with self-confidence. Under stress, her inner critic can make her life extremely difficult by repeatedly telling her that she is not good enough or smart enough to be taken seriously. By working with a coach, Linda realized that the critical voice playing in her head came from her childhood. To manage the voice, she called it "Little Linda," and she made a decision to send Little Linda to Disneyland. Every time the voice arose, she told herself, "Little Linda, you're in Disneyland enjoying yourself. I don't need you here anymore."

Using visualization is another way to tame your inner critic and enable you to focus on your real desire.

Visualize Your Success

Visualization is a powerful technique that can help you achieve your goals. While it is used by athletes and actors, visualization is still relatively uncommon in the business world, although more and more executives are discovering its benefits. So what do we mean by visualization? Basically, it is the process of creating a mental picture of what you want to achieve. Visualization works best when you use as many of the senses as possible. The more you repeat the visualization, the more you can train your mind and body to perform in the way you have imagined.

Early Russian studies of visualization indicated that those athletes who spent 25 percent of their time engaged in physical training and 75 percent of their time mentally training had greater success than those who used only physical training. For visualization to be effective, it must be as detailed as possible, focusing on what you see, hear, feel, think, and even smell, and it must be as frequent as possible.[25]

Top soccer player Didier Drogba shares how he mentally rehearses goal scoring. "I actually think about the way I am going to score my goal," he said. "I close my eyes and try to imagine it and sometimes it doesn't happen. But most of the time when you get it in your head that you are going to score a certain kind of goal, it happens. It's funny, but you create something in your head, a desire to score, an attitude, and everything can go like this in the game."[26] His view is reinforced by former top Italian player and soccer club manager Gianfranco Zola, who has been quoted as saying, "The success I have from free-kicks is 5% skill and 95% successful imagery."[27]

A visualization study on basketball was undertaken at the University of Chicago with people split into three groups. The people in each group were tested to see how many free throws they could make through a basketball hoop. Then those in the first group practiced free throws every day for an hour, those in the second group were told to visualize making free throws, and those in the third group were given no instructions and did nothing. After 30 days, the people were tested again. Unsurprisingly, those in the third group had not improved at all. However, while those in the first group, which had actually practiced, improved 24 percent, those in the second group, which had used visualization techniques, actually improved by 23 percent. "Not only does a visualized experience condition the human brain," says Dr. Judd Blaslotto, sports psychologist, world-class power lifter, and author of a number of books on mind control, "but it will also program the human body."[28]

When you use visualization techniques, you build new neural pathways in your brain; this makes whatever act you are visualizing easier to perform. The more you repeat the visualization, the more your brain becomes wired to act in a certain way, and the action can become second nature. According to chef and TV personality Gordon Ramsay, "Every chef uses visualization. You have to visualize what you're going to put on the plate before you do it. I visualize the completed thing, then work back mentally, thinking and visualizing textures and contrasts... I cook from noon to 3 p.m. and from 7 to 11 p.m., and it's usually then at the height of things, that I visualize and create the best dish."[29]

According to psychologist Steve Bull, author of *The Game Plan: Your Guide to Mental Toughness at Work*, "We all engage in visualization and self-talk. They are everyday habits. The challenge is making them work for you, rather than against you. Visualization and self-talk must be used in a facilitative rather than debilitative manner. Rather than focus on what might go wrong, it is critical to focus on a successful outcome." Nasser Hussain, the former cricket captain of England, refers to the visualization techniques taught by Steve Bull and says, "Remembering a good inning, or even just a very good shot you've played, just before you go out to bat helps you to focus the mind and get rid of nerves."[30]

Andrew, a senior HR executive, set himself a goal of reducing his anxiety concerning his feelings of conflict avoidance that arise when he has to have difficult conversations. He used visualization techniques to prepare himself for sensitive meetings with employees who might be in an anxious state because of some perceived loss of status. Says Andrew, "I picture myself in the room with the employee. I am feeling calm and compassionate. I try to create a sense of containment in discussing sensitive information in an empathetic way." By visualizing these types of situations over and over, Andrew found that he was able to reduce his own anxiety and manage these meetings in a much more supportive and productive manner.

The next time you have an important presentation, business meeting, or critical dialogue, why not spend some time visualizing the event to see if this method can help you, too, in supporting a positive outcome?

Stepping Out of Comfort Zones

In order to sustain a goal focus, you will inevitably need to leave your comfort zone. This zone is a state in which you perform at a steady level with a feeling of safety and without the anxiety created by taking risks. When you are in your comfort zone, it is likely that you apply behaviors you have used many times before. In order to achieve your desire, you will need to step out of your comfort zone and into a certain amount of anxiety. Anxiety can play a role in keeping you focused. A level of anxiety can be like the lubricant in a car—it helps the machine work. Robert H. Rosen talks about having "just enough anxiety." If you have too little anxiety, you may have ineffective energy. If you have too much anxiety, it produces chaotic energy, and, over a prolonged period, it can lead to physiological and neurological wear and tear known as "allostatic load." With just enough anxiety, you are harnessing productive energy.[31]

It takes courage to step out of your comfort zone. But it is entirely necessary if you wish to stretch, challenge, and grow yourself. It is about taking a risk—a risk of failing, but also a risk of succeeding. In the words of the late Steve Jobs, "Remembering that you are going to die is the best way I know to avoid the trap of thinking you have something to lose. You are already naked. There is no reason not to follow your heart."[32] Obviously this does not mean taking life-threatening risks, but this insight shows us how those daily "step out of your comfort zone and go for it" risks help you to embrace, expand, and enjoy your life.

After stepping out of a successful career in corporate banking, Sonia followed her desire and set herself the goal of pursuing a career in coaching and leadership development. In order to build her new business, she had to force herself to approach people in a way that was entirely new to her, without the backing of a large company or an impressive title. Overcoming her initial reluctance, she forced herself to list some daily actions she needed to take, including reaching out to new contacts to create connections, share ideas, and potentially get new business. Although the initial response was slow, the time that Sonia invested led to her involvement in an international network, resulting in some significant business and, most important, increasing her confidence in her own ability to succeed.

While it is far easier to stay "safe" in your comfort zone, this also keeps you trapped in your own limitations. Every day, take a small risk by doing something that you would normally prefer not to do or would procrastinate on. By taking action, you empower yourself. With each step you take, you expand both your experience and your confidence. Stretching your comfort zones becomes easier, even if you may still have some residual anxiety or fear. As long as you are taking regular, small risks that take you into a space of "unease," you enhance your feelings of competence and self-worth and move to a place of power.[33] So, take a moment right now to decide what small stretch you can take that will move you one step closer to your goal.

The Use of Symbols

Symbols can play a powerful role in supporting the achievement of your desire. When you create a symbolic object, it becomes a visual reminder of your goal. The brain thinks in visual images. If we ask you to close your eyes and think of a horse, what you see is a horse, not the word *horse*. Therefore, associating the achievement of your goal with a visual image or symbol can provide a powerful external reminder. The Olympic rings are a powerful symbol that many athletes use not only to motivate them to make the Olympic Games but also to symbolize their achievement in representing their country at the event, providing them with motivation to continue to achieve. Participants often wear an Olympic ring, and in recent years, many athletes have had the image of the Olympic rings tattooed on their upper torso.

One symbol that is in widespread use in Japan is the Daruma doll. Made of papier-mâché and frequently red in color, it always pops back to an upright position when it is knocked down, making it a symbol of optimism, good fortune, and determination. The dolls come with blank eyes. Once you have decided upon your goal, you color in one eye. The Daruma then sits wherever you place it, watching you with one eye to keep your focus on attaining your goal. When you achieve your goal, you then color in the second eye.

Logistics executive Martine Kok handed out Daruma dolls to four close business associates with whom she had undertaken a leadership journey and kept one for herself. They each colored in one eye when they had set their goals and then placed the dolls on their desks. When they met one year later, three of the five had already colored in the second eye, indicating that they had completed their goal. The other two expected to reach their targets within the next six months. Another international executive, Brian, who uses a Daruma doll for goal completion, not only places it on his desk at home, but has also taken a photo of it and has it as his wallpaper on his phone. Then, no matter where he travels, his goal symbol goes with him and reminds him of the actions he needs to take.

Help yourself to stay focused on your goal by associating it with a symbol that you keep visible to remind you of your target.

Your Goals Need STAMINA

In order to increase your chances of success, it is important that you frame your desire and make sure that your goal has STAMINA—that is, that it is specific, time-stamped, achievable, measurable, inspiring, narratable, and actionable. To maximize your chance of success, your goal needs to be specific and as descriptive and detailed as possible. It must be time-stamped; you need to be clear about the time frame within which you want to achieve the goal. It must be achievable—it can certainly be a stretch goal, but it should also be feasible. You need to make it measurable, meaning that you know the stages and milestones along the way (and take time out to celebrate the quick wins). It has to be inspiring; it is important that you gain energy just by thinking about your goal. In the words of Richard Olivier, "You can't hope to inspire others if you can't inspire yourself." Make it narratable: what is the story that you can tell yourself and others in relation to the goal? We all remember stories. Building one that you tell yourself concerning your desire will help you to stay focused. It must be actionable: our goals are achieved through the small daily steps we take, so ask yourself every day, "What can I do today to work on my goal?" Using the elements of STAMINA, you may want to go back and revise the vision statement you wrote earlier for the Beliefs House exercise.

Jason viewed himself as an anxious presenter. After critical feedback from his boss, he decided that he wanted to change his own mindset concerning his ability to present. While he had a reasonable level of presentation skills, his nerves often got the better of him, and he would lose confidence, particularly during question-and-answer sessions. Jason set himself a goal of improving his presentation ability over a 12-month period. He worked with a coach, his boss, and two colleagues to identify the areas where he needed to improve and then to focus his practice, using visualization and rehearsals and adjusting over time based on feedback. He also set himself a number of milestones to achieve along the way. One year after he started, and numerous presentations later, Jason reached his goal: he delivered a presentation at his company's annual conference and felt fully confident throughout, describing himself as being "in the zone." His talk was highly rated, as evaluated by the participants. He has now changed his own view of his ability and carries that confidence forward, incorporated into his learning and his skill set.

Another important factor is to frame your desire in the present tense, as opposed to the future. The brain does not have to respond to the future thought, "I will be x, y, z." Framing the goal in the present as "I am x, y, z" means that your brain is more likely to act in concert with the belief. Writing down your goal is also an important action. When you write down your goal, it becomes a visual image for your brain. It is also helpful in reaffirming your goal. When you write something down, it is more likely that you will be able to recall it. It is reported that Richard Branson carries a notepad with him at all times so that he can jot down thoughts, ideas, and feedback as well as capture his goals and experiences on paper.[34] Many business executives also use the notes function on their phones to record their goals succinctly and clearly.

So, you have made a conscious choice. You know what it is that you desire. You have a clear goal that you believe in, and you have visualized your success. The next step is for you to apply the *discipline* required to achieve that goal.

Key Points to Remember

- Use the power of belief to help you achieve your goals. Understand your limiting beliefs so that you can work on addressing them.
- Learn to disassociate from your inner critic; embody the voice in a fictional character and focus on what you want to achieve as opposed to what you want to avoid.
- Practice using visualization techniques, making them frequent, as detailed as possible, and using all five senses.
- Take small daily steps outside your comfort zone and enjoy the feeling of the stretch.
- Use symbols to remind you of your desire; place them where you will see them regularly.
- Make sure your goals have STAMINA; they must be specific, time-stamped, achievable, measurable, inspiring, narratable, and actionable.

CHAPTER THREE

Discipline

What Are Your Small Steps to Big Success?

We are what we repeatedly do. Excellence, then, is not an act, but a habit.

—Aristotle

Dᴉsᴄɪᴘʟɪɴᴇ ᴄᴀɴ ʙᴇ one of our toughest challenges in achieving any goal. Our desire may be clear, but applying the necessary discipline takes energy, focus, and considerable effort. Many of us start an initiative but stop when we find it too difficult to sustain the effort. This is the reason why fad diets and quick-fix pills make so much money. However, there's a different path—a harder one—that is defined by the reality that the more you do some-thing, the more you practice, the better you get. This applies to all types of practice, from exercising to golf to managing change at work.

We each have the same amount of time in every day. It is how we choose to use that time that determines whether we can improve and grow or whether we fail. There is a story that the famous violinist Itzhak Perlman was approached by a fan after a concert one evening. The fan gushed to Perlman, "Your playing was wonderful. I would give my life to play as beautifully as you do." To which Perlman responded, "I did. I gave my life. That's why I am so good." You may not become Perlman-like in whatever your profession may be, but without discipline, you'll never know how good you can be.

Shortcuts are easier and more tempting than sustained, applied effort. The definition of *discipline* is "training or conditions imposed for the improvement of physical powers, self-control."[1] When change is involved, the essence of discipline lies in asking yourself the question: what can I commit to do on a daily basis to achieve my goals? In this chapter, we look at several approaches that will help you build up the discipline you need if you are to achieve your change goals, including one daily action that, if carried out, can make a signif-icant difference. Discipline involves a number of aspects, including habitual

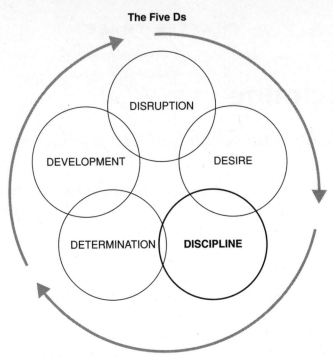

The Five Ds

Source: Goldsworthy

behavior, developing willpower, looking after your mind and body, and practicing mindfulness. We'll first discuss the importance of making small steps—of changing your behavior incrementally and repetitively.

Leading and Living Change: Pierre Deplanck

French executive Pierre Deplanck has lived in Asia for 20 years. Formerly the CEO of Guardian Health and Beauty, Singapore, Deplanck moved to the Philippines in 2013 to take up the role of chief operating officer in a joint venture between Dairy Farm and Rustan's Supercenters Inc. (RSCI). Pierre's use of the disciplinary skills he learned in the French Army has helped him to achieve success in business and in his leadership journey.

> *In the retail industry, we often say: "Retail is detail." It is true, and for the past 22 years, I have been practicing it. However, by looking only at the details, I have sometimes lost the big picture. I spent seven years in China, and the best piece of advice I got from the people working with me was a Chinese saying, "Yi bu, yi bu," which translates as "step by step," one thing at a time. Simply said, it means to focus. I have a tendency to chase too many things at one time, and*

therefore I do not get the results I expect. This style affects the people around me who are exhausted or just confused by not knowing what they should focus on. It has an impact on our results as well when resources are spread too thin across too many projects. It has an impact on me, as I get frustrated when I do not see progress as fast as I expected it or, even when I see it, when I did not set the priorities well enough. Although I keep catching myself wanting to do more, now that I am aware of it, I have made some progress. Focusing on a few key projects or key people has given me better results. I do not totally forget the new ideas I may have; I just schedule them over a period of time.

Discipline has helped me to keep learning. I believe the capacity to learn is a key attribute of a good leader. The world is changing, and the speed of change is accelerating year after year. We need to "learn, delearn, and relearn." What was true a few years ago might not apply anymore. In the 1990s, retailers used to put the most sellable items at the end or the back of the store so that shoppers had to cross the whole store in the hope that they might buy something they had not planned to purchase. In those days, the concentration of retailers was not what it is today. Now, shoppers have so many choices that retailers have to deliver what customers want and do it as fast as possible.

As to my own leadership journey, I continue to focus on developing my cognitive empathy. Becoming more aware of and attentive to people's emotions and listening more has helped me a lot. I am also working on increasing my mindfulness. I have made good progress on staying calm and intervening in my own amygdala hijacks. When I feel one coming, I breathe deeply, place my hand on my stomach, and wait until I sense the calm returning. Then, and only then, do I respond. Applying discipline with regard to diary management has been another successful tool—making time to prepare and follow up, and scheduling two hours weekly for strategic reflections. My personal assistant ensures that we schedule no more than five meetings a day. I am conscious that my progress in these areas requires daily application and focus. Viewing leadership as a journey rather than a destination has liberated me to embrace and enjoy the daily steps.

Taking Small Steps to Success

Learning the discipline required to make change work for you is first about taking small steps. Indeed, research by Elliot Berkman shows that a person has more success in achieving a goal when it is broken down into small steps.[2] If you decided to run your first marathon, you would be unlikely to sign up and participate the next day, and you would be somewhat unwise if you did so.

You would plan at least eight to nine months in advance and then start small, perhaps with a one-kilometer or two-kilometer run. Then you would build up gradually, increasing your mileage week by week, and also allowing time for rest and recovery. And so it is with achieving any desire. You know what you want, but it is not going to happen overnight. If it were that easy, you would already be doing it.

Every day, you have the opportunity to do something that brings you closer to your goal. It can be small steps—*yi bu, yi bu*, as in Pierre's story. These small daily steps build day after day, week after week, month after month, until they become habits. The effect is like a snowball: Once you get it rolling and keep it rolling, the momentum reinforces the forward movement. A body that is at rest tends to stay at rest, and a body that is in motion tends to stay in motion. That's why you need discipline to fight the inertia that is so inviting when you face a major change. Developing momentum is a critical aspect of successful change at both the individual and the organizational levels. And every small win that you achieve builds up your confidence that greater goals are reachable.

When Susan climbed Kilimanjaro with family and friends in August 2013 in honor of their friend's 50th birthday, the guides were experts in turning the group's minds away from the enormity and complexity of the challenge and on to the next immediate step. With the top of Mount Kilimanjaro in the far distance, looming above the clouds, Ake Lindstrom, the summit leader from Adventure International, focused everyone on the walking to be done in the next few hours. When people asked him "How much farther?" he would respond, "You are getting closer with every step." Pole, pole (meaning slowly, slowly in Swahili), step by step, minute by minute, hour by hour, and day by day the team trekked closer to their goal. Through this process, they were able to reach the top and celebrate both the mental and physical achievement.

So, take a moment to be in the present and think, "What can I do today to move closer to my goal? What small step can I take?" We all fully accept that if we train our bodies, they get fitter and perform better. Why not apply that same logic to our minds? Advances in neuroscience demonstrate that if we learn better ways to train our brains, we can radically improve our mental performance, too.

Many people are familiar with the research by Anders Ericsson, Michael Prietula, and Edward Cokely, cited in Malcolm Gladwell's book *Outliers*, showing that there are three elements to becoming an expert. The first is to practice (the famous 10,000-hour figure), the second is to do deliberate practice (continuing to learn and grow in areas that you don't yet know), and the third is to have a coach, mentor, or third party who gives you feedback.[3] Now, there is no need to panic over the thought of the 10,000 hours. That is the number required to become an expert. A different way to frame this is to say that every hour you practice will help you to improve, step by step. Instead of viewing your performance as good or bad, think about it in terms of improvement. In the words of Aidan, one of our interviewees, "As you broaden yourself, you learn to be a little less digital, a little less black and white."

Tony Dungy, Super Bowl–winning head coach of the Indianapolis Colts and now a commentator for the NFL Network, once said, "Champions don't do extraordinary things. They do ordinary things, but they do them without thinking, too fast for the other team to react. They follow the habits they've learned."[4]

As mentioned in Chapter 1, habits involve a three-step process: cue, routine, and reward. The cue creates a craving that is met by the routine, which then releases the reward. The trick to altering habits is to maintain the cue and the reward, but to change the routine.[5] This approach has been confirmed by study after study and forms the basis for many programs in which changing habits is necessary, such as Weight Watchers and Alcoholics Anonymous.

Redoing routines is now recognized as an effective treatment for people with obsessive-compulsive disorder (OCD). Author, research psychiatrist, and OCD specialist Jeffrey Schwartz shares a four-step process to help you let go of unwanted habits and replace them with healthier ones. The first step is to relabel: to identify the unhelpful brain messages and accompanying uncomfortable sensations and call them what they really are. The second step is to reframe: to change the way you view the thoughts, urges, or impulses by recognizing that they are false messages from your brain. They are not you; they are just your brain responding habitually. The third step is to refocus: to direct your attention away from the unhelpful and false messages, thoughts, or sensations and replace them with more productive and positively supportive messages. Finally, the fourth step is to revalue: to clearly see the unhelpful, deceptive messages as just that and to let go of any value or worth that you have attached to them. Methods of refocusing include participating in a substitute, healthier activity, using your breathing to self-regulate, or practicing mindfulness.[6]

If you train yourself to implement different routines, you will see a gradual and sustained change result. An important part of change is understanding that patience and practice are required to become skilled at anything in life. Whatever your goal, you can achieve it if you are willing to go through the sometimes tedious and painful process of applying daily discipline. Research by

NASA shows that it takes between 21 and 46 days for astronauts to rewire the neurological pathways in their brains to adapt to a zero-gravity atmosphere and relearn basic tasks like brushing their teeth and eating. Maxwell Maltz, the plastic surgeon who discovered the cybernetic mechanism, conducted extensive studies on why brain circuits take what he called "engrams" (memory traces) and produce neuropathways when they are bombarded for 21 days in a row.[7]

This means that when you repeat something over and over, and do this, it would seem, for at least 21 days, you can potentially replace an old habit with a new one. The more you can create rituals that make your actions into routines, the greater your chance of success. Turn those things that you do every day, no matter what, into nonnegotiable actions. One way to help yourself is to apply your new ritual alongside an existing one, as you are then leveraging your existing routines.

The Stages of Competence

Insight into the stages of competence[8] (see Figure 3-1) will help you navigate major transitions, both at an individual level and at team and organizational levels as well. As you develop discipline for new behaviors, you may experience frustration with your own pace of learning. You may wonder whether you will ever succeed.

Figure 3-1   Stages of Competence

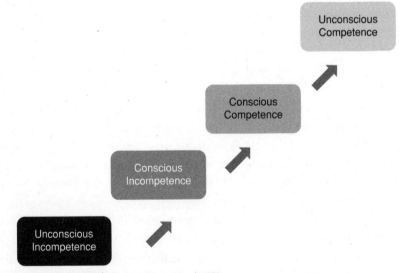

Source: Noel Burch, Gordon Training International, 1970s

Understanding the stages of competence can help you see that everyone experiences stalls and setbacks, as well as progress, because of the nature of our brains. There are four stages. The first is *unconscious incompetence*; this is when you are unskilled or untested at something and are blissfully unaware of your inability. If you have no consciousness of your incompetence, there can be no improvement. You then try the activity, and you become *consciously incompetent*: Now you know that you aren't good at it. This stage creates discomfort in the brain and evokes one of two responses as you realize that you are unskilled: Either you never try it again or you practice, practice, practice.

If you follow the latter path, eventually you become *consciously competent*: You know you can do it, but you have to think about it. After significantly more practice, you eventually become *unconsciously competent*: You can perform the activity without consciously thinking about it. Remember what happened when you learned to drive a car. Before you ever tried, you assumed you would be able to do it. Then you started driving and, after stalling the engine or needing to reverse on several occasions, you realized that you lacked the necessary skills. So you practiced and took lessons, and you improved. However, you still had to concentrate when you were looking in the mirror and changing gears. Finally, after many hours, you drove home from work and could not even remember the details of the journey. You could then drive with a minimum of mindful brain energy. So it is entirely possible to become better at anything you choose, if you are willing to put in the practice and get feedback. However, it is necessary to apply willpower.

Exercising Willpower

To keep yourself focused and moving through the stages of competence requires willpower. From his research, Professor Roy Baumeister observed that willpower is like a muscle: It can become tired from overuse, resulting in ego depletion, but it can also be strengthened through exercise. An effective way of handling temptation is to avoid situations in which you have to exercise restraint. By using self-control to plan habits and routines that support your goals, you can reduce stress and the need to apply willpower. This helps to set you up for success.[9] This is another reason that it is important that you set yourself small, daily steps toward achieving your ultimate goal. Go for achievable chunks of application and build in breaks and small rewards (a cup of tea or coffee) along the way. The lasting technique for conserving willpower is creating habits. When you repeat something over and over, it becomes a routine to the point where it eventually happens automatically.

For example, Martin, an introvert by nature, found himself in a leadership role that required him to approach people he did not know well and speak to them. To practice his ability to connect, every day he would make a point of talking with people he did not know in a more direct and caring manner, using eye contact and, where appropriate, the person's name. He ensured that he greeted the receptionists by name every day. When he traveled, he practiced conversing with the airport staff in an interested and engaged way. While this felt very strange at first, over time Martin became much more comfortable in his interpersonal relationships, leading to an increased ability to inspire those around him.

Another option is to use the "if/then" technique to help you manage your brain and make dealing with temptation easier. The if/then technique is simply a script you can run in your head that says, "If I am doing this (undesired behavior), then I will do that (desired behavior) instead." "Set up cues that prompt your planned behavior," observes Professor Mark Conner of the University of Leeds. "For instance, 'If I feel hungry before lunch then I will eat an apple, not a chocolate bar.' Conserving willpower in this way also means you'll have more left over for other things."[10]

In the late 1960s, Walter Mischel conducted the renowned marshmallow tests with young children and showed that their ability to delay gratification by waiting to eat a marshmallow when they were left alone in a room, based on the promise that they would receive a second marshmallow later, correlated strongly with their success later in life in a number of areas, including higher SAT scores, better social skills, and less substance abuse.[11] Willpower is the key to your success, and you have the power to work on your own ability and improve it through practice.

Sister Madonna Buder, known as the Iron Nun, is a wonderful example of applying discipline to achieve a goal. She started running in 1978 at the age of 48 at the behest of Father John Topel, who told her what a joyful release it was to harmonize mind, body, and soul. He also told her that the benefits of running included helping to diminish depression, diabetes, addictions, and stress, and that it could increase concentration. "Nothing could be that good," responded Sister Madonna. "I have been active all my life, but I can't just go out there and run for no reason. I need a goal." "In that case, go out and run between those two eddies without getting wet," replied the priest, smiling and looking at the beach. It was April 1, 1978 when she took that first run on the beach. Sister Madonna completed her first triathlon at age 52 and her first Ironman event at age 55, and she has continued ever since. In August 2012, at 82 years of age, she became the first woman over 80 years old to reach the finish line of an Ironman triathlon when she completed the 2.4-mile swim, 112-mile cycle, and a full marathon in a time of 16:32:00 at the Ironman Canada in Penticon, British Columbia. Says Sister Madonna, "Honor the smallest steps—even the most insignificant action adds to the grand scheme of life."[12]

Ordinary people demonstrate extraordinary discipline every day. In 1995, Jean-Dominique Bauby, a French journalist and editor, suffered a massive heart attack, causing him to go into a coma for 20 days. When he awakened, he found that he had a very rare neurological disorder called locked-in syndrome, in which a paralyzed body houses a perfectly normally functioning brain. Jean-Dominique could move only his left eyelid. He wrote the book *The Diving Bell and the Butterfly* by blinking when the correct letter was spoken by a person who slowly recited the alphabet over and over again. Imagine it. Bauby had to compose the book entirely in his head, and convey it one letter at a time. A testament to phenomenal discipline and willpower, the book was published in France on March 7, 1997. Bauby died just three days after the publication of his book.[13]

Try the present self/future self exercise; it can assist you with being more disciplined by externalizing your important goals so that you acknowledge them consciously and pay attention to them. In the present, you write a message to your future self, saying what actions you have taken in the present to make life easier for yourself in the future. For example, you may leave yourself a note saying, "Dear Future Self, I am working on the presentation this week so that when you read this next week before the board meeting, you can feel confident about the work I have done to prepare you." University student Ian uses this technique: he leaves his future self a note by his bedside, along with a glass of water and an aspirin, to help himself recover from a hangover after a late night out.

Michael Watkins, bestselling author of *The First 90 Days*, suggests using structured reflection about any situation as a good way to maintain goal focus. Structured self-assessment can be designed in whatever way works best for you, whether it be taking notes, answering some key questions, or following a template.[14] In fact, creating a routine structure for your discipline, as Pierre did with his schedule in the opening story, can increase your willpower and your success.

Improving your willpower also delivers another important benefit: it has a positive impact on your heart-rate variability, which is the physiological phenomenon of variation in the time interval between heartbeats. Research studies have shown that people with higher heart-rate variability are better at ignoring distractions, are more able to delay gratification, and can deal more successfully with stressful situations. Applying willpower and focus not only helps you get the job done, but can also improve your general well-being.[15]

The Discipline of a Healthy Body and a Healthy Mind

The concept of discipline is central to the struggles we have had as a species since the beginning of time. We often sabotage ourselves and interfere with our own success. Way back in 1919, Dr. Frank Crane, a minister, speaker, and columnist, wrote a short essay, "The Body and the Automobile," that provides food for thought in today's world, where unhealthy food options and lifestyles are the stuff of convenience. Dr. Crane wrote,

> There's my automobile. I hire a chauffeur to take care of it . . . He is always washing it, polishing it, tightening a screw here and regulating a valve there, nosing around under the hood—even when we're riding he listens to its purr as a doctor listens to a man's heart.
>
> Why do I have this piece of machinery so looked after? Because I want to get all the use out of it there is in it.
>
> Well, if I were twenty-one I'd take as good care of my body as I do my automobile. And for the same reason: to get a hundred per cent efficiency and fun out of it. The body is the most important machine a man has, and certainly he's a fool to neglect it, as I've neglected mine, I'm sorry to say.
>
> I'd watch what I put into it, for one thing. I'd cut out eating as a form of diversion. . . .
>
> It's queer how a man goes along abusing his body, loading it up with waste, letting it get rusty and rattly. What if he did that with his two-thousand-dollar car? What if he left that out in the rain, and let the carburetor get dirty and the cylinders full of carbon and paid no attention to it generally? Wouldn't he be a fool?
>
> Well, he's fooler when he doesn't keep his body in order. For his body's more than a two-million-dollar machine, and has more to do with his happiness or misery than any contraption of steel and brass.
>
> Yes, sir; if I were young again I'd take as good care of my body as I do of my automobile.[16]

How many of us take as good care of our bodies as we do of our cars? Are you spending more time and attention on maintaining an inanimate object than on maintaining your own body? Are you aware of how much your brain influences your body and vice versa?

Diet, exercise, and sleep are the three key practices that deliver immediate improvement in the performance of your brain, thereby helping you to have more discipline during any type of change, be it personal or business. During organizational changes, it is easy for you to feel more stressed than usual, and therefore there is an even greater need for you to consciously manage the type of food you are eating, the amount of exercise you are doing, and the hours of sleep you are getting. To perform at your best, you need to be disciplined in these three basic areas.

Brain expert and teacher Terry Small talks to audiences around the world about the benefits of eating "brain-friendly" food to manage our stressful, 24/7 lifestyles. Terry shares the importance of optimizing health and managing stress by choosing what you eat. "Food has the power to heal the brain. Good nutrition can balance and support healthy brain chemistry, without drugs. The results can be felt within minutes," says Terry.

I have been telling people for years that what we consume directly influences our thoughts, feelings, and actions. Research shows that food can influence your mood, optimize brain function, provide the fuel for cellular renewal and protect your brain from free-radical damage. When stress becomes chronic, or unmitigated, it can damage your brain and impair memory. Prolonged stress will release surges of cortisol and adrenaline. Too much of these hormones is toxic to nerve cells in your hippocampus. The long-term consequences are not great. In the words of Hippocrates, "Let food be your medicine."[17]

What type of food can busy executives consume to help their brains? Apart from the obvious advice of eating a well-balanced diet with plenty of fresh vegetables and ensuring that you are drinking enough water so that your brain is not dehydrated, two simple foods can help you with energy and stress during the day: nuts (walnuts are particularly good for brain energy) and dried fruit (prunes are extremely high in antioxidants). To ensure healthy snacking, carry nuts and dried fruit with you for when you travel or for when you get hungry in the office.

We often hear stressed executives bemoaning the fact that they do not have time to exercise. Extensive research shows that people who exercise outperform those who do not on a series of brain activities, including long-term memory, reasoning, attention, and problem-solving tasks. Exercise increases your brain's resistance to stress and has been shown to reduce the risk of brain impairment, strokes, dementia, and Alzheimer's.[18] The key here is to reframe what you mean by the word *exercise*. Does this mean finding the time to go to a gym, or does it simply mean finding ways to choose exercise in everyday life? Office buildings have stairwells, as do airports. Using the stairs rather than the elevators or escalators is a surprisingly simple way of increasing your exercise on a daily basis. A Dutch research study found that if you burn the same number of calories, standing and walking over the course of a day is better than an hour of intense exercise when it comes to improving cholesterol levels and preventing diabetes.[19] When you have a choice to use your body, do so. Be aware of your choice point, that 0.2 seconds, and make simple daily exercise choices, such as taking the stairs, to boost your body and your mind.

Some managers view going without sleep to deliver business results as a necessary price to pay for success, and many make a point of bragging about their toughness. Make no mistake: Without sleep, you will lose mental and physical function and eventually do tremendous damage to your system. There is evidence indicating that lack of sleep has a negative impact on attention, executive function, working memory, mood, quantitative skills, logical reasoning, and even motor dexterity. Have you heard of the benefits of a power nap? Research supports the idea that napping makes you more productive. One such study showed that a 26-minute nap improved NASA pilots' performance by 34 percent, and a 45-minute nap gave them a boost that lasted for more than six hours.[20] However, other research has shown that napping for just 10 minutes can have a substantial benefit in terms of alertness and performance, both immediately after the nap and up to three hours later.[21] In fact, sleep deprivation can be more lethal than food deprivation.[22] Do you get enough sleep? If you have difficulty falling asleep, build in a short bedtime routine to ensure that you are relaxed and ready to unwind. And think about building a short nap into your daily routine.

Noticing the "Here and Now"

Living in the moment is an opportunity to be more conscious and present in your own daily life. We often spend our time thinking about what has happened or what is going to happen. In the words of Terry Small, we are either "pasteurizing or futurizing."[23] Rarely do we hold ourselves in the moment—the here and now.

Henrik Schurmann, an executive in a privately-held global company, shared this insight, "When I was two to three years into my first manager position, my boss told me something like: 'It is fine that you are ambitious, but don't spend your energy on looking for the next job possibility. That will only distract you. Spend 100 percent of your energy on outperforming in your current position, then the opportunities will come automatically.' Whenever I have found myself in a similar situation over the last decade, I have always thought of and then followed his advice. And every time, some interesting possibilities have arisen."

Mindfulness is defined as awareness of one's present thoughts, emotions, and actions.[24] According to Professor Ben Bryant, "here and now" awareness contributes to mindfulness by liberating mental energy and allowing you to pay heed to your immediate experience in the moment when it happens. Rather than losing energy and becoming caught up in what should be or what could have been, you learn to free your mind and focus on what is happening right now. Bryant says,

> When you are in the "here and now," you notice whether you are bored, tired, or energized. And you notice if you feel threatened or competitive, aggressive or protective toward others. "Noticing" means being able to take in impressions without immediately attaching meaning or judgment to them—this means stepping back from your own agenda and watching with unblinkered eyes. When you practice being mindful, you actively choose rather than automatically react on the basis of mindless (unreflective) habits and assumptions.[25]

Leaders who wish to develop in the area of discipline, as well as in other areas linked to self-awareness, are strongly encouraged to consider mindfulness. Not only will this help with individual change, but it will help with organizational change, too. In fact, to improve performance, make mindfulness a priority.

Make Mindfulness and Meditation a Priority

If this book could tell you a surefire way to improve the quality of your daily life and your level of happiness, would you leap at the chance to apply it? Well, the good news is that mindfulness and meditation will do exactly that. Through countless scientific studies and data, meditation techniques have been proven to significantly improve your ability to perform in a number of areas. And the even better news is that you do not have to change your life, move to a monastery, or spend hours every day to do so! The only thing you need to do is apply the discipline to practice mindfulness and/or meditation for several minutes each day. Numerous studies have shown that mindfulness meditation can improve our ability to sustain attention.[26] Four days of training for just 20 minutes per day can help on a battery of cognitive tests. Mindfulness meditation practitioners performed particularly well on tasks with time constraints, suggesting that mindfulness could be useful for any of us who have to work to deadlines, according to studies by Fadel Zeidan and colleagues.[27]

As Richard Davidson, director of the Laboratory for Affective Neuroscience at the University of Wisconsin, said, "Attention is the key to learning, and meditation helps you voluntarily regulate it."[28]

Gordon, a successful Dutch executive in a global trading and service company, was keen to improve his leadership ability. He had also bitten his nails for the past 30 years. As part of his development, he underwent an eight-week mindfulness program that ran alongside his daily work. Part of the program involved short daily relaxation and meditation exercises. During one of these sessions, Gordon became aware of his hands as an extension of himself. He felt a sensation in his hands and fingers that focused his mind in a different way. Since that program, whenever this trigger occurs, Gordon focuses for a moment on his hands resting on top of his thighs and then continues with his normal activity. He has not bitten his nails for nine months. What Gordon has done is replace his previous habitual routine, chewing his nails, with another routine, "sensing" his hands while resting them on his thighs. Not only has he stopped chewing his nails, but he has also improved his ability to control his emotions.

Medical researcher, doctor, and professor Craig Hassed has said, "We found the more mindful you are, the more activation you have in the right ventrolateral prefrontal cortex and the less activation you have in the amygdala. We also saw activation in widespread centers of the prefrontal cortex for people who are high in mindfulness. This suggests people who are more mindful bring all sorts of prefrontal resources to turn down the amygdala. These findings may help explain the beneficial health effects of mindfulness meditation, and suggest, for the first time, an underlying reason why mindfulness meditation programs improve mood and health."[29]

Matthieu Ricard is a French Buddhist monk and the coauthor of a study on the brains of long-term meditators, including himself. He is a board member of the Mind and Life Institute, which is devoted to collaborative research between scientists and Buddhist scholars and meditators, and the author of *Happiness: A Guide to Developing Life's Most Important Skill*. Ricard shares a story of a disruptive moment for him on a train in India that helped him to realize the true benefits of meditation.

The windows of the train were all broken. I sat down on a wooden bench. I put my laptop above the seat in a well-protected place and somehow someone, with a wire I guess, pulled up my laptop and stole it. Then, I had a terrible back pain. That evening, all the lights went off. Suddenly, in the darkness with this back pain and my computer stolen, I felt so good. I felt a sort of inner peace and serenity to the point that I started laughing. The outer condition was so horrible and yet I felt extremely peaceful, joyful, serene, and satisfied. I suddenly had a glimpse that it really depends on your state of mind. When you feel extremely angry and therefore very disturbed, you are angry, but then you look at anger as if you are looking at the fire burning or the volcano and you look and look at it. Now what will happen? You look at anger as a phenomenon. And as you look at it, it is sort of melting away like the morning frost in the rising sun. It just vanishes and disappears. We feel that there is extraordinary potential in every human being. You can act on the causes and conditions that change your mental landscape. We are born with certain traits. People are more or less joyful, more or less depressed, but this is just a blueprint. Even our genetic inheritance is just a blueprint, if you don't do anything about it, it must follow its own course, but the point of mind training is that gradually with diligence you change the landscape of your mind and acquire the quality that brings you this deep sense of well-being.[30]

What is clear is that mindfulness is the key to discipline, and discipline is the key to mindfulness. The scientific evidence is growing all the time. No matter what your predisposition, you always have the power to choose to act.

Mindfulness Exercise

Some executives struggle with the idea of meditation. In their busy, stressful, 24/7 days, they ask, "Where am I supposed to find the time to meditate?" They feel like hamsters trapped on a wheel, running furiously and going round and round, but not moving forward and exhausting themselves in the process. What does it take to step off the wheel? The answer appears to be practicing mindfulness techniques or meditation for as little as 10 minutes a day. Make it one of your daily nonnegotiables. Andy Puddicombe, a former Buddhist monk, has a clear desire: to demystify meditation and make it accessible and relevant to as many people as possible. Andy encourages people to make simple meditation part of their everyday lives in order to reap the benefits, which research shows to be huge. At the heart of meditation is the intention to rest in the moment, remaining focused and relaxed. All types of meditation have two component parts: concentration (which provides a sense of calm) and clarity (which provides a sense of insight). Using your breathing as the primary support for your meditation allows you to practice anywhere, anytime.[31] Start by setting your alarm for one minute, sitting comfortably, and just focusing on your breath. Observe and feel your breath, resting your attention on where the air enters and leaves your body, either through your nose or through your mouth.[32]

By focusing on your breath, you can experience a sense of calm that slows your racing mind and allows clarity to arise in its own time. You cannot force clarity. As soon as you try to do that, you are thinking and consciously controlling the process. Clarity is about a steady unfolding of the mind, providing an increasingly direct insight into what's happening. Now, it will take practice to achieve this state. In the beginning, it is likely that your mind will wander constantly, pursuing the endless thoughts that come to you. That's OK. It doesn't matter if your mind wanders; just notice it and bring it back to your focus on your breath in the here and now. When it wanders again, notice it and bring it back again. No self-criticism. Your thoughts and feelings are transient. They come into your mind, and they go out of your mind. You have the choice as to whether to focus and act on them or dismiss them. So just notice any distracting thoughts, allow them to float away, and return to the focus on your breath. You can start with 1 or 2 minutes a day, and then gradually build up to 10 minutes a day. Just 10 minutes out of the 1,440 minutes you have each day—a small investment with a massive payoff.

Says Bill George, author, Harvard Business School professor, and former CEO of Medtronic, "When I started meditating, I was able to stay calmer and more focused in my leadership, without losing the 'edge' that I believed had made me successful. Meditation enabled me to cast off the many trivial worries that once possessed me and gain clarity about what was really important. The important thing is to have a set time each day to pull back from the intense pressures of leadership to reflect on what is happening. I try to do twenty minutes, twice a day."[33]

There's a Purpose in No Purpose

Relaxing, chilling, hanging out with family and friends, snoozing—all these activities may feel as if they serve no great purpose. However, while it is important that you take a disciplined approach in applying the steps toward achieving a desire or a goal, it is also critically important that you build in downtime for rest and recovery. Part of being disciplined is knowing when to take a break. According to Michael Watkins, it is important that you work hard at recognizing when you are at the point of diminishing returns and then take a break of whatever sort refreshes you.[34] So being disciplined is not just about applying yourself to achieve your goal; it is also about being disciplined to achieve your goal smartly and to allow yourself downtime to rest and recover. This is obvious when you think of the sports analogy. Athletes train, build themselves up, taper off, perform at an event, and then rest and recover before repeating the cycle. Resting is an important part of successful goal achievement. Research has shown that unconscious thought and incubation time are conducive to better decision making and insight.[35] And, according to Dr. Stuart Brown at the National Institute for Play, playfulness enhances your ability to innovate, adapt, and master changing circumstances. He says, "It is not just an escape. It can help us integrate and reconcile difficult or contradictory circumstances. And, often, it can show us a way out of our problems."[36] The research reinforces what we all know to be true: sometimes our best ideas come when we are in the shower, walking, driving, or doing something other than working.

Rachel Bamber, founder of a coaching and training business, Brighter Thinking, and one of the first people to be awarded a postgraduate qualification in the neuroscience of leadership, shares this insight about taking breaks.

Research suggests that people who engage in multitasking often do so not because they have the ability, but because they are less able to block out distractions and focus on a singular task.[37] I often have to force myself to "focus to the finish" on certain tasks. I have been known to start washing up, then move on to another activity before it is finished! However, despite this, I consistently achieve goals and complete projects. Applying knowledge from neuroscience, I am now more aware of my own habits, and I am alerted to my brain's need for distraction, so I purposely take breaks to look out the window or go into another room to make a drink. The difference is that I now see this as a positive method to help my brain to refocus and get the job done, rather than berating myself for stopping. When I share this approach to dealing with the brain's limited attention and focus with clients, they report that they have a greater sense of achievement and job satisfaction, are more in control, and, importantly, feel less stress.

Therefore, being "always on" may not be the most productive way to work, as the brain is being forced to be on "alert" far too much.[38] When the brain regularly experiences this overarousal, the cortisol and adrenaline levels in the blood rise, increasing the allostatic load and causing significant stress.[39] Giving yourself regular breaks is good not only for your brain but is good for your relationships, too.

In a wonderful speech, Brian Dyson, the former CEO of Coca-Cola, said,

Imagine life as a game in which you are juggling some five balls in the air. They are Work, Family, Health, Friends and Spirit, and you're keeping all of these in the air. You will soon understand that Work is a rubber ball. If you drop it, it will bounce back. But the four others— Family, Health, Friends and Spirit—are made of glass. If you drop one of these, it will be scuffed, nicked, damaged, even shattered. And it will never be the same.

Work efficiently during office hours and leave on time. Give proper time to your family and friends, and take a decent rest.

Value has a value only if its value is valued.[40]

As you work on these areas for yourself, you will also create a positive climate for those you work with by modeling the behavior you want to see in yourself and others.

When you apply the necessary discipline, you will be well on your way to achieving your goal. A vital next step is to be able to overcome the inevitable obstacles that you will face and to show *determination* to stay the course. And this is the focus of the next chapter.

Key Points to Remember

- Discipline is a practice: the more you do it, the better you get at it.
- Break down your goal into small, achievable daily steps.
- Apply rituals as daily nonnegotiables to turn your actions into routines.
- Make some healthy brain choices with regard to food, exercise, and sleep.
- Notice the here and now; mindfulness is a proven way of reducing stress and providing significant benefits.
- Build in ways to switch off and relax. Downtime is essential to recharge the brain and the body.

CHAPTER FOUR

Determination

How Can You Embrace the Setbacks?

Success is not final, failure is not fatal: it is the courage to continue that counts.

—Winston Churchill

D ETERMINATION IS ABSOLUTELY necessary if you are to overcome obstacles in your change journey. No matter how focused and disciplined you are, you may get sick, have an unexpected work emergency, or experience personal problems that interfere with your progress. Setbacks will happen, and when they do, you need to have *determination*, defined as "firmness of purpose; resoluteness."[1] When enacting change in your life, the essence of determination lies in asking yourself the question: how will I deal with setbacks and failure?

There are numerous stories of famous people who were discounted, who faced failure, or who were told that they would never succeed. Walt Disney was fired from a newspaper for "lacking imagination" and "having no original ideas." At age 30, Steve Jobs was fired from Apple, the company he had founded. As any actor knows, rejection is part of the game—you need to view it as feedback and learn not to take it personally. When Edison was inventing the lightbulb, he is rumored to have failed more than a thousand times. When a colleague implored him to give up, saying that he had failed so many times, Edison reportedly responded, "I haven't failed, I've just found a thousand ways it doesn't work."[2]

Living and Leading Change: Alan Murray

Determination has become something of a watchword for Alan Murray, the CEO of NextFoods. When we interviewed him for this book, Alan told us how, when he was growing up in South Africa and was the smallest child in the class, he quickly

The Five Ds

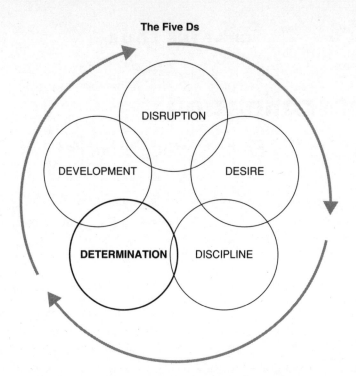

learned to work with what he had and to use his wits to survive and thrive. He grew up in a family in which survival and achievement were expected. "At one stage," says Alan, "you have to stop whining, stop externalizing the problems and looking for excuses, and work with what you have." This philosophy has followed him throughout his life. Through application and persistence, he became good at sports, representing his state in judo and tennis. His parents also expected him to deliver solid academic performance.

At a young age, he adopted the belief that failure is not an option. "Whenever I face a challenge, I think about the end state and ask myself, what would nirvana look like amidst all the chaos, and what's stopping us from getting there? Once we have identified the obstacles, we can work out a way around them—there's always a way." Appointed managing director of Tetra Pak USA in 2001, he was determined to make the American market a success. Although this market had historically been less successful for Tetra Pak, the U.S. employees were feeling happy with their performance, as their operations had turned a small profit under the previous managing director. To disrupt their sense of complacency, Alan compared the U.S. company's performance with that of companies in every other Tetra Pak market. He discovered that, on a number of parameters, the U.S. company was the second worst performer, behind Bangladesh. "So I shared this information with them. We are the second worst *in the world. This is an embarrassment for the United States," said Alan. At first, he faced resistance and denial, with many of the problems being externalized to the headquarters or to the product offerings. "I told them that, at the end of the day, we had to work with what we had. I was very direct with the management team. I said that if they didn't think we could achieve success, then they should leave. If they believed we could turn the business around, they were welcome to stay." Along with his management team, Alan set an ambitious goal: to triple the bottom line within five years.*

Recalls Alan, "I went to my boss and told him our target, and he smiled and suggested that I go tell the CEO. I went to the CEO, and he smiled and suggested that I go tell the board. When I presented to the board, one of the members started laughing, and another told me that I was the fourth person who had promised to deliver in the United States, and why did I think I would succeed where others had not. I said I was glad I had gotten their attention, I believed we could do it, and I would keep them updated." Not only did the U.S. market triple its bottom line, but it did so earlier than expected. The results were considered so successful that the company wrote a case on it with Ashridge Business School and used it to train managers within the company.

Later, when Alan first joined NextFoods, the company was facing a lawsuit that, if successful, could bankrupt it. At his first board meeting, many of the board members were complaining about the unfairness of the lawsuit. After listening for half an hour, Alan intervened, saying that he would take charge of the problem, as he was the only person who was not emotionally involved with the issue. "I remember thinking, it is what it is. Complaining is not going to make it go away. We have to work within the system and deal with what we are facing as best we can." When Alan went to court, he saw the plaintiff and approached her to apologize for any perceived wrongdoing, stating that it was not the company's intention to mislead anyone with its product labeling. The pair bonded through dialogue, and when the lawyers and the judge arrived, they agreed to move ahead quickly, and the lawsuit was settled then and there at a fraction of what had originally been asked. Shares Alan, "When faced with incredible hurdles, there are two key questions that go through my mind: how can we treat people with respect, and how can we solve the problems?"

> *For our product GoodBelly, we offer our consumers a 12-day challenge—take the product for 12 days in a row, and if you don't feel better, you get your money back. In 2010, we had a couple of hundred consumers signing up each month online for the challenge. We conducted interviews with over 5,000 people, and 83 percent said that they noticed a difference, while 71 percent were still buying the product a year later. During 2011, we experimented with our approach, refining what worked and what did not. Basically, we*

measured everything—if it worked, we continued it; if it didn't work, we stopped it. It is important to be determined in your approach and to follow it with discipline. Over the course of 18 months, we refined the 12-day challenge, and by 2012, we peaked at 1,000 people signing up every day.

Alan's goal as CEO is twofold: to play a part in the education of people with regard to improving their health and to take this company from a start-up phase to a more mature company phase. He is inspired by NextFoods's founder, Steve Demos. "When Steve founded the company, he wanted to have a science-based food where people could feel the effect and the benefit. Our GoodBelly drinks are organic and vegan and can really boost the immunity in your gut. I am passionate about the product and about bringing greater awareness of the benefits to a broader audience."

Alan is aware that there is a price to be paid for his dogged determination and focus on success. "I am really bad at celebrating the quick wins and small steps along the way. However, I know how important it is to do this, and so I outsource celebration to a member of my immediate team, to someone who is good at it. Fundamentally, I believe that everyone wants to succeed. The role of management is to set the direction, communicate intently, remove the obstacles, and then empower the people around you to make it happen."

Alan's life view, "work with what you have," has influenced the way he has approached all aspects of his life and enabled him to apply the same level of determination to any challenge he has faced. While he may not express it in scientific terms, Alan's high self-awareness allows him to use his choice point when threats occur.

People are wired to become defensive when they are faced with failure, as it is viewed as a threat, and any threat can be perceived, at a base level, as a challenge to our survival. When we get defensive, we can revert to denial and blame, be it on ourselves, others, the situation, or even life itself. Using your choice point—that is, catching yourself consciously in the moment—allows you to refocus and reframe the situation. When setbacks occur, ask yourself two questions: how can I get back on track, and what can I learn about the conditions or situations that led to the setback?

Building Your Resilience

Resilience, the ability to recover quickly from change or misfortune, is an essential ingredient of determination. It is about accepting the reality, learning from it, and moving on from the setback. According to Diane Coutu, author of the *Harvard Business Review* article "How Resilience Works," resilience is "merely the skill and the capacity to be robust under conditions of enormous stress and change." She continues, "Resilient people possess three characteristics: a staunch acceptance of reality; a deep belief, often buttressed by strongly held values, that life is meaningful; and an uncanny ability to improvise. You can bounce back from hardship with just one or two of these qualities, but you will only be truly resilient with all three."[3] It is also helpful to keep a sense of humor and to view events and experiences from a detached perspective while still finding meaning and a sense of purpose.[4]

Steve Jenner is a former senior civil servant in the British justice system and a global expert on benefits management. His experience illustrates how resilience sees people through the experience of making unpopular but necessary decisions in order to make needed change strategies work. Jenner told us,

> I worked on a major cross-government IT portfolio where difficult decisions needed to be made to address significant cost escalation and uncertain business benefit. The CEO came to my desk one day and said, "Steve, we've just had the prime minister's advisors visit us. They told me, 'People may not like what we're doing, but they respect us.'" I replied, "Respect us? They hate us." And my CEO replied, "I'm quite relaxed about it; they don't hate us, they hate you!" But he was right; it wasn't a popularity contest. We continued to receive funding at a time when most areas of government were facing severe cuts, and two years later, the most senior program directors, who had opposed us at the time, publicly gave their support to our approach.

Steve said, "Determination, resilience, not giving up, and staying the course are crucial in embedding change—whether organizational or personal. Some might call it bloody-mindedness, but I prefer to see it as the single-minded pursuit of a desired end state."

Allan Lam, a senior executive based in Singapore, shared his perspective on the importance of resilience.

> In a 36-year career, I have received a lot of very good advice along the way. Some I have implemented; some I have forgotten; and a few are always deep in my heart. One piece of advice that I have always kept and that is probably the one that has affected me the most came from my father. When I was 16 and his business had just gone belly-up, he said to me one evening, "Son, all of those around you can give up on you. It is all right. As long as you don't give up on yourself,

you can always be the last man standing." This conversation is always fresh in my mind, even after 37 years. It is not 100 percent true that I have been the last man standing in all situations, but this has helped me through many, many down moments and in making strong comebacks. I believe that this advice has driven a lot of my endurance and resilience.

Resilience includes mental skills that you need if you are to perform in difficult circumstances and overcome obstacles. Only a decade ago, it was far easier for executives to switch off from the hectic pace of life simply by leaving the office. Now, with the dramatic technological advances in mobile Internet and telephony, we can all be connected—all the time and everywhere. While this accessibility brings advantages, a major disadvantage is that there is now very little separation between work and home. Therefore, the onus is now on you, the individual, to manage your own boundaries. We find that many executives struggle with the challenge of saying no and can easily be drawn into an e-mail addiction, with work taking priority at all times. In times of change, it can be even more difficult to maintain your boundaries. Building your own resilience is a powerful way of taking charge of yourself.

It is important that you practice the behaviors that build your capacity for resilience, so that when you are facing change, you will have equipped yourself with the capacity to deal with the stress and uncertainty. The Resilience Institute, founded by Dr. Sven Hansen in 2002, defines *resilience* as a learned ability to bounce back from adversity, thrive on challenge, reach our full potential, and have a positive impact on others. It has undertaken extensive research and created a diagnostic tool to assess resilience in five key positive areas: mastering stress (being calm, staying alert, and having an engaged presence), energizing the body (maintenance of strength, endurance, and flexibility), engaging the emotions (self-knowledge, empathy, and resonance), training the mind (being optimistic, maintaining focus, and making effective decisions), and having spirit in action (experiencing flow and joy in what you do and feeling compassion). Through a series of questions, this tool will also show you where you may be in the spiral of six key negative areas (see Figure 4-1): confusion (a state of overload, agitation, and mindless busyness), disengagement (loss of attention, daydreaming, worry), withdrawal (loss of energy, avoidance, isolation), vulnerability (indifference, self-neglect, and fatigue), distress (stress symptoms, sleep problems, illness), and depression (loss of interest,

Figure 4-1   The Resilience Spiral

Organizational		Individual
Sustainable world-class business	Spirit in Action	Meaning, flow, joy, and compassion
Flexibility and fast execution	Train Mind	Optimism, focus, and effective decisions
Engaged, resonant leadership and culture	Engage Emotion	Self-knowledge, empathy, and resonance
Organizational vitality and well-being	Energize Body	Maintenance of strength, endurance, and flexibility
Stable, focused clarity	Master Stress	Calm, alert, and engaged presence
Agitated and unfocused operations	Confused	State of overload, agitation, and mindless busyness
Lost productivity	Disengaged	Loss of attention, boredom, and worry
Low morale and engagement	Withdrawn	Loss of energy, avoidance, and isolation
Absenteeism and presenteeism	Vulnerable	Indifference, self-neglect, and fatigue
Regrettable talent loss	Distress	Stress symptoms, sleep problems, and illness
Organizational death	Depression	Loss of interest and sadness

Source: Sven Hansen and the Resilience Institute, 2002

sadness).[5] The questionnaire also assesses organizational resilience. (To find out more about the tool, visit www.resiliencei.com.)

Working to improve your own resilience involves a three-step process: (1) gaining awareness of where you are today, (2) intervening in your daily routines and habits to make a change, and (3) getting the necessary support from others to help you to make it happen.

Resilience Actions

Resilience is essential in times of change. You can put some healthy habits in place as a matter of routine that will help you increase your resilience quotient and will stand you in good stead in times of stress caused by change. While resilience and managing stress warrant an entire book by themselves, we share five simple actions that, if turned into daily nonnegotiable rituals, may make a difference for you:

- Take four deep breaths at least once every day. Whenever you feel anxious, practice this technique.
- Practice mindfulness for just one minute a day. You should be totally open to the moment and engrossed in it. This can be as simple as savoring a cup of coffee or tea or watching a bird in a tree.
- Choose to use the stairs in the office, at the shops, and at airports as an excellent and efficient way to increase your exercise.
- Prepare for a good night's sleep by having a brain cooldown 45 minutes before going to bed. Avoid the stimulation of phones, laptops, or television. Instead, read a book or listen to relaxing music.
- Make a conscious effort to focus on what has been positive about your day, what you are grateful for, and where you have felt a connection to someone else.[6]

The science supporting good practice is clearly established. Appropriate exercise, relaxation, sleep, nutrition, and social connection dramatically shift your well-being potential. The individual benefits are obvious. However, think also of the massive increases in productivity, reduced healthcare and welfare costs, more vibrant community life, and enhanced happiness.[7] Improved resilience works at both the individual and the collective levels. Adopting a healthier lifestyle also improves your immunity significantly: by 47 percent with exercise, by 45 percent with relaxation, and by 44 percent with sleep.[8] And the good news is that the steps necessary to do this are all within your control.

Determination, Motivation, and Meaningful Ambition

Patricia Alireza started college when she was 31 and completed her PhD at 45. In 2009, she became the first and only grandmother to receive the prestigious L'Oreal-UNESCO fellowship for promising women scientists. Interviewed for *O, the Oprah Magazine* and now in her mid-fifties, Patricia said, "Little by little, I went from being a housewife studying on the side to being a scientist. It wasn't easy, but when you really want something and you're determined and dedicated, you can do it."[9]

Motivation involves "a feeling of enthusiasm or interest that makes you determined to do something."[10] Ambition is an earnest desire for some type of achievement or distinction and the willingness to strive for its attainment.[11] The object of your ambition is often something that is difficult to attain and therefore represents a challenge. In times of difficulty, an ambition that is tightly linked to a meaningful purpose (such as the desire you established in Chapter 2), will give you the motivation to carry on even when you feel like giving up. As we have seen, a meaningful purpose is a key component of resilience.

Danny McCarthy, a general manager for an Australian mining company, Thiess Pty Ltd., has committed himself in past years to a series of cycling challenges with fellow riders in order to raise money and awareness for cancer research. In early 2013, he completed the Smiling for Smiddy Cycling Challenge, cycling 630 kilometers in four days. Says Danny, "This was an emotional and personal journey for me, having watched my father, Peter, battle and beat bowel and bladder cancer over the past five years and having experienced the deeply sad loss of my wife's mum and my great friend Hilary to aggressive cancer some years ago. But through the cold, wet, and challenging terrain, I knew I was riding for a cause, and both Peter and Hilary were in my thoughts and kept me motivated. While I was excited by the physical challenge of this ride, I was also determined to do my part in funding research into curing cancer."

His most recent challenge was to cycle the 1,600 kilometers from Brisbane to Townsville in eight days to raise funds for research on melanoma and prostate cancer as well as complementary therapies for cancer patients.

In order to prepare for these challenges, Danny had to commit himself to a grueling training schedule. There were many days when, after a hard day's work, he would have rather gone home to relax. However, by keeping his goal in mind, he was able to get back on his bike and put in the required miles. "Of course, I enjoy cycling, and it also keeps me fit," shares Danny. "However, knowing that I am combining my hobby with a meaningful contribution to a valuable cause gives me a different type of energy and reward. Interestingly, I also feel that I have improved as a leader in the process. I am calmer, more self-aware, and more focused, qualities that I believe not only make me more accessible as a leader at work, but also enable me to be more connected with my family. And I could not achieve any of the results I have without the support and love of my wife. Her commitment gives me the strength to maintain my determination, dedication, and drive to raise awareness and funds to beat cancer."

By aligning his passion with a purpose and applying determination in order to succeed, Danny is proving to be an inspiration to those around him, both at home and at work. His story also demonstrates that there are many ways to define success—and volunteering can be one way to contribute beyond the self. Many people choose to contribute to their communities and actually increase their own well-being and emotional health through doing things for others.

Managing Transitions

Aidan, a seasoned executive in one of the world's leading building materials companies, told us,

> Change starts with yourself. If you're not motivated, then why should your team be? In difficult times, I often tell my folks, there may be dark clouds in the sky, but the sun is still shining somewhere beyond them. I don't see myself as a sore loser, but I do indeed hate to fail. When I fail, I truly want to find out why and see how to correct the problem or at least draw learning and experience from it. I guess this stems from my training as an engineer, where I learned the practice of "root cause analysis."
>
> I ask myself: why did I fail, what went wrong, and what can I learn from knowing the true origin of the problem? Aircraft do not regularly fall from the sky because that industry is obsessive about examining the root cause of failure. If you don't understand why you failed, you can't correct it, and it will catch up with you again later. It's important to be curious about understanding your less successful decisions, so that you can explore and reflect upon what you could have done better. Ironically, success is a poor teacher. Failure is the best thing to learn from. Rarely do we do a root cause analysis on our successes. We just celebrate and move on, perhaps not really understanding *why* the success came our way in the first place. This is an area where I think we could maybe spend some more time.

> Change is about dealing with transitions successfully. We all face transitions in our lives as a natural part of aging, and all transitions involve loss of a certain type. They can arise not only because of a negative event, but also as a result of something positive, such as your child leaving home to go to university, your receiving a promotion or taking a new job (and thereby saying goodbye to colleagues or a company), or your moving to another house (and saying goodbye to your old home and a stage of your life). Transition is all about letting go of somebody or something and entering a period where we allow confusion and potential chaos to be, before preparing to let something new or different come in the future. The mantra of "let go, let be, and let come" is most helpful in dealing with transition difficulties (see Figure 4-2).

Figure 4-2   Managing Transitions

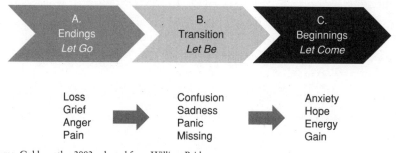

Source: Goldsworthy, 2002, adapted from William Bridges

Understanding what is happening during a change can help you deal with what you may feel or experience and support you in staying focused when you face failure or setbacks. When Alastair Robertson, the chief human resources officer for a global logistics organization that operates in more than 80 countries worldwide, was appointed, he was given the task of implementing an HR transformation. This goal had an additional challenge: he was the fifth HR director in ten years to attempt it. The organization did not know exactly what it wanted or needed, and the HR team had become demoralized through being sidelined and discounted over time.

Alastair worked with his team to devise a five-year HR change strategy with clear milestones. The plan met with a mixture of passive resistance, active resistance, cynicism, and disinterest. The team started with a lot of communication, but quickly realized that actions speak louder than words and sorted out some quick wins to build momentum. Alastair said,

> At times, it was very easy to be derailed or distracted by other people's inertia, but part of what we did was draw a map as we went along. That way, in our monthly meetings, we could judge whether the distraction was taking us away from our objective or whether it was only a slight detour. If the distraction amounted to only a detour, then we could live with it if that was what the organization needed at that time. However, if the distraction could derail the strategy, we often just stopped doing what we were doing and faced up to what was driving the derailment. Through our determination to stick to our principles of integrity, honesty, and transparency, and never embellish the facts, we won over many detractors. Sometimes we did have to let go of a step, work out why it didn't work, learn from it, and then get back on track. We also worked to keep up the momentum, communicate progress, and

celebrate success, and to focus on looking for the solution rather than the problem.

It was a tough journey, with many twists and turns, but we pulled it off. Belief in what we were doing and the determination to succeed were both vital elements in our journey.

When you're going through change, you tend not to go from endings to new beginnings. The endings involve the need to let go. When you're changing a behavior, the letting go can be related to the loss of the comfortable and the routine. The change may involve some elements of loss, anger, grief, and pain. The important aspect is to remain conscious that these are normal feelings during this stage. Work by Nobel Prize winners Daniel Kahneman and Amos Tversky showed that people are far more motivated to avoid a loss than to achieve a potential gain. Kahneman sees loss aversion as a part of behavioral economics, with people being disproportionately influenced by fear of feeling regret and often forgoing benefits to avoid even a small risk of feeling that they have failed.[12] However, it is possible to override this natural fear and train your mind to embrace the pain in order to achieve the gain it will eventually deliver. Acknowledging and expressing your feelings of loss can actually reduce the level of emotion in the amygdala. This can then make it easier for you to let go and move on.

If you stay in the endings stage, it becomes harder to move ahead to the new state of growth. When you let go of an old habit or an old way of thinking, you create space and release energy for something new to come. "Getting over a painful experience is much like crossing monkey bars. You have to let go at some point in order to move forward," noted C. S. Lewis. The visual imagery of the monkey bars and change is a powerful one. You first have to stretch yourself to reach up and place both hands on the first rung. Then, to move forward, you have to let go with one hand and stretch forward to reach the second rung. As you do this, there's a risk that you may not make it. However, without facing the risk and uncertainty, you cannot move forward. Once your first hand reaches the second rung, you then need to let go of the first rung in order to move ahead. Otherwise, you get stuck between the first and second rungs. It takes a lot of energy to just stay hanging in one place. Moving forward releases productive energy. By letting go and reaching out with one hand, straddling yourself for a short time between the two rungs, and then having the courage to fully let go by moving the other hand, you progress forward.

Classical concert violinist Miha Pogacnik also endorses this approach by using music to demonstrate the principles of renewal and change within corporations. He says, "You have to let go in order to let come."[13]

Consultant Ayin Jambulingam shares advice he was given on embracing uncertainty and the unknown. "I read recently that we are not afraid of the unknown, because, how can we be afraid of something we have no idea about? Instead, we are afraid of letting go of the known. Since adopting this advice, I have come to believe that one of the roles of leaders is to contain uncertainty and the unknown for their employees, to allow them to feel safe enough to let go of the known, and to discover new territories."

Once you have let go, you don't arrive at the new state immediately. There is a stage of confusion in which the unknown remains unknown and the uncertainty can be upsetting. Your brain can deal with good news, and it can deal with bad news. What the brain finds most difficult is uncertainty, a sense of not knowing. A sense of uncertainty about the future and a feeling of being out of control both generate strong limbic system responses, says David Rock, author and founder of the NeuroLeadership Institute.[14] During this in-between stage, you may feel a longing for the past and want to return to your earlier circumstances, where you felt more comfortable. This feeling of discomfort is actually a very positive sign that you are growing and evolving. Growth is uncomfortable, even painful, as you leave behind the familiar and risk the unknown of the future. However, when you overcome your fears and take full responsibility for your life, you realize that change is not something to be feared. Rather, you can welcome change with open arms and encourage it, as it is only through change, through the death of a cycle, that rebirth, regeneration, and rejuvenation can occur.[15] Walk into that feeling of discomfort with confidence and optimism, in the knowledge that you are making progress. "Chaos is actually a fertile state, a creative state, a state of pure energy and great potential," said William Bridges, author of *The Way of Transition*.[16]

As you move into the new beginnings, you will inevitably experience a mixture of feelings: some anxiety about what might be (remember that a certain amount of anxiety creates enabling energy), balanced with some hope and optimism that releases positive energy and helps you to focus on the gain from the pain. In our practice, we recommend a phrase for helping people who are dealing individually with these transitions from endings to beginnings: "pride in the past, passion for the present, and faith in the future."

What has happened has already happened. It is part of what has made you the person you are today. It may have been difficult, but you have learned from your mistakes and moved on. Today is about living in the moment and being fully present and committed to whatever you are doing. And, based on all the actions you are taking, it is about having the belief that things will work out for you in the future. We recommend the same mantra for organizational change with a slight adjustment: "pride in the past, passion for the present, and *focus* on the future."

Sara Mathew, chairman and CEO of Dun & Bradstreet, shared this story of learning from failure.

> I had been with P&G for about 10 years, when I became the head of Investor Relations. Since I have this intense need for change, I decided we should communicate directly to investors through a web cast. This was a first for P&G, and I got the CEO's buy-in to proceed. And then, everything went wrong.
>
> For starters, our results that quarter were lackluster, but by the time I was done talking, I had destroyed about three billion of P&G's market cap in one fell swoop. As I reflected back, it was clear that my somewhat casual communication style had failed miserably. It was my idea, my script and definitely my fault.
>
> As the week progressed the stock dropped further and I found myself struggling to make it in to work. Failure is tough. Public failure is devastating. By weekend, the solution was clear. We needed to stay with web casts, and get it right the next time. I now had a plan.
>
> Unfortunately, P&G's CEO had other ideas; I came to work on Monday to find a neatly handwritten note—A "Dear Sara" note— saying we should never do a web cast again, since the "old" approach worked better.
>
> I knew this was a mistake, so I went back and pled my case. Looking back, it was clear my CEO did not want to try this AGAIN, but after listening to my impassioned plea, he agreed to give me a second chance. The second time was magic. And today, this is how P&G communicates with investors. . . .
>
> I failed very publicly. I was quoted in the *WSJ*, on CNBC—I even made the papers in India! Everyone knew I messed up! But I learned so much from this experience—I learned to pick myself up and try again. And my biggest learning—failure teaches you much more than success ever will.
>
> This became apparent when I decided to leave P&G to join D&B. I called the CEO to say goodbye. This was a man who gave me a second chance. It was this second chance that made me the person I am today.

I thanked him for that. Imagine my surprise when he could not remember the incident. All he said was that when he thought of Investor Relations, he thought I set the benchmark for excellence!

So today, I am not afraid to fail. I realize that people who fail just take more risk than you and me.[17]

As Sara's experience demonstrates, it is how you react to failure that makes the difference. Failure is an important component of success. Knowing the stages in a transition can help you to be aware of where you are in the process and deal with the resulting emotions and feelings accordingly.

It is said that in Africa, to stop monkeys from stealing crops, farmers place a gourd on the ground. They then cut a hole in it, large enough for a monkey to place its hand inside (as monkeys like the seeds). When the monkey places its hand inside and grabs the seeds, it cannot remove its hand because its full fist is larger and becomes trapped. To free itself and escape, all the monkey has to do is let go of the seeds. What are the seeds you are holding on to that stop you from moving forward?

Transition Exercise

Try this exercise, that we call "Write, Walk & Waste," to help you with letting go and moving forward. Take a piece of paper and write down everything that you are unhappy or upset about. Make sure to put down specific details and cover every emotion you are feeling. Use bad language if you wish. Take your time doing this to make sure you have written down every part of what you feel. Then put the paper down and go for a walk or do some exercise. When you are ready, come back to the paper and make the decision to free yourself from the negativity it contains. If you have a fireplace, burn the paper and watch as the words are licked by the flames and consumed. If not, tear it into small pieces and throw them into the waste bin. Then, physically place some tape on the floor (or you can use a belt or a piece of string) and take a deep breath. When you are ready, step over the line and say, "I am leaving the negativity behind and moving into my new future." Do this only when you are ready. This symbolic act enables you to let go of the negative emotion and free yourself from what is holding you back. Then, the next time the negative thought arises, you can recognize it and recall the symbolic ritual you undertook to say goodbye to the old pattern, freeing yourself to move forward.

The Power of Proactive Acceptance

There is a famous prayer, often referred to as the Serenity Prayer, that goes as follows: "God grant me the serenity to accept the things I cannot change; the courage to change the things I can; and the wisdom to know the difference."[18] When you are dealing with change, these are wise words. Reflecting on what you could have done differently from the perspective of learning is helpful; however, wallowing in a pool of self-blame and criticism is not. We cannot control the external circumstances of our life, but we can control how we react to them. Refusing to accept the way things are is a process of denial that takes an enormous amount of energy and keeps you locked into the pain. When you choose to accept a situation, you release pent-up energy and enable yourself to harness that energy toward positive action.[19]

Acceptance is not a passive act. It is about working with the flow of life rather than fighting against it. We call this *proactive acceptance*, as you are accepting from a state of high energy and moving forward rather than staying stuck. "The only place where you can experience the flow of life is the Now, so to surrender is to accept the present moment unconditionally and without reservation," advises Eckhart Tolle.[20] Proactive acceptance is a stage that can help you move forward. However, it can be more of a challenge to accept a situation when you feel it to be unfair. Perceptions of unfairness are associated with negative impacts on physical and mental health, particularly in those situations where the unfairness breaches a psychological contract held by group members.[21]

When Philip, a global innovation strategist, was made redundant by his employer as a result of a global directive to reduce headcount, he initially found the news hard to bear. He felt angry and frustrated, as he had been working for three years on a highly successful project and was rated as outstanding in all of his performance reviews. At first, he was stuck with these feelings of unfairness. However, by recognizing that the decision was not personal, but instead was related to a corporate initiative, he was able to work through his feelings, and he eventually came to accept the situation and refocused his mind on seeking out new employment opportunities.

A perception of unfairness can generate strong threat responses, which may include activation of the insular, a part of the brain involved in intense emotions such as disgust.[22] Reframing the situation can reduce the intensity of the emotional reaction and help you let go of feelings of unfairness and instead move toward proactive acceptance.

The Change Time Lag

Another reason that we often see change fail is that the person starts working on a different approach, but then does not immediately gain external recognition for the effort. Imagine that a behavior of yours is labeled X, and that everyone knows you do X. This could be any number of behaviors—for example, a tendency to micromanage, lose patience, or take control. After the disruption and desire stages, you start applying the discipline to introduce a new behavior, labeled Y.

Now, introducing the new Y behavior takes a great deal of energy; it involves the prefrontal cortex, as opposed to the more routine basal ganglia activity which directed the old X behavior. So, you make this big effort, but no one rewards you. Either your colleagues are cynical ("Oh, he's just taken a course; give it a week or two and he'll forget"), or they simply do not notice your efforts. They expect your behavior to be X and they look for occasions where you demonstrate X. At this stage, many people seeking to change simply become frustrated, give up, and say, "I knew it wouldn't work." However, if you keep going through this period, gradually your new Y behavior will become stronger than your old X behavior, and people will start seeing and commenting on the signs of the new Y behavior. Eventually, your behavior and the perception of your behavior by others will become aligned and the change will be recognized (see Figure 4-3). However, it does take time, persistence, and determination to get the benefit.

Senior executive Joanna returned to work reenergized after attending a leadership training program. She had a clear action plan for working on some areas identified through a 360-degree feedback process. During those first weeks

Figure 4-3   The Change Time Lag

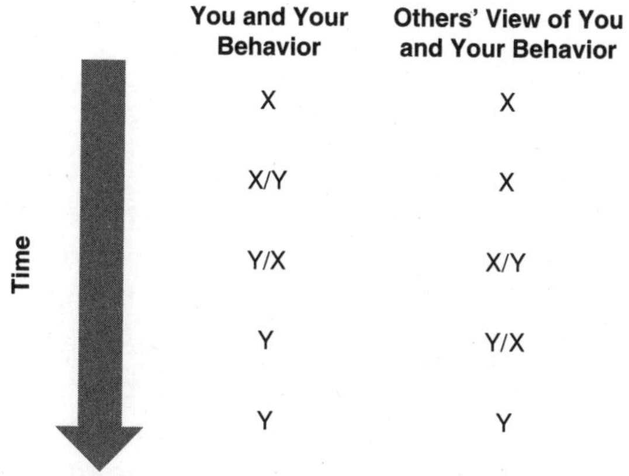

	You and Your Behavior	Others' View of You and Your Behavior
	X	X
	X/Y	X
Time	Y/X	X/Y
	Y	Y/X
	Y	Y

Source: Goldsworthy, 2009

back at the office, she was full of good intentions and was eager to apply her new learning. However, the response from her direct reports was less enthusiastic. It took considerable effort for Joanna to sustain her leadership change, and she was disappointed by the lackluster response that she received. However, because she had learned about the change lag, she was able to stay focused, not be derailed by the reaction, and stick with her action plan. In her six-month follow-up 360-degree report, Joanna's employees recognized her efforts and appreciated the change. Joanna realized the power and need for being consistent in her application.

As you develop, you must also be aware of the impact that change may have on those around you. In the words of Professor Jean-François Manzoni,

> The "old you" was part of a system that had reached some form of equilibrium. You and the people you interacted with had come to a modus vivendi. It was a more or less happy one, but it had come to some form of equilibrium. Your "ongoing professional and personal development efforts" are disturbing this equilibrium, and you may have to allocate some time and attention to help some key individuals to accept the changes and to become willing and able to learn to behave differently so they can support it. Hopefully, they all will become willing and able to help. But if some individual proves unwilling and/or unable to do so, you will have to decide how much of a problem this is for you and how you want to deal with the disconnect.[23]

Determination is a necessary part of success. Knowing that in the early stages your efforts may not be fully recognized or rewarded by those around you helps you to manage your own expectations and stay on track.

Andreas, a senior vice president and managing board member of a leading consumer brand, was known by his direct reports as being something of a micromanager, interfering in the smallest details on a regular basis. Following feedback from his team and working with a coach, Andreas realized the negative impact of his behavior on the motivation of the team and resolved to step back and empower his team more. He refocused his attention and energy on a different part of the business. He also stopped checking on his team every day. At first, he did not receive any positive feedback from the team. However, he stuck with his new approach and persisted. Eighteen months after he began his modification program, he was given direct feedback at an off-site meeting with his management team. They all acknowledged the clear difference in Andreas's leadership style. He had moved from micromanagement to empowerment, even to the point where, on occasion, the team felt that he had moved a little too far out and asked him to step back in a bit more.

Change takes determination. However, determination is less about the one grand gesture and more about the small, daily, quiet steps of courage that lead to a larger, more visible result.

Understanding that you will have setbacks and failures in your pursuit of change can be liberating. Awareness of the process of change and the confusion that is a natural part of any transition then frees you to keep focused and determined to achieve your goal. You can now move on to the fifth and final part of our change process: *development*.

Key Points to Remember

- Determination is necessary if you are to achieve your goal. Expect failures and setbacks and reframe them as opportunities to learn and continue to grow.
- Resilience can be built by improving your mental, physical, emotional, and spiritual well-being.
- Letting go is necessary in order to move ahead. Let go, then let be, in order to let come.
- All change involves a period of doubt or confusion; awareness and acceptance of this makes it easier to move forward rather than retreat.
- Feeling discomfort during change is a sign that you are making progress.
- Be patient; it may take longer for other people to recognize and reward your change efforts.

CHAPTER FIVE

Development

How Will You Keep Growing and Who Will Help You?

Intellectual growth should commence at birth and cease only at death.
—Albert Einstein

THE LAST OF the Five Ds is vital for ensuring that not only do you succeed with your original change goal, but you also approach your present and your future with a mindset of learning and growth. Life is a wonderful opportunity for continuous development. The only absolute for every single one of us is our mortality. Once born, everything dies—the only unknown is exactly when. As we saw in the previous chapters, fear and uncertainty are inescapable; they are natural components of your growth journey. It can be quite liberating to begin to see your whole life as an opportunity to develop and grow. Living organisms are either growing or decaying—there is no such thing as a static state. The choice is yours as to which category you fall into. *Development* is defined as "the act or process of growing, progressing, or developing."[1] The essence of development for change lies in asking yourself the question: how can I continually learn and grow? Adopting a mindset of continuous improvement is the best way to maximize your potential for continuous success.

In this chapter, we'll discuss the thinking skills and behaviors you must develop if you are to strengthen this frame of mind and apply it to leadership and to life. These include knowing when to go back to and practice the basics and knowing how to let go of perfectionism, maintain humility, align intention with impact, give and receive nonthreatening feedback, and seek out secure bases that challenge you and hold you accountable.

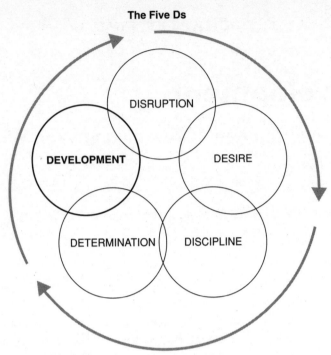

The Five Ds

DISRUPTION

DEVELOPMENT

DESIRE

DETERMINATION

DISCIPLINE

Source: Goldsworthy

Leading and Living Change: Tom Miller

Tom Miller is a leader who exemplifies many of these insights. He founded the Miller Company, a consultancy that focuses on recognition and reward systems, in 1992. Several years ago, he became concerned that the business, although successful, was not growing quickly enough to keep itself relevant in the future. In searching for a way to make the company stronger, Tom decided to embark upon a master's program in consulting and coaching for change that was offered jointly by two of Europe's most prestigious academic institutions, Oxford University in the United Kingdom and HEC in Paris, France.

When I looked at the program modules, they lined up with my hypothesis about what the marketplace in my line of business needed. I felt that if I became more expert in change management, the company would be able to help our clients more. And indeed this was one of the results. However, the big surprise for me came on Day 2 of the first module when I realized that the growth required was not in terms of knowledge for our clients but actually my own growth and the growth of the company. The real challenge I faced was to answer the question, "How do I want to live inside my company, and how do the other employees want to live?"

Tom realized that if he wanted his company to change and adapt, he would have to change and adapt. As the founder and owner of the company, he had created a culture in which everyone waited for him to do something before acting.

When he returned from the first module, the company faced a business issue. "I knew it could be better handled by other people, but they were all looking at me to give them the answer. Frustrated, I stood up, announced that I was going for a two-hour bike ride, and told them that I wanted to hear their proposal when I got back." It was a symbolic moment in which Tom turned his words into action.

"I realized that, for the good of the company, I had to break that cycle. At first it was painful. I had to release some of my power, and as I learned to do that, not everyone was ready for the change, as many had not been trained to deal with the empowerment I was offering them. It was an emotional experience. In the process, I found out where my blind spots are, and I found skills in other people who could do what I could not and could thereby give me the time to concentrate on what I am good at."

As part of the transformation journey, Tom also decided to change the name of the business from the Miller Company, named after himself, to Symbolist. The group members also determined a set of values as a guide for the way they wanted to work.

Says Tom, "The Symbolist brand was created to provide the foundation for doing what we do best: helping our clients offer better places to work. We wake up every day and work to live our own values: to be sustainable, relevant, and inter- ested in what we can do to have an impact on the companies with which we work. Our favorite question is, 'What's possible?' Tomorrow's work will be different from today's. We want to not only be ready for innovation, but also search it out, invite it, and embrace it."

Tom sees his personal leadership transformation as a journey. He has changed from the person who was always leading from the front to someone who creates the right environment so that the business can run smoothly whether he is there or not. He has developed talent and brought in systems and processes to help the business. "The thing I am most proud of is that our employees can spend their entire working life with us if they so choose. Yes, people must perform, but the system works because people feel responsible—even to the extent that our vacation policy is that you take what you need."

As Tom's journey continues, he relies on feedback from a close group of friends and business associates. "Usually, the higher up in the organization you go, the less truth you get. I worked on changing that. I now get feedback when I am being too con- trolling and when I am abdicating responsibility too much."

It is no surprise that as Tom and his people grew, so did the benefits to the clients, too. Tom is now hooked on learning. "It's a journey," he says. "There is no endgame to transformation."

The beauty of a continuous improvement mindset is that you can apply it at any time of your life. In fact, the earlier in life you begin, the greater the benefit to you and to those around you.

While studying for an MBA at IMD business school in Switzerland, Fabian Chessell reflected on the personal growth required for leadership. Said Fabian,

> As well as learning more conventional skills, such as finance, strategy, and marketing, it has been fascinating to develop a deeper under-standing of myself. Only by understanding how my behavior affects others, and how others' behavior affects mine, can I begin to explore and change how I interact with others. To connect with and motivate other people, I've learned the importance of understanding and remaining connected with my own goals and motivations. Learning about myself continues to be confronting, but each insight helps me leave behind old habits and cycles. I am genuinely excited about applying these new skills in my career going forward.

Psychologist Carol Dweck encourages people to have a growth mindset, instead of a fixed one.[2] If you have a fixed mindset, you are less likely to be curious, playful, and exploratory. You are more likely to have a rigid approach to life and a black-and-white binary approach. With a growth mindset, you are more likely to approach life with a more open frame, alert to possibilities.

Dr. Bertrand Piccard, record-breaking "around-the-world" balloonist and the president and initiator of the Solar Impulse Project, shares the story of how he became aware of a learning difference between bees and wasps. When he was sitting in his conservatory, he noticed that there were dead bees on the floor, but no dead wasps. Intrigued, he watched them to see what was happening. The bees constantly flew against the windows again and again until they died of exhaustion. However, the wasps that were also trapped in the conservatory explored every angle and eventually managed to find the opening and fly out. After he and copilot Brian Jones had successfully flown around the world in a hot-air balloon, he was asked how they had managed to beat the other teams, some of which had far greater financial backing. In ballooning, fighting against the winds is not always successful, and they beat other better-equipped competitors by changing their strategy and accepting the prevailing winds. Piccard said, "We had the strategy of the wasps. Our competitors had the strategy of the bees. To succeed, it is important to step out of comfort zones, try new strategies and think outside of the box."[3]

Move Ahead by Rediscovering the Basics

One thing that all successful people have in common, no matter what area they have become successful in, is that they were not successful when they first began. For people who have been successful in one field (for example, athletes who enjoy success when they are young), it can be difficult to let go, go back to the beginning, and become successful in a different walk of life. It is sad to see people who achieve success early in life remaining trapped in that success and living as if the future were nothing more than a memory of the past. However, if they apply the learning that made them successful the first time round, are willing to go back to basics, and can work with the Five Ds, they can enjoy success again.

Henry Nwume has packed a great deal into his 36 years of life. At Oxford University, where he studied medicine, he was awarded an Oxford Blue (for competition at the highest level) in rugby. He also played for one of the best rugby teams in the United Kingdom, the Wasps rugby team, winning Europe's greatest club rugby prize, the Heineken Cup, against Toulouse in 2004. He joined the army and served as a medical doctor in Afghanistan. While working at army novice camp, he was introduced to the bobsled, and he realized that his combination of power and speed made him a natural for the sport. Applying himself in the same way as he had done in becoming a successful doctor and rugby player, he began training for the Winter Olympics as a member of the four-man bobsled team. On his second day at the Olympic training camp in 2006, he ruptured a ligament in his ankle, an injury that could have cut him out of the squad. Henry saw this as his biggest setback. However, he was determined to recover and participate in the Olympic Games. As Henry told us in an interview,

> Just after I'd decided to commit to bobsleigh, and dared to set myself the goal of competing in the next Olympics, I'd gotten injured. I slipped on the ice in a training session and badly tore the ligaments in my ankle. Suddenly all the excitement and energy I'd felt upon committing to that goal were suddenly converted into feelings of despair and loss. To feel driven by a new goal is a wonderful thing, and just when I'd gotten used to enjoying that sense of purpose, I had to confront the feeling of losing it. Now my confidence had been replaced with uncertainty and self-doubt and all the anxiety that comes with that.
>
> For about 12 hours I was devastated. It really was a feeling of loss. But with a bit of time came clarity; I had overcome injury before, and so I would again. I pushed to be flown home as soon as possible so that

I could be scanned and diagnosed. Then I knew exactly what I was dealing with and how long my recovery might take. With that information, I could start planning and making choices. Getting injured was out of my control, but by making choices, I could reexert my control. Despite what had happened, there were still opportunities. There are always opportunities. Why couldn't I come back stronger, faster, and better? And so I sat down and wrote down my weaknesses. I sought out expert objective help from my coach and my physiotherapist. Some of what I was told hurt. But to be strong enough to accept objective criticism is the first lesson I had to learn in order to improve.

That's one of the benefits of being an athlete: you are surrounded by people who are highly motivated to help you improve. I had a great doctor, a great physiotherapist, and a great coach who all bought into my goal and wanted to help me as much as they could. I think that's why being injured can be such a positive experience for an athlete, a real lesson in goal achievement. If you're disciplined and you work with focus and structure, your hard work pays off. Every week I would set myself new goals, and more often than not I was able to reach them, and there is nothing more motivating than systematically reaching and surpassing your goals. This is what energizes you and improves your confidence. And once you have done this multiple times, you recognize what you can achieve despite adversity. You become confident in your own self-efficacy, and you realize that this is transferable to any situation. So when the next setback comes, which it inevitably will, you have the tool kit to deal with it.

In 2010, Henry achieved his goal, representing Great Britain at the Vancouver Olympics. At the 2012 Olympics, he was involved in a program to mentor young athletes who were keen to make the 2016 Games in Rio de Janeiro. He is currently training to be a GP (a general practice doctor). "All my previous achievements don't make a difference in helping me achieve this goal," says Henry. "The examining board is not going to give me a free pass because I went to Oxford or played rugby or competed at the Olympics. I have to earn the right to be a GP by passing the exams just like everyone else. Once people get to know me, they are often impressed by my background, but it is not something that I expect to open doors for me." Henry applies the same process to everything he attempts in life, whether it be an academic or a sporting achievement. One of the reasons for his repeated success is that he is willing to go back to the basics to learn new talents, time after time, and to be open to feedback from those around him to help in his development.

Development Is Personal

Development requires you to dig deep within yourself and start the change process from within. American Society of Training and Development (ASTD) president and CEO Tony Bingham says, "A great step forward in performing change better lies in leading it better, and the best place to start in leading change is with yourself."[4]

Virtually anyone can develop the capacity to lead more effectively through practical learning and development, says leadership and organizational behavior professor Jack Wood. "Responsible leadership takes practice— involvement and the willingness to question yourself. Meaningful behavioral learning occurs only as a result of a strongly felt need and a deep personal commitment to develop oneself. Anyone who wants to run a marathon in under three hours has to spend months practicing. Leadership is a practice, like medicine and law. Executives who want to develop their capacity to lead must get their hands dirty and actually 'do' leadership."[5]

José Maria (Pepe) Gonzaléz has enjoyed a rich and varied international career. More than a decade ago, he led the creation of an in-house academy at a large global packaging company with the goal of tying the corporate strategy to the development of the competencies necessary to achieve it faster and more efficiently. Working with external providers and a large network of internal top executives, the academy was so successful that not only did it train more than 3,000 people in record time, but it is still in existence today. "I particularly enjoyed the fact that as I grew and developed, so did the people within the company in terms of skills, knowledge and competencies," said Pepe. "All of the learning was linked to the achievement of the company strategy, and so it benefited both the individuals and the organization."

Today, Pepe runs his own successful consultancy, lectures at business schools, and consults on a number of topics. He has also created and runs several in-house academies for large multinational companies. In the words of one of his clients, Pepe is "very skilled at getting to the bottom of the real business needs and then creating innovative, powerful learning." Adds Pepe, "Learning is fundamental to change. By helping individuals to grow and develop, the organization can help itself to grow and develop. The combination of individual and organizational change is something I feel deeply passionate about. And I can help others learn and grow only if I remain open to growth and learning for myself."

When Nick Shreiber took over as CEO of Tetra Pak, he was humble enough to realize that he had to grow into the role, even though many people in the organization expected him to act as the CEO immediately. At a Q&A session during an internal conference, one participant asked him how his first four weeks had been. He responded that it had been like going back to college, as even though he knew a fair amount about the company, there was still so much to learn. He also said that the CEO role was very different from his previous role as regional president. The next day, the employee sent him an e-mail saying, "Dear Nick, it is so wonderful to hear that a CEO can still be open to learning as opposed to claiming to know everything."

In *Managing Your Self*, Jagdish Parikh talks of two types of learning: additive and subtractive. Additive learning is the more traditional approach, where you learn more and add to your knowledge sequentially, over time. However, after a certain amount of time, you need to pursue subtractive learning as well in order to continue to develop. Some of the knowledge you have accumulated and the beliefs and attitudes you have acquired over time may need to be chiseled out, as they may have become obsolete or even function as barriers to your further growth. By being open to objectively reviewing and considering altering some of your mental and emotional constructs, you can sculpt your real learning and growth.[6]

When you pursue a life of continuous learning and development, you open up to opportunities and never quite know where the path may take you. That's the humility and openness to learning that we see in Nick's approach, and it also helped Robyn Renaud create a business as a successful executive coach. Robyn has enjoyed many reincarnations in her career, and each time she has embraced the learning, challenges, and growth that each very different opportunity had to offer. Although she has enjoyed a wide variety of roles, from teaching secondary school chemistry and biology, to working in special education with autistic and then dyslexic children, to providing physiotherapy for Maasai children with polio, to being a leader in the Africa regional office of the World Health Organization, to being a senior-level executive coach, all these roles have had one thing in common: her desire to help people to fulfill their potential.

For many years now, Robyn has worked with individuals, teams, and organizations to help them to grow and develop. Her most recent learning journey has involved her becoming certified to work with horses to help business executives recognize the power of their unspoken intentions and attitudes, overcome their fears, and stay mindful and in the present. Says Robyn, "If I keep myself open to learning, I am better equipped to help others learn. The attitude and the practice start with me."

The learning person demonstrates five key attributes: self-knowledge, self-acceptance, self-respect, autonomy, and the seeking of both solitude and

company. With self-knowledge, you are able to assess your own abilities, apti-
tudes, and motives realistically. With self-acceptance, you are able to affirm the
essential validity of your own being or reality and recognize and acknowledge
your own feelings and reactions. With self-respect, you are able to think well
of yourself regardless of your particular achievements or possessions, and you
feel adequate, lovable, acceptable, and worthy. With autonomy, you are able
to accept your own need for others, but you are also emotionally independent,
believing that you have the emotional resources needed to handle life's opportunities and crises. Finally, when you seek both solitude and company, you are
willing to spend time alone and also with others.[7]

The attitude of helping others through development of self is demonstrated by the author of the *New York Times* bestseller *Uplifting Service*, Ron
Kaufman. Passionate about learning, Ron made the decision many years ago
to dedicate his life to service, which he defined as taking action to take care of
someone else with the aim of serving a larger social purpose. That desire has
been at the core of his intentions and his actions for more than two decades.
When interviewed for this book, he said,

> The most important ingredient for development and new learning is
> curiosity. There is a fixed way of looking at development that is about
> getting certified, passing tests, and generally proving oneself to build
> credibility and provide a sense of achievement. This view addresses the
> question, "Am I good enough yet?" But there is a very different and
> more open orientation toward development that stems from a mindset
> of genuine curiosity and addresses the questions, "What is possible?
> What is emerging? What am I becoming?" When I'm curious, I am
> naturally open to learning. Curiosity is a mood of wonder, coupled
> with a natural sense of ambition and purpose, even if that purpose is
> not yet defined. Development emerges from approaching life with a
> curious nature.

Ron's approach epitomizes a learning mindset, aiming high for himself
and those around him by remaining open, curious, and ambitious.

Letting Go of Perfectionism

In our experience working with senior executives, many of them often fall into
or close to the perfectionist category, holding themselves and those around
them to unrealistic standards. Perfectionists often have a fixed mindset; that
is, they think about their goals in terms of black or white, pass or fail, good

or bad. This binary mindset typically involves attaching a judgment to the outcome. This approach can lead to a fear of failure, and so perfectionistic people avoid trying something new because if they do not achieve it, they will then be judged a failure. This tendency can be particularly acute during major change experiences.

Perfectionism hampers success and is often the path to depression, anxiety, addiction, and life paralysis, says Dr. Brené Brown, author of *The Gifts of Imperfection*.[8] She points out that there is a huge difference between healthy striving and perfectionism. Healthy striving is about growth, potential, and self-improvement. It is self-focused and prompts asking, "How can I improve?" Perfectionism is, at its core, about trying to earn acceptance and approval. When they were raised, most perfectionists were rewarded for their accomplishments in terms of results. This is why perfectionists are other-focused, always asking, "What will they think?"[9] Perfectionism is self-destructive and stimulates a great deal of unhelpful mental self-flagellation.

According to Ginka Toegel and Jean-Louis Barsoux, perfectionists can fuss over details while losing sight of the big picture. Executives with this tendency need to ask themselves, "Is this a high-leverage activity, or could my time be better invested elsewhere?" Perfectionism has another unfortunate consequence: sensing that their boss is inclined to get too involved or to micromanage, employees may grow reluctant to flag issues. If you are a perfectionist, put on your coaching hat and switch to questioning mode so that your input comes across as help, not control.[10] This advice is relevant whether you are talking to yourself or to others.

How can you notice if you have perfectionist tendencies? The following list from Resilience Institute consultant Madeleine Shaw shows some of the ways in which perfectionist thinking may manifest itself:

- The inability to celebrate your successes, focusing only on what went wrong rather than on what went right
- Putting off doing certain things because you fear that the result will not be good enough
- Not knowing when to say, "That's good enough," and so spending a disproportionate amount of time and effort on finessing something that already meets its needs
- Getting down on yourself for not performing "perfectly" and letting this affect your mood and your relationships with others
- Projecting the impossibly high standards you hold for yourself on to those around you, and then being critical when they fail to meet them[11]

Now, of course, this does not mean that you do not want to get things right. We all want the pilot of our plane or the doctor who is performing our surgery or the financial advisor who is investing our money to be accurate and highly competent. It is important to function at the necessary standard, but it is also important to be realistic about what that standard actually is.

In the change you are working on, seeking perfection is not the goal. You are human, after all. Steve Jobs was known for his unpleasant outbursts and bad behavior in terms of the way he treated other people. Fired from his own company in 1985, he returned in 1996 not as a changed man, but with enough control over himself to refocus on making Apple the success it became.[12] Steve Jobs knew that he had to change his behavior and have the courage to face his demons in order to fulfill his dreams. Although he changed, he by no means became a model of a caring leader. However, he did improve enough to make his leadership workable. As you embark on your journey of change, while it is helpful to have ambitious goals, it is also important for you to make sure that your small steps have STAMINA, as discussed in Chapter 2.

Another way to manage perfectionism is to rediscover your "playful child," that part of you that is curious and joyful. Playfulness involves your imagination, releases creativity, and is vital for innovation. The opposite of play is not work but rather depression, says Dr. Stuart Brown, founder of the National Institute for Play. "Respecting our biologically programmed need for play can transform work. It can bring back excitement and newness to our job. Play helps us deal with difficulties, provides a sense of expansiveness, promotes mastery of our craft, and is an essential part of the creative process," says Brown. "In the long run, work does not work without play."[13] Play facilitates learning. The joy of play stimulates the reward centers in the brain and is associated with the release of dopamine, which facilitates the establishment and consolidation of new neuronal pathways, which in turn is important for creativity and memory.[14]

So, rather than distracting you from your goal, embracing the playful part of yourself can actually help you in achieving it. Being a healthy striver is important for success; however, you can also be a healthy player and still achieve. Say farewell to the false lure of perfection.

Intention Versus Impact

When you see a behavior or receive some feedback you don't appreciate, it is all too easy to take it personally and then become defensive. Knowing how instantaneous this response can be, exercise your choice point the next time you find yourself looking at someone else and feeling aggressive or defensive.

Stop and ask yourself, "What is this person's intention?" When they wake up in the morning, most people do not think, "How can I ruin someone else's day?" Most people wake up and think about themselves and want to do the best they can that day. Their intention is positive and is often related to themselves. Unfortunately, for many reasons, the impact of our choices is often not aligned with our intentions.

Our intention is rarely to be personally damaging or insulting. For most people, we are the centers of our own universe. Unconditional positive regard (UPR), a phrase coined by psychologist Carl Rogers, is the basic acceptance and support of a person regardless of what that person says or does. Rogers believes that unconditional positive regard is essential to healthy development.[15] It is the profound and yet simple act of one individual accepting all the traits and behaviors of another individual, as long as this does not entail causing significant harm to oneself. Just as you can think about the intentions of others as being distinct from their impact, it is important to think about your own intentions the same way. This can be particularly useful for leaders during change, when the stress of new roles and routines can lead to confusion and suspicion about intentions. Aligning attention (your focus) and intention leads to a more positive impact.

Sometimes you may block your awareness of your impact. You may be too focused on your future success and fear that an examination of the present may lead to a "discovery" that can prompt failure. You may be too reliant on external validation. You may be too cocooned within your own comfort zones, and you may be trapped in the illusion of control. In any of these cases, you may interpret feedback through the biased filter of your own belief about yourself. It is for this reason that it is so important to have other people to work with you on your development journey.

Having Secure Bases to Support You

Research by Benjamin Bloom and colleagues shows that the top performers in many fields were not outstanding from birth; in fact, they were quite average.[16] What made the difference in their success appears to be that there was a parent, coach, teacher, mentor, or manager who believed in their potential and set the bar high in terms of possibility. This then created a self-fulfilling prophecy by inspiring them to engage in more deliberate, frequent, and ongoing practice in a focused way.

As leaders rise through the ranks, it becomes harder for them to find out the "truth." They may be told what they want to hear rather than being told what is actually happening or how people are really feeling. In medieval times, the king would have a court jester, someone who was no threat to the throne, who would tell him what people were saying and how things were being viewed. You can support your own change success by having people around you in the court jester role. In 1994, British Airways even appointed Paul Birch to the position of court jester to listen to people, involve them, and then provide feedback to senior management.[17]

Says Ron Kaufman, global expert on customer service,

> I've been fortunate to have excellent people guide and coach me in my life. One deeply influential person is Dr. Fernando Flores. I had the privilege of becoming his student in the late 1980s, and we are still collaborating on new projects today. He is a living example of lifelong personal development, and I learned many things from Dr. Flores, including the power of the beginner's mindset. When you declare yourself a beginner, you can then seek coaching and support, whether it be through a person, a workshop, a book, or a development community. A beginner says, "I am curious. I am ready. And I want to learn." Everybody wants to play in this life. I have found that when you give people enough feedback, encouragement, and opportunity, they will rise to the occasion, often surprising you with their commitment and contribution. Dare to stretch the boundaries of what's possible and you can redefine the way the game itself is played. Your development is then of benefit to everyone else's development, too.

In the lead story of this chapter, Tom Miller mentioned that feedback is essential to keep him on track. In the words of the seventeenth-century poet John Donne, "No man is an island." Never underestimate the importance of working with secure bases like mentors and coaches whom you trust enough to allow them to challenge you and hold you accountable in your personal development journey. British tennis player Andy Murray was renowned for being a second-rate world-class player—always the bridesmaid but never the bride. Year after year, he steadily rose up the global tennis rankings and managed to reach a number of finals as well as semifinals and quarterfinals. However, it seemed that he could never quite achieve victory in a major championship. In 2012, former champion Ivan Lendl became Murray's coach.

Since then, the progress in Murray's game has been clear. He has improved his forehand and second serve, but Lendl seems to have had the most effect on Murray's inner game, instilling a belief in Murray that he could better manage his emotions and maintain a positive approach. Fast-forward to Wimbledon

2012 and the finals against Roger Federer, where after taking the first set, Murray lost the match in four sets. Several weeks later, he faced Federer again, this time in the finals of the 2012 Olympic Games. Murray defeated Federer in straight sets to win the gold medal in the men's singles, becoming the first British champion in more than 100 years. He also won a silver medal in mixed doubles. Just over a month later, at the 2012 U.S. Open, he became the first British player since 1977, and the first British man since 1936, to win a grand slam singles tournament when he defeated Novak Djokovic in five sets.

Andy Murray's success is a wonderful example of the Five Ds in action and of his continuous development. In his desire to reach his full potential, he accepted that he needed to work on certain aspects of his behavior, he remained focused on his goal, he put in the practice required to compete at the very top of his chosen sport, he remained determined to improve and overcome defeat, and he continuously sought outside support to help him to grow and improve.

Seasoned business executive Alastair Robertson recalls, "I have used several coaches and mentors, each with a slightly different role to play, from content experts to leadership coaches with whom I could talk through my next steps, to out-and-out visionaries. In the sometimes lonely position of chief human resources officer, it is very comforting to have people around you whose judgment and feelings you trust telling you that you are doing OK at times and guiding you when you feel the world is against you."

Steve Bennett, former CEO of Intuit, says, "At the end of the day, people who are high achievers—who want to continue to learn and grow and be effective—need coaching."[18] Another senior executive who endorses the importance of coaches is William R. Johnson, CEO of H. J. Heinz Co. "Great CEOs, like great athletes, benefit from coaches who bring a perspective that comes from years of knowing [you], the company and what [you] need to do as a CEO to successfully drive the company forward. Every CEO can benefit from strong, assertive and honest coaching."[19]

In 2012, working with George Kohlrieser and Duncan Coombe, Susan coauthored an award-winning book on secure base leadership which demonstrated the importance of having trusted relationships with others in order to fulfill your potential.[20] Leveraging the doctoral research of Dr. Coombe, the book outlined the need for all of us to have secure bases in our lives, people who can stretch us and challenge us to go further than we may have thought possible, as well as nurture and support us. Secure bases can tell you things you may not want to hear but, because of the strength of the bond between you, you will listen to them and even act upon their advice, no matter how reluctant you are. One reason for the importance of secure bases is that you cannot see yourself as others do.

Says benefits management guru and author Steve Jenner,

> Continuous learning is something that we all sign up for, but it is something that is harder to achieve in practice. The issue here is that, as psychologists have shown, we suffer from a number of cognitive biases, including what is termed confirmation or expectation bias. In short, we tend to recognize evidence that confirms our preconceived opinions and ignore anything that runs counter to them. The result is that we mistake perception for reality until it eventually, and unexpectedly, bites us. The solution: we need to be open to feedback, to the unexpected and the insight that it brings. In turn, this means taking deliberate steps to ensure that it happens. For example, on one major cross-government program, I included sections in the monthly program report for "Things we could do better" and "Things not going as well as anticipated." The red warning flag for us was when these sections were blank. As our program director said, "If we haven't identified and shared any areas for improvement, then we're not looking hard enough."

The Necessity of Feedback for Success

We all have blind spots, and we require feedback from others to become aware of them, particularly during major change events, when the pressure is greater. Shares senior executive Aidan,

> Once, during leadership training, I was filmed with a group as part of an exercise on team behavior. At the end, the video was replayed, and I saw that I had totally ignored someone sitting right next to me who was trying to make an important point. Without the video evidence, I would have vehemently denied that I had ignored anybody, as I had no memory of the incident. It was a complete blind spot for me. When you reflect on your own behavior, it is impossible for you to see yourself clearly. You need a "mirror," a third-party reflection to help you. In my case, the combination of the video and a skilled coach helped me enormously. Being self-aware is pivotal, but often you need a close friend or a trusted mentor or coach to tell you some brutal facts about yourself!

The Johari Window was invented in 1955. The word *Johari* comes from the names of the two psychologists who created it, Joseph Luft and Harrington Ingham.[21] It is used to help people better understand their relationship with

Figure 5-1 Johari Window

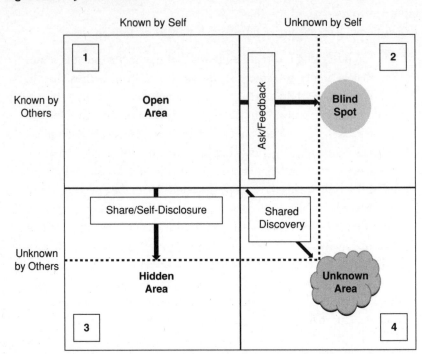

Source: Adapted from Alan Chapman 2001–2004, based on Ingham & Luft's Johari Window concept

themselves and with others. We regularly use a version of this model to share the process of continuous learning and development, and the building of trust. You can use the diagram in Figure 5-1 to initiate and stimulate a rich dialogue with another individual or amongst a team.

Square 1 is the open area; this represents those things that everyone knows upon meeting you—basics such as your gender, age, ethnicity, and extroversion or introversion.

In square 2, we have the blind spot: the things that are known to others but unknown to you. These are the things that people say about you at the coffee machine when you are not there! Complacency, at both the individual and the organizational level, indicates an excess of self-confidence that may make you blind to the need to change. The way you find out about your blind spots is to ask for and receive feedback.

The third square is the hidden area; these are the things that you know about yourself but that others find out only if you share the information. Now, some thoughts should probably never be shared. However, by sharing some hidden information about yourself, you show vulnerability, and this can create closer relationships with other people. The combination of squares 2 and 3, the asking and sharing, creates the process by which trust can be built.

When you enter into a process of soliciting feedback and disclosing information about yourself, you then expand your open area into square 4: unknown area. The process of shared discovery helps you to expand your self-view and embark on a lifelong journey of growth.

So, when do you expand to fill the full window? How long do you think that will take? Well, the answer is that you'll die first. Even the Dalai Lama hasn't reached the fullness of the window. That is the beauty of the gift of life that we all have—the only day when we can no longer develop and grow (at least in this life) is the day that we die. The Johari Window works equally well for growth journeys whether it is looked at from the individual or the team perspective.

Making Feedback FAIR

As shown by the blind spot area of the Johari Window, feedback is a vital element of the development stage/learning mindset. However, our brains can be quite defensive about inputs that they may perceive as a threat. Exchanges that are thought to be unfair generate a strong threat response.[22] Fairness is a hot button for your brain. The FAIR feedback model is a brain-based approach to giving and receiving feedback in a way that makes it most likely to be received, accepted, and acted upon. As an individual and a leader, creating a climate of open feedback can accelerate growth and performance for both you and your team.

The F stands for focus: when you are giving feedback, it is important for you to be specific about what behavior you liked or did not like. It is critical that you separate the person from the problem and provide input about the action as viewed from your perspective (when you did a, b, c, I felt like x, y, z), rather than label the person (you are lazy, stupid, or incompetent). This is important for both positive and negative feedback. Rather than just saying "good job," let your counterpart know why it was good. This helps the person understand exactly what she did well and hence increases her opportunities to consolidate and replicate the positive behavior. Being specific about what you did not like in a behavior increases the person's ability to know exactly what behavior is not appreciated.

The A stands for approach: this is linked to the connection between words, tone, and body language. When you are giving feedback, it is helpful if you are viewed by the person receiving it as being reliable, credible, and having the person's best interests at heart. The results of research by Daniel Goleman, Richard Boyatzis, and Marie Dasborough showed the impact of performance review feedback on two groups. The first group was given negative feedback, but with positive tone and body language, while the second group was given positive feedback, but with negative tone and body language. After the feedback, the participants were asked how they felt. Those in the first group understood that they clearly needed to improve but felt that they were supported and that others believed they could do it. Those in the second group were rather suspicious and hesitant, as what they had heard was positive, but the way it was delivered was at odds with the content.[23] Their brains noted an "error detection," and it made them feel uneasy and suspicious, as error signals are closely related to our brain's fear response. It is important to align your words, your tone, and your body language.

The I stands for intent: what is the purpose of the feedback? Is it viewed as helping the person grow and develop, or is it seen as diminishing or discounting the person in some way? Or is it more about the giver wanting to show how clever he is? Feedback says as much about the giver as it does about the receiver. The person receiving the feedback must have faith in the person delivering the feedback. She must believe that the other person has her best interests at heart; if she does not believe it, the feedback will be discounted. This is why others whom you trust are important for feedback. You are more likely to listen to potentially confronting and conflicting input if you trust the intentions of the person giving it to you.

The R stands for repetition: the best feedback occurs frequently and in the moment—what we call "coachable moments."[24] This is how sports coaches work. They see the play in action, and then they give immediate feedback, again and again, on what to correct in order to do better. Can you imagine a coach letting an athlete train every day for months and giving him no feedback until the end of a six-month review period? Or a coach giving an athlete a piece of feedback once, but then not mentioning it again? Clearly, this would be madness, as the athlete would have been practicing incorrectly for six months and wiring in some bad habits. Why should the same thing not be true for business feedback? If you want someone to help you to correct a behavior, it is useful for him or her to catch you in the moment and then repeat the feedback whenever they observe the behavior.

When you create a feedback climate, people are much more open both to giving you feedback and to receiving inputs themselves. A mindset of continuous improvement changes feedback from a potential threat to a potential gift, designed to improve the performance of the individual and the team.

In *The Wisdom of Teams*, Jon R. Katzenbach and Douglas K. Smith refer to high-performing teams as "a small number of people with complementary skills who are equally committed to a common purpose, goals, and working approach for which they hold themselves mutually accountable. Members are also deeply committed to each other's personal growth and success. That commitment usually transcends the team. The high performance team significantly outperforms all other like teams, and outperforms all reasonable expectations given its membership."[25] The ability to give and receive feedback is a fundamental part of that success.

Supported by Dun & Bradstreet, Sara Mathew created a social platform, daretolead.org, to enable Indian women to share their stories so that a new generation of women leaders can learn from those experiences and be inspired to follow in those footsteps. She says, "To become a better leader, you have to open yourself up to feedback, even criticism, and commit to do better every day."

Alastair Robertson also stresses the importance of being open to feedback.

When implementing our HR transformation, we realized that we needed to be open to feedback. To go that extra mile and really deliver globally, you need to listen to all corners of the globe, not just the head office. However, we also realized that while you must listen, there is no escape from the reality that not all feedback can be acted on and choices have to be made.

There is also no escape from another fact of life. To improve means to do something different or new, or to stop doing something. It means that, as a leader, you need to look in the mirror and recognize who you see. Sometimes, it is necessary to bypass your own ego and then make the internal adjustments. This is something I have learned throughout my career.

The Practice of Gratitude

Gratitude is a powerful tool—feeling grateful and expressing it is good for you and for those around you. Our intellect, our will, and our feelings are all engaged when we are grateful. It is a wholehearted response.[26] Gratefulness puts us in touch with what is really important in our lives. It is the simple, daily things that we are often most grateful for. If you ever take a walk around a cemetery and read the inscriptions on the headstones, they refer to the familial relationships that people had rather than their job titles. Gratitude helps you to maintain a healthy perspective in your life.

Self-confessed perfectionist Michael has found that applying the daily gratitude exercise has helped him to let go of an overly critical inner voice and to feel better about himself and his life. "Before going to bed, I have made it a habit to stop and reflect upon what I have been grateful for during that day. It takes me only a couple of minutes, but it actually makes me feel good about the day and able to go to bed more relaxed. It also makes me a better leader."

Cultivate a practice of gratitude by carrying out this simple and quick gratitude exercise every day.

Gratitude Exercise

Either in the morning or at the end of the day, take a moment to ask yourself the question, "What am I grateful for?" Reflect upon three things that you appreciate; perhaps even write them down. By making the gratitude exercise a daily part of your life, you can help frame your thinking toward the benefits in your life and the things for which you are truly grateful.

Pulling It All Together

Now that you have read each of the chapters relating to the Five Ds framework, as outlined in the Introduction, you are well equipped to continue your own change journey. Remember, meaningful, lasting change is an iterative process in which discoveries and changes in one part of the model will help you go deeper into practices in another aspect. Throughout our lives, we move among the Five Ds like the ebb and flow of the tide. By following the Five Ds process and by applying the techniques and tips outlined in this part of the book, you have it within you to really work on and achieve the change you want to make.

Let us reflect upon the Five Ds:

Disruption. What has made you aware of the need to change? What conscious choice will you make? What is your motivation?

Desire. What do you really want to change? How serious are you about making it happen?

Discipline. What are your small steps to big success? What are you willing to do differently to make it happen?

Determination. How will you deal with setbacks and failures? How resilient are you?

Development. How will you continuously improve, and who will help you?

The Five Ds

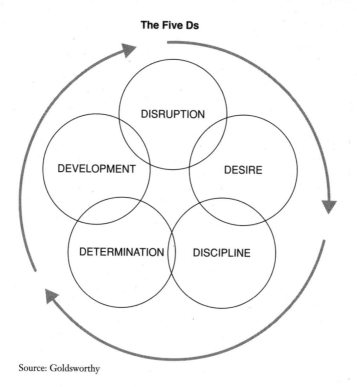

Source: Goldsworthy

How will you know when you have been successful in your change journey? What will success look like, feel like, and sound like? What are the quick wins along the way? Think of the metaphor of a duck on a pond. On the surface, it looks as though the duck is just hanging around. Underneath the surface, the duck is paddling against the currents. Ducklike status refers to the fact that whenever anyone is good at something, people tend to say things like, "Oh, well, he's a natural," or, "It comes easy to her." What they forget is that when anyone is any good at anything, that person can make it look easy (the unconscious competence stage); however, behind the scenes, he or she has prepared thoroughly. The hard work happens out of sight of most people. It is the performance that people see and remember. Take a moment and think about your ducklike moments. What will it look like, feel like, and sound like when you have achieved your goal? What will you hear people say?

Following the Five Ds helps you to choose change and make it happen, day in and day out, at the individual level. However, the same framework can also help your organization to choose a change-focused approach and make it happen, day in and day out. Personal development is essential to creating dynamic, vibrant, and innovative companies. Change-focused organizations are populated by change-focused people across all levels. Turn to the second part of this book to find out how to successfully choose ongoing and sustainable organizational change.

Key Points to Remember

- Cultivate a growth mindset. Be curious to learn and develop.
- Be conscious of the difference between your intentions and your impact.
- Perfectionism is a killer. Embrace your imperfection; be a healthy striver instead, and free your playful child.
- Find secure bases who can support, stretch, and challenge you in the achievement of your goals.
- Create a feedback climate to encourage growth for yourself and those around you and to build trust.
- The practice of gratitude is powerful. Reflect upon what you are grateful for every day.

Bridge

Moving from a Change-Focused Leader to a Change-Focused Organization

Part II of our book has two purposes. The first is to improve your ability to lead organizational change efforts through sharing insights from our study of effective change strategy, the experiences of accomplished leaders in the field who we have interviewed, and our own experiences. The second is to help you build into your organization more capability to change in the future. In the five chapters that follow, we make recommendations focused on helping you achieve both purposes.

Part II provides an array of recommendations for leading large-scale organizational change and includes topics that often come up during organizational change efforts, but that are seldom—if ever—discussed. Here are a few examples.

One of our recommendations in Chapter 6, "Disruption," is to "create a guiding philosophy." We recommend that senior executives meet and define "what change is and how we conduct it here." To put it another way, executives should define the "ends" and "means" of organizational change. Through our interviews and experience, we have learned that senior executives seldom take the time to create such a philosophy. They brush the idea aside, claiming that it isn't necessary because they already have a guiding philosophy—but they don't.

Our interviews and experience indicate that each executive has different ideas about what organizational change is and how it should be carried out. These differences cause misunderstandings, conflicts, and delays as change efforts unfold. If you can build a guiding philosophy among your senior team and tie it to your organization's core values, you will ease many of the necessary transitions during organizational change efforts.

One of our recommendations in Chapter 7, "Desire," may sound familiar: "create an organization-wide communications strategy." However, our approach differs from what you have read or heard about in most other books. We draw on neuroscience to show that rational arguments and threats are largely ineffective in persuading and motivating the workforce to desire organizational change. The most effective change leaders do not use communications to threaten or persuade. Instead, they use communications to inform, inspire, and involve. Instead of merely persuading, these leaders take action to build an environment that is less threatening to the brain and fosters better thinking.

In Chapter 8, "Discipline," we focus on creating management structures that help to guide and sustain organizational change—but with a new twist. We suggest that managing great change isn't just about creating detailed change plans and oversight structures. In fact, too much management control can rob change efforts of the creativity and original thinking that complex change requires. Instead, we recommend a management process that balances control and flexibility to ensure that the change effort stays on schedule and inspires the best thinking of the workforce at every step.

In Chapter 9, "Determination," we speak about something that all change efforts experience: setbacks. We suggest that great change planning anticipates setbacks before they occur and provides the structures needed to reduce—or even exploit—their effects. We also suggest ways to better manage the current competitive environment, which we describe as volatile, uncertain, complex, and ambiguous (VUCA).[1]

In Chapter 10, "Development," we discuss the importance of enabling your organization to constantly improve at carrying out organizational change efforts through continuous learning. The ability of your organization to learn from, and remember, the lessons of change is at the heart of a change-focused organization and creates real competitive advantage.

In moving through Part II, we focus on one particular kind of large-scale organizational change, one that we call *revolutionary change*. Revolutionary change is defined as change that is unexpected, affects all parts of the organization, and threatens the organization's existence. We chose revolutionary change as our focal point because it is the most complex form of organizational change, and the stakes are highest. However, our recommendations are also relevant to other forms of large-scale organizational change.

Finally, we address the reader as a "change leader." However, we have not focused our comments on any particular position or organizational level. It is our hope that whether you are the CEO, a senior executive, a middle manager, a first-line leader, or a member of the workforce who wants to help your organization lead change better, there is something here for you. Regardless of who you are, choosing to lead great change in your organization begins with choosing to lead great change in yourself.

The
Change-Focused
Organization

CHAPTER SIX

Disruption

Balancing Challenge and Opportunity

We are continually faced by great opportunities brilliantly disguised as insoluble problems.

—Lee Iacocca

IN CHAPTER 1, we defined *disruption* at the individual level as "a problem or action that interrupts something and prevents it from continuing." We noted that although disruptions are difficult, they can provide you with a real opportunity for personal growth—if you choose to embrace them. Simply said, leading real change in yourself requires both a disruption in your thinking *and* a conscious choice to use the disruption to bring about change.

Our definition of disruption also works at the organizational level, although the ways in which organizations experience disruptions are both similar to and different from the ways in which people experience them. A big reason that organizations experience disruption differently is related to the intensity of twenty-first-century competition. Organizations in many industries are experiencing more competitive disruptions and view these as real threats to their survival—and for good reason. There's significant data showing that disruptions can threaten the very existence of an organization, in spite of its best efforts to adapt and change.[1]

In the spring of 2010, Michael Tushman of the Harvard Business School and Charles O'Reilly of the Stanford School of Business delivered the Leading Change and Organizational Renewal course at the Harvard Business School campus. Present were 90 executives from over a dozen countries who had one thing in common: like you, they each wanted to do better at leading organizational change. As the course began, the screen at the front of the classroom came to life. On it was a long list of large companies—several whose names

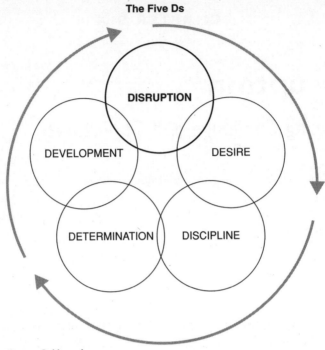

Source: Goldsworthy

were household words. Tushman asked the group: "What do these companies have in common?" The answer was: they had led their industries, experienced a significant competitive challenge, and failed to make the changes needed to survive—often in spite of their best efforts.

In terms of similarity, a disruption can elicit great performance improvements in both people and organizations. The disorienting effects of disruption can trigger the deep reflection and changes in perspective that are required for leaps in learning and performance.[2] We have seen this occur in individuals and organizations during revolutionary change efforts, and the executives we interviewed also mentioned it. Let us return to the Harvard Business School story for a moment.

Immediately after showing the list of great companies that failed to survive a competitive disruption, the image on the screen changed to a different list of companies, many with very familiar names. Tushman repeated the question: "What do these companies have in common?" The answer was: they led their industries, experienced a competitive disruption, and continue to thrive today. Then Tushman asked one more question: "What did the surviving companies do differently?" The answer was: they were able to lead change in themselves.

Tushman and O'Reilly noted that a key factor in the ability of these organizations to change successfully was their ability to develop great change leaders—leaders who don't fear disruption. Instead, they know that a well-led disruption can elicit performance improvements in people and organizations that are far greater than anyone expected—or believed possible.[3]

An important difference, therefore, between leading change in yourself and leading change in your organization is the nature of the choice you must make. To lead change in yourself, you must choose to *act* on a disruption—to use it for personal growth. To lead change in your organization, the choice is not *whether* you will act on a disruption, but *how*. The purpose of Part II is to guide you in how to lead revolutionary change in your organization. Your first step is to quickly and effectively reframe the competitive disruption as the opportunity it can become.

Leading and Living Change: Kimo Kippen

Kimo Kippen, the chief learning officer of Hilton Worldwide, assumed his role in the midst of the largest competitive disruption in the firm's 100-year history: its acquisition by The Blackstone Group. Kimo's role was to design and implement new structures and processes to improve the learning and performance of the global workforce. Three years into the acquisition, organizational performance has increased, and improved workforce performance is heralded as a key reason why. Kimo used the disruption as an opportunity to enhance Hilton's overall standing in the hospitality industry. In Kimo's words:

> *The rich history of Hilton Worldwide dates back nearly a century to 1919, when Conrad Hilton purchased his first hotel in Cisco, Texas. Since its founding, the company has distinguished itself as a leader in the hospitality industry. In 2006, the company's international and U.S. brands came together for the first time in 40 years. The following year, a merger agreement between Hilton Hotels Corporation and affiliates of The Blackstone Group was finalized and we became a privately held organization.*
>
> *In 2009, we made the strategic decision to relocate our world headquarters to McLean, Virginia, and, on the heels of this move, launched our new Hilton Worldwide corporate identity to better represent who we are today and our aspirations for the company going forward. This period represented the largest-scale transformation in the company's history and also included changes in senior leadership and our brands, new strategic initiatives, and a fresh approach to learning and development. This time period represented*

a profound change for Hilton Worldwide and provided the company with an opportunity to embark on one of the most powerful evolutions in its long history.

In 2010, Hilton Worldwide hired me as the new chief learning officer, and the story of Hilton Worldwide University (HWU) began. Before HWU, learning was delivered on an as-needed basis, and the corporate learning and development team (L&D) lacked the structure and process required to run learning as a partner and strategic provider to the business. The learning function was turned around by the creation of HWU, which is made up of five colleges and a number of specialty schools. Each college is led by a dean and supports a specific team member audience and business need. HWU offers thousands of e-learning options, virtual training sessions, and classroom instructor-led learning opportunities. The branding, communication, and outreach of HWU to hotels and corporate team members showcases ongoing initiatives to consistently keep learning opportunities fresh, innovative, and in the forefront for team members across the globe.

HWU was founded to address five mission-critical areas: strategy, structure, people, process, and systems. Learning had to show that it could contribute to driving market share and profitability as well as deliver a best-in-class solution that met the needs of the business. Our leadership team's relentless focus on ensuring that we had the right strategy in place, people to implement our plans, and the process and systems to support our initiatives became the foundation upon which HWU was built.

The launch of HWU came during a particularly challenging economic climate. As the economic crisis, which began in 2008, worsened, executive support for learning became even more critical. To achieve maximum support for the role of learning, each college created close ties to the business via an executive sponsor and a learning council. The councils consist of team members in diverse roles and divisions that provide input on the needs of the business and contribute ideas as to how the college can support these needs. Council members influence the curriculum, the program design, and the overall strategy and direction of the individual college.

The executive sponsorship and learning council are the building blocks for creating learning solutions that deliver impactful results to the business. The insight, feedback, and perspective brought by these team members help to keep the learning content fresh, relevant, and appealing. It is important to note that sponsorship started out small and grew with the addition of learning councils. For sponsorship to succeed, the direction must be scalable, be effective, and make sound use of technology along with solid metrics to demonstrate the impact of learning.

Since its launch, HWU has continued to extend its reach into the heart of our business, and the response by the organization has been overwhelmingly positive. From mid-2011 to mid-2012, HWU delivered more than five million hours of training to our team members. The recent launch of a new learning management system, establishment of partnerships with leading universities, and creation of cutting-edge programs have earned our corporate university an overall team member satisfaction rating of 9.57, compared to an average corporate university satisfaction rating of 8.64 at other companies. Furthermore, a relentless effort to support the growth of our learning professionals through ongoing development opportunities exemplifies how the L&D team sets a strong example for individuals in the organization to embrace learning and own their development.

In closing, perhaps the most critical takeaway from the HWU story is that to be successful an organization's response to a true disruption must be accompanied by a sense of urgency, leaders that can quickly adapt to change, and a product that can drive results for team members and the business.

Like Kimo Kippen's, your role in leading revolutionary change is not to "get your team and organization through the change effort," but to use the effort to take yourself, your team, and your organization to a higher level of performance.

Competitive Disruption and Revolutionary Change

As mentioned, competitive disruptions are periodic occurrences in modern organizations that are unexpected and so significant that they threaten the very existence of the organization. Because competitive disruptions threaten survival, organizations take them seriously and often respond with large-scale change efforts that we refer to as revolutionary change. The goal of the revolutionary change effort is to quickly and effectively address performance gaps and make the organization more competitive.

Organizational change comes in many forms, from simple process changes to large-scale mergers and acquisitions and revolutionary change efforts. A revolutionary change effort is the most complex form of change and the one with the highest stakes for people and organizations—this is why we chose it as our focal point. As a change leader, leading a successful revolutionary change effort is a crucial part of your role.

Note that when we refer to you as a change leader, we don't specifically define your organizational role. You could be the CEO, a member of the executive team, a middle manager, a frontline leader, or a member of the workforce who is interested in leading change. Regardless of your formal position, you assume a new set of responsibilities when you take on the role of change leader, and you must be prepared for them.

The executive interviews conducted for this book, our ongoing research, and our personal experience all underscore the importance of the early stages of revolutionary change for the ultimate success of the effort.

This chapter is about helping you lead the initial stages of revolutionary change efforts, and it addresses the period of time just after a competitive disruption has occurred. The goal is to help your organization quickly reframe the disruption from threat to opportunity. We make specific recommendations for leading the early stages of revolutionary change efforts. For now, we want to set the stage for that discussion by exploring the nature of competitive disruptions in more detail.

Characteristics of Competitive Disruptions

Disruptions can affect organizations and people in profound ways—particularly in the early stages. The first step in leading change is to understand the nature of competitive disruptions and these five characteristics. Competitive disruptions:

- Are inevitable
- Are unexpected
- Affect the entire organization
- Threaten the organization
- Can foster a false need for urgency

Competitive Disruptions Are Inevitable

Organizational scholars have concluded that periodic disruptions are now a normal part of organizational evolution.[4] In this view, organizational growth and development occurs in two important ways. The first is through periods of relative stability in which change is evolutionary. The second is through brief periods of revolutionary change triggered by a disruption.[5]

Organizational scholars also assert that an emerging set of factors is forcing twenty-first-century organizations to change more and faster than ever before, and in different ways.[6] One result of this phenomenon is an increase in the frequency and number of competitive disruptions. Put another way, the most complex and difficult kind of organizational change—revolutionary change—is happening more often.[7] For this reason, the organizations (and change leaders) that are best prepared to lead these efforts will have a competitive edge. The executives we interviewed agreed that the ability to carry out organizational change better, faster, and with fewer resources would provide real competitive advantage.

Competitive Disruptions Are Unexpected

Competitive disruptions often arrive as a surprise—in spite of your organization's best efforts to predict and/or mitigate them. Even when there is some form of early warning, it is often inadequate for detailed planning and preparation. This fact has several implications for you as a change leader:

- Disruptions can hit your organization hard, causing immediate confusion, anxiety, and even fear.
- Anxiety and fear can foster poor initial decision making, which can set the change effort on the wrong course.
- Focusing on urgency as the primary goal of the change effort is a bad decision. Great change leaders balance reflection, collaboration, and urgency. They think before they act.

The temptation to act with too much urgency is something that you should resist and is discussed in more detail later in this chapter.

Competitive Disruptions Affect the Entire Organization

Competitive disruptions are not specific to any one geographic area, business unit, or function. They affect all or most of the organization in a profound way. One implication for you as a change leader is that you need to try to manage the simultaneous reactions of the entire organization to this unexpected threat. Managing the reactions of the workforce is a particularly important consideration because you need to keep the workforce supporting and actively engaged in the change effort. The workers' collective expertise, insight, and experience are essential ingredients in successful change.

Competitive Disruptions Threaten the Organization

The word *threat* is often used in discussions of organizational change. The idea is that change efforts—and particularly revolutionary ones—can threaten the very existence of an organization and the livelihoods of every person in it. We know some executives who believe that the threat fostered by disruption is a good thing and is invaluable in leading change efforts. Their idea is that threats to the organization motivate people to embrace organizational change. To these executives, leading change is about communicating the next threat in order to "motivate" the workforce one more time. We think this approach is misguided for several reasons, but a key one is that it exhausts the workforce and deprives the organization of its best, most creative thinking.

The high levels of uncertainty, anxiety, and performance pressure that characterize competitive disruptions can foster a reaction in the brain called a "threat state." As Rock and Tang noted, a threat state involves more than just fear.[8] It includes anything that the brain seeks to avoid, including sadness, anxiety, lack of safety, and depression. When their brains are in a threat state, members of the workforce:

- Are less creative
- Are overwhelmed by problems
- Have fewer ideas for action
- Have a narrower perceptual view
- Are less likely to take action
- Collaborate less
- Lose control more easily

To put it another way, competitive disruptions can impair the best thinking of the workforce just when that thinking is most needed—and therefore hinder revolutionary change. This helps to explain why organizations experiencing a disruption are sometimes unable to change even when their survival is at stake. Your ability to foster and sustain a "brain-friendly" environment during a competitive disruption is critical in taking your team and your organization to a higher level of performance.[9] We speak more about how to create a brain-friendly environment in Chapter 10.

Competitive Disruptions Can Foster a False Need for Urgency

Successful revolutionary change requires everyone's urgent and focused attention. Earlier, Kimo Kippen noted the importance of a "sense of urgency" in successful organizational change at Hilton. However, we have found that too much urgency can be as bad as too little.

As noted earlier, competitive disruptions can arrive so surprisingly and with so much anxiety that urgency is replaced by panic. As a result, revolutionary change efforts can begin badly. The fear that disruptions elicit can cause leaders to act too quickly and without adequate collaboration and reflection. This causes a sort of "negative urgency" that can jeopardize the success of the change effort before it begins. We focus our comments on this negative urgency because it is seldom discussed—and because it was mentioned frequently by the executives we interviewed.

In our experience, organizational leaders most often use the excuse "There just wasn't time" to rationalize bad decisions made during change efforts. Specifically:

- There wasn't time to build clarity and consensus among top leadership about the specifics of the change effort. As a result, the effort lacked clear direction.
- There wasn't time to engage the workforce in a meaningful way. As a result, the effort missed out on the workers' collective experience, insight, and creativity.
- There wasn't time to establish and use metrics to monitor performance. As a result, the change effort frequently got off track, and its purpose and progress were unclear.
- There wasn't time to use the change as an opportunity for staff development. As a result, no new capacities and capabilities were developed.
- There wasn't time to share pockets of learning (from success and failure) across the organization. As a result, nothing was learned from the effort.
- There wasn't time to work together better, to deepen professional relationships, or to build trust. As a result, the bad memory of this change effort will impede the next one.

The executives we interviewed repeatedly stressed the importance of not getting "caught up" in a false need for urgency. They suggested that the early days of revolutionary change are about careful consideration and collaboration—not reaction.

Taken together, these five characteristics of competitive disruption can create an environment in your organization that is characterized by confusion, anxiety and/or fear, poor thinking and decision making, and urgent pressure for action. As a change leader, your job is to guide your organization through all this. Here, we provide specific recommendations to help you.

Recommendations for Leading Through Disruption

The initial steps of leading revolutionary change are about refocusing your organization away from the fear and uncertainty of competitive disruption to the opportunities it always brings by taking fast and considered action. We recommend that you:

- Create a guiding philosophy
- Establish a change leadership council
- Formulate a change strategy
- Initiate communication

Recommendation: Create a Guiding Philosophy

An important and overlooked tool for building the positive discipline needed for change is the creation of a "guiding philosophy." In this era of continuous complex change, it makes sense for your organization to create a formal statement about what great change is and how it is achieved. The guiding philosophy is a sort of "core values" for organizational change, and it should be informed by the organization's overall core values. The guiding philosophy for organizational change works best when it is created by the senior executive team in close collaboration with the workforce. The goal is to build an organization-wide consensus on what great organizational change is and how it is implemented. The collaborative creation of a guiding philosophy will contribute to the overall desire for change.

The guiding philosophy addresses the "ends" and "means" of organizational change by answering two questions:

- What is great organizational change in our organization?
- What are the most important considerations for achieving it?

What is great organizational change in our organization? This question is about the ends. The answer defines what successful change is in your organization. For example, does success mean achieving the primary goal of the change effort on time and within budget, or is more expected? Does your organization want to use the opportunity provided by change to accomplish other goals, such as developing staff members, creating new capabilities, and/or improving organization-wide learning about change? A guiding philosophy provides a clear definition of what great organizational change is in your organization.

What are the most important considerations for achieving it? This question is about the means. Its answer informs your actions as a change leader and establishes boundaries. For example, is leading great change in your organization about fostering compliance or about solving complex problems? Is leading great change about maintaining a tight focus on personal responsibilities or about collaborating and crossing boundaries? A guiding philosophy provides a clear statement of how change is led in your organization.

The guiding philosophy should be created in advance of a competitive disruption—that is, as soon as possible. In creating it, you should ensure that it is tightly linked with your organization's overall core values. Once it is created, the guiding philosophy should inform every decision in managing revolutionary change.

Recommendation: Establish a Change Leadership Council

Quickly creating a high-level management structure to lead and oversee the change effort is a critical first step in leading revolutionary change. The structure reassures the workforce that top leadership is focused on the disruption and is taking positive action to lead the organization through it. We recommend announcing the creation of the structure as soon as possible after the competitive disruption occurs. This helps minimize the confusion that a competitive disruption can cause.

Depending upon the size of your organization, the management structure should include two specific groups. We will refer to the first group as the *change leadership council*. The council is chaired by the CEO or equivalent and includes the most senior leadership team and other relevant members as needed. The change leadership council defines the nature and scope of the change effort and sets goals that are in line with organizational strategy.

The council provides direct leadership of the revolutionary change effort and meets regularly for the duration of the effort. Its duties include:

- Formulating the overall change strategy
- Chartering a change implementation team and selecting a leader
- Guiding the creation and execution of the change plan
- Approving modifications to the change plan
- Ensuring that the change effort stays on schedule
- Approving resources for the change effort
- Conducting periodic performance reviews of the change effort
- Resolving high-level issues or conflicts in executing the change plan
- Assuring everyone that the change effort is a top priority

It is crucial that the CEO chair the change leadership council and demonstrate active leadership of the revolutionary change effort. The CEO's leadership makes the importance of the change effort clear to everyone, enables fast resolution of conflicts, helps keep the change effort on schedule, and helps keep the workforce calm and focused on the opportunities provided by the change effort.

We will refer to the second group as the *change implementation team.* This team has two key roles: it creates the detailed change plan, and it leads the change effort after the plan is approved by the change leadership council. In leading the change effort, the team coordinates and integrates all change-related activities across the organization.

We will say more about both groups in Chapter 8. For now, our recommendation is focused on creating the groups and defining their roles as quickly as possible. The creation of these groups is a critical step in leading your organization through revolutionary change.

Recommendation: Formulate a Change Strategy

An initial task for the change leadership council is to create a change strategy. A great change strategy is brief, clear, and inspirational. The change strategy is important because it helps build desire for the revolutionary change by increasing organization-wide understanding of the change effort, why it is important, and how it will unfold.

A key feature of the change strategy is its alignment with the overall organizational strategy. The concept of aligning all organizational interventions—including change efforts—with organizational strategy is regarded as a "best practice" in organizational performance.[10] Aligning your change strategy with your organizational strategy will make your change effort easier and more effective for several reasons. First, aligning the change effort with organizational strategy sends a clear message to everyone that the effort is a priority. Because the change effort is positioned as "strategic," the workforce understands that this effort has the full attention and support of top management.

Second, alignment helps the workforce understand why the change is needed. One of the executives we interviewed mentioned that this action "helps connect the dots for people." That is, explaining the need for revolutionary change in the context of organizational strategy helps the workforce understand how the change will help the organization achieve its goals.

Third, alignment with organizational strategy ties the change effort to your organization's core values.[11] This is important because it reassures the workforce that the change effort is subject to the same rules as all other organizational endeavors. Finally, it reassures the workforce of continuity. The change effort won't change the essence of what the organization is and aspires to be. In fact, great organizations use revolutionary change efforts as a way to reaffirm who they are.[12]

Formulating the change strategy is a great opportunity to involve members of the workforce. This involvement makes the change strategy better, sends a clear message that the organization is serious about involving the workforce, and is a great opportunity to mentor people in a key business skill.

Recommendation: Initiate Communication

In the next chapter, we recommend the creation of a comprehensive organization-wide communications strategy for the revolutionary change effort, and also discuss communications in more detail. We do that because the communications strategy is so important in building the desire for change. For now, we note that the executives we interviewed underscored the importance of great communications in the early stages of change, when anxiety and confusion are highest.

The executives specifically noted three key elements of communications in the early stages of change: they should begin as soon as possible; focus on informing and integrating the change effort; and be frequent, detailed, and personal. The last point—making communications personal—is worth more discussion.

The executives emphasized the importance of making change-related communications personal, particularly at key moments in the change effort. At key moments, such as the early stages of change, those in the workforce don't want to hear about the change from communications experts via canned presentations—they want to hear from you. They want you to inform them of the change, explain why it's important, and challenge them to engage. They also want to hear from you about opportunities to achieve personal development goals—and to make a difference in shaping the future of the organization.

Leading Revolutionary Change: The Bigger Picture

In the Introduction, we noted that some 75 percent of organizational change efforts fail. We attribute this dreadful performance to several things, but the primary one is the continued reliance on an antiquated approach to leading organizational change: the linear, sequential change process. A quick review of the websites of leading organizational change consultants reveals a continued reliance on this approach. We believe that leading great organizational change isn't about inventing a better kind of linear, sequential process. It's about inventing a better kind of organization—one that is optimized for change and changing. We refer to such an organization as *change-focused*.

The executives we interviewed noted that the competitive environment of the twenty-first century is driving organizations to change more, faster, and differently than ever before.[13] The current environment, characterized by continuous, complex change, overwhelms any linear, sequential process. Modern organizations will not be able to change by having external consultants apply linear, sequential processes. They will change through the efforts of internal change leaders who can build new kinds of organizations that align structures, processes, systems, and culture with a strategy of continuous change. Organizational change must become something that organizations *are* rather than something that they *do*.

We have just made four recommendations for getting you off to a good start in leading a successful change effort. However, the current competitive environment demands more from you as a change leader. It demands that you do two difficult things at once: lead successful change today and simultaneously build the capabilities of your organization to bring about change better tomorrow. We have structured Part II to help you accomplish both of these things.

To help you lead successful organizational change today, we will use the same format as Part I. That is, we will use the Five Ds and move from disruption to desire, discipline, determination, and development. Each chapter will conclude with recommendations for leading revolutionary change in your organization. Our goal is to take you through a complete cycle of revolutionary change, from the disruption that initiates it through the development that ensures that your organization continuously learns and improves its ability to bring about great organizational change.

To help you build the capabilities to bring about change better tomorrow, we now introduce eight actions that are foundational in helping your organization become change-focused. We will refer to these eight actions as *foundational competencies*. We recommend that you focus on them continuously—not just during periods of large-scale organizational change. These foundational competencies will help you avoid getting lost in the immediate chaos of change and guide you in navigating the immediate disruption. They will also allow you to use the current change to build capabilities for handling the next change.

In the concluding section of each chapter, we will explain how each of our recommendations complements one or more of these eight foundational competencies:

- Make change strategic
- Integrate change into the business
- Create a cadre of change leaders
- Develop people constantly
- Model collaboration in everything
- Foster better thinking
- Ensure organization-wide learning
- Lead change in yourself

Make Change Strategic

Making change strategic means taking actions to make organizational change a formal part of organizational strategy. In this context, the ability to bring about change faster, better, and with fewer resources is viewed as a source of real competitive advantage. The idea of aligning the full power of the organization with a particular business strategy is not new. We've seen organizations rise to prominence based on their ability to align their organizations with a strategy of least cost,[14] customer service,[15] innovation,[16] or process.[17] In each case, the organizations' strategies, structures, processes, and other systems were aligned to support and reinforce the strategy. Making change strategic builds change into your organization's DNA.

Integrate Change into the Business

Integrating change into the business means taking actions to ensure that change happens constantly across the organization and becomes a routine part of doing business. This has several advantages for the organization. First, by making change less "special," the organization stops overreacting to change (and adding to the overall anxiety). Second, by integrating change into normal business operations, the organization empowers the workforce to continuously take action to deal with small and midsize changes. This ability to act can increase job satisfaction throughout the workforce and build the desire for change. Third, this action makes small and midsize change efforts faster and more efficient, as they are immediately addressed at the working level. Finally, this action enables senior management to focus on more strategic aspects of change, such as building processes to better anticipate competitive disruptions and seizing opportunities for industry leadership.[18]

Create a Cadre of Change Leaders

The executives we interviewed highlighted great leadership as being essential to successful change. They often shared examples of how a great leader made all the difference during a critical change effort—sometimes even "saving" the organization. The executives also noted that, in spite of this, organizations frequently underinvest in developing change leaders. A number of the examples given in Part I discussed how senior executives made a significant difference during times of change.

It's hard to overestimate the value of high-quality leadership in successful revolutionary change. We speak in greater detail about how to create a cadre of trained change leaders in Chapter 8.

Develop People Constantly

Change efforts provide many opportunities for an organization to improve its performance, but a key one is the opportunity to develop people. Because change efforts are viewed as significant, high-priority, and unfamiliar events, people are particularly open to learning during them. You can use change efforts to build important new capabilities into your team and your workforce. Change efforts are a great forum for focusing on performance shortfalls and other developmental needs and can help improve the business performance of your team and your workforce.

Doing this while leading a change effort isn't easy. You will be incredibly busy with many other things, and you may be tempted to let the development of people slip. You can't let this happen. Your personal attention in developing people is critically important to them and to the change effort. In fact, your investment in people may be the only thing that contributes to desire, discipline, determination, and development.

Model Collaboration in Everything

Collaboration provides energy and problem-solving power in revolutionary change efforts. A key goal for a change leader is continuously collaborating across boundaries—and modeling this behavior to everyone. It's important to note that by "collaboration" we mean both giving and receiving help and information. Recognizing and using the good ideas of others is at least as important as sharing your own good ideas with them. Great collaboration enables the organization to access the experience, knowledge, and insight of everyone and apply it in powerful new ways.

Collaboration is also an important first step in building new capabilities for collective learning. An increasing number of organizational scholars are asserting that the collective knowledge and insight of a highly diverse workforce can provide effective solutions to the most complex organizational problems.[19] Your ability to focus and unleash the collective problem-solving power of your team and your workforce is critically important to the success of the change effort and provides your organization with real competitive advantage.

Foster Better Thinking

An important contribution of neuroscience is its focus on how the organizational environment influences the quality of thinking. A key part of that environment is the actions of leaders. Your actions as a change leader—what you say and what you do—affect the ability of your team and your workforce to perform great original thinking and complex problem solving.[20] The thinking environment you create during organizational change efforts (and at all other times) is a key factor in your team's performance. In Chapter 7, we talk more specifically about how you can make your organization a better place to think.

Ensure Organization-Wide Learning

It's easy to get lost in the "busyness" of a large-scale change effort, but you can't allow this to happen to you or your team. You have to stay focused on ensuring that the whole organization benefits from the lessons of the change effort—both successes and failures. In Chapter 10, we discuss how to create formal processes to ensure that the whole organization learns how to carry out change better.

Lead Change in Yourself

An important step in carrying out change better is leading it better. Great change leaders don't become great by taking a last-minute course on "change management." They focus first on learning to lead change in themselves. We believe that the ability to lead change in yourself is compulsory for leading organizational change. That is why we began this book with a discussion of the change-focused person.

In our experience, something happens during the leadership of change efforts that isn't often discussed: leading change changes you. Leading change will refine you as a leader and build new capabilities in you that are available in no other way—if you are open, are prepared, and have the courage to truly explore your own growth and potential. Part I is all about building the ability to lead change in you. Once you master the techniques for applying change in yourself, you will then be better equipped to teach, share, and inspire that ability in others.

Disruption Summary

From an organization's perspective, disruptions are a paradox. On the one hand, they are a threat to the organization's survival that evokes high levels of anxiety and fear. On the other hand, they provide the opportunity to make deep improvements in performance and competitive advantage that are available in no other way. It's your job to navigate this paradox by quickly reframing the disruption as the great opportunity that it always is.

This chapter focused on preparing you to lead the important initial stage of revolutionary change—the time period just after the competitive disruption. We recommended that you take four actions for getting your revolutionary change effort off to a good start:

- Create a guiding philosophy
- Establish a change leadership council
- Formulate a change strategy
- Initiate communication

Creating a guiding philosophy unites the senior leadership in a common definition of the means and ends of organizational change. This helps avoid conflict and misunderstanding as change unfolds. Establishing a change leadership council provides the high-level leadership needed to reframe the disruption as an opportunity. The CEO's leadership of the council is crucial. The council's first task is to create a strategy for the revolutionary change effort and align it with organizational strategy. This underscores the importance of the change effort and makes it easier for people to understand. Finally, change-specific communication should be initiated. Taken together, these four actions help you mediate the initial effects of a competitive disruption and quickly refocus your workforce on the opportunities that disruption brings.

This chapter was also about helping you build the capabilities needed to carry out change better over time—to help your organization become a change-focused one. Our recommendations help you build several of the foundational competencies:

- Creating a guiding philosophy contributes to both *making change strategic* and *modeling collaboration in everything*.
- Establishing a change leadership council contributes to both of the competencies just noted and to *integrating change into the business*.
- Formulating a change strategy contributes to *making change strategic*.
- Initiating communication contributes to *modeling collaboration in everything* and to *ensuring organization-wide learning*.

In the next chapter, we focus on helping you build the *desire* of the workforce for revolutionary change.

Key Points to Remember

- Organizations periodically experience major shifts in their competitive environment called competitive disruptions.
- Competitive disruptions are inevitable, unexpected, affect the whole organization, threaten the organization's survival, and can foster a false need for urgent action.
- Organizations respond to disruptions with revolutionary change efforts focused on ensuring that the organization adjusts to new competitive demands.
- A key part of your role as a change leader is leading the important initial stage of revolutionary change.
- The focus in leading the initial stage is on quickly refocusing the workforce from the threat created by the disruption to the opportunities it brings for people and for the organization.

CHAPTER SEVEN

Desire

Building Motivation to Change

Our chief want is someone who will inspire us to be what we know we could be.
—Ralph Waldo Emerson

I N C H A P T E R 2, we defined *desire* as "a wish or longing" and noted that a desire for change arises from a disruption. We also noted that a mere wish or longing for change isn't enough. Making deep changes in yourself requires transforming a wish into a more powerful "want." To put this another way, you must choose to build in yourself a desire that is strong enough and sustainable enough to fuel real change.

At the organizational level, your ability to build a strong and sustainable desire is also essential if you are to achieve real change. However, a disruption does not create a desire for change. In fact, as we noted in Chapter 6, competitive disruptions threaten organizations and can hinder the desire for change. For this reason, we focused our attention in that chapter on leading the initial stage of revolutionary change—the period of time just after the disruption. Our aim was to help you refocus your organization from the threat of disruption to its many opportunities.

The focus of this chapter is on helping you lead the next stage of revolutionary change: building a strong and sustainable desire for change in your team and your workforce. Your ability to do this is essential to the success of the change effort. Uniting people around a common desire for change can be inspirational and can create positive energy and momentum for change.

What is a "strong and sustainable desire for change," and why does it matter? You have probably noticed in the organizational change literature or in practice that people use different words to describe the phenomenon of increasing people's desire for organizational change. These phrases include "reducing resistance to change," "building support for change," "increasing

The Five Ds

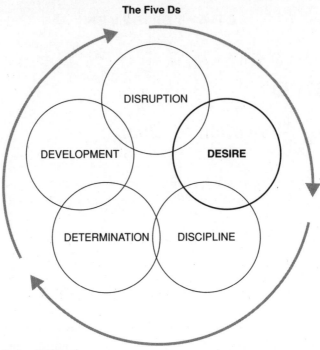

Source: Goldsworthy

engagement in change," and "commitment to change." Let's briefly discuss each of these phrases and clarify what we mean by *desire* in the context of revolutionary organizational change:

- *Reducing resistance to change.* This concept considers the role of the workforce during revolutionary change efforts to be passive. The workforce is not expected to actively support the effort or to add value to it. The only expectation is that employees will not resist. Unfortunately, this idea has become popular in the last two decades.[1] We think this idea of "reducing resistance" undermines the role of people in change and has contributed to the dismal performance record of change efforts.

- *Building support for change.* This concept implies that increasing the "support" of the workforce during change efforts is a good thing—and we agree. However, the mere support of the workforce is not enough. Success at revolutionary change demands the active participation of the workforce in every stage of the effort.

- *Increasing engagement in change.* This concept is better, and we see it as the minimum standard for successful change. The best change efforts we've seen actively engage everyone. Employees in the workforce are treated as full partners rather than as impediments or spectators. In this book, we define *desire* in the organizational context as "the active and meaningful engagement of the workforce in every stage of revolutionary change."

- *Commitment to change.* We view building the commitment of the workforce to change as the highest expression of desire—and it's compulsory for you as a change leader. The executives we interviewed consistently described great change leaders as being "absolutely committed" to the success of the change effort. Nothing less will do.

Leading and Living Change: Ron Kaufman

Ron Kaufman is a global consultant who focuses on improving customer service; he is also the author of the *New York Times* bestselling book *Uplifting Service.*[2] Ron was engaged by the government of Singapore to lead a multiyear effort to change Singapore's business culture into one of providing world-class service. Ron's success in reshaping a national culture has been repeatedly acknowledged internationally. How does an American lead successful national-level change in an Asian nation? Ron says building strong desire within himself and others was key. In Ron's own words, this is how he "harnessed the desire to uplift a nation":

I moved to Singapore in 1990 to help raise service standards in the nation. Manufacturing was migrating to lower-cost factories in China, and back-office processing was moving to India. Singapore's leaders could see that the nation's economic future would require the delivery of higher-value services: financial services, legal services, medical services, education, hospitality, conventions, research, logistics, and the like. However, most of Singapore's population had been carefully trained to succeed in a factory environment, delivering zero defects on budget and on time. This rigorous approach works well when customer requirements are consistent, as in manufacturing, but it falls short when customers present a wide variety of interests, needs, and preferences for service.

Reeducating a national workforce to embrace this change and deliver higher-value service is a massive undertaking that can succeed only if there is unrelenting ambition, commitment, and desire. The government and people of Singapore shared an ambition to be ranked among the finest countries and cities in the world. The national government had a driving commitment to succeed and the budget to back it up. But desire does not come from competitive rankings or from budgetary allocations alone. Desire comes from within people who want to make a difference.

My desire to serve others and make a positive difference found expression in my younger years though global sports and citizen diplomacy events. But it was this national service education project that fueled my desire to contribute powerfully and deeply, and that has kept the fire burning for more than two decades. Meanwhile, Singapore's desire to achieve this necessary change has been more challenging and complex. The national commitment to service improvement finds logical expression through investments in infrastructure and workforce skills training. But the emotional commitment to creating a great service experience requires more than skill sets and measures; it requires a collective mindset of generosity, compassion, and genuine interest in the concerns and well-being of others.

Today Singapore is wrestling openly with this service improvement effort. The nation's desire to serve others well is facing a struggle from within. Accuracy, speed, and technical standards have accelerated to world-class levels. But as these standards have risen, so have the cosmopolitan nature of the country and the cost of living. Singapore citizens today are struggling with conflicting desires: to protect their own well-being and to be genuinely welcoming to customers from all over the world. The tension between "What's in it for me?" and "What can I do for you?" is an example of the challenge of desire that all of us face each day.

I am confident that Singapore will continue to improve, and that you will get a little more each time you are served in Singapore. I also know that this result will not be achieved by government policies and investments alone. This socially uplifting result will thrive only on the harnessed desire of the people who make up this nation.

The remainder of this chapter is about helping you lead the next stage of revolutionary change: building and sustaining desire for change in your team and the workforce. Like Ron Kaufman's, your role is to foster strong desire for change "within people who want to make a difference."

Perspectives on Building Desire for Change

One of the most powerful assets in any organization is the collective talent of its workforce. When people focus their combined experience, insight, and creativity on an organizational problem, great things happen. In fact, the ability of an organization to focus and apply the collective talent of its workforce is a powerful way to solve the most complex problems—including revolutionary change.[3]

Building a desire for change in a workforce following a disruption is difficult—and something that change leaders often fail to accomplish. In fact, a review of the literature on organizational change reveals that the ability to build the desire for change has been a problem for decades.[4] For this reason, we use this section to explore desire in more detail.

The thinking on how to build and sustain a strong desire for change has evolved and continues to do so. Two recent themes of this evolution are the increasing role of "strategic communications" in building desire for change and the introduction of neuroscience principles. Here, we reflect on the following three themes:

- Traditional perspectives on building a desire for change
- The rise of strategic communications
- The neuroscience perspective on building a desire for change

Traditional Perspectives on Building a Desire for Change

Our discussion here focuses on three approaches to building a desire for change. We see forms of these approaches in practice, and they were also mentioned by the executives we interviewed. The approaches were first mentioned in the famous book *The Planning of Change*,[5] and they have been widely used and discussed ever since. They are called *power-coercive*, *empirical-rational*, and *normative-educational*. The power-coercive approach says that a workforce supports organizational change only when it must. Therefore, during change efforts, leaders should use formal power to coerce the workforce to comply with the goals of the effort. During the current economic downturn, we have seen more evidence of this approach being used around the world. As one senior leader in the finance industry said:

> We have to get on with this [change]. Our expectation is that in this environment, with unemployment so high, the workforce will quickly get on board. They better.

The power-coercive approach seeks to build compliance through the threat of retaliation: those who don't comply will be fired. We found no evidence that this approach has improved the success record of change efforts, and it can make matters worse. Introducing coercion into an organization that is experiencing competitive disruption further increases the anxiety of the workforce and could push their brains into a threat state. As discussed further later in this chapter, this adversely affects employees' performance by reducing the brain's ability to do its best, most complex thinking. We have seen evidence that coercion can "motivate" the workforce to comply with a change effort in the short term. We have seen no evidence of coercion inspiring the best performance of the workforce during revolutionary change.

The empirical-rational approach says that the workforce supports organizational change only when employees understand how doing so advances their self-interest. In this approach, change leaders seek to build a desire for change by explaining to the employees "what's in it for them." We see this approach being used a lot in current practice. In fact, it is often the centerpiece of a strategic communications campaign. However, its use has not improved the success rate of change efforts. One reason is that factors besides self-interest are important in building the desire for change. A great example is people's need to contribute to a higher purpose—to help shape the future of their organization.

The normative-educational approach says that the workforce supports organizational change when employees are personally involved in making changes that affect them. In this approach, leaders actively partner with the workforce and involve the employees in every aspect of revolutionary change. This involvement helps transform the perspectives and, ultimately, the behavior of the workforce. Although there are examples of this approach in practice, we have seen fewer of them in recent years. The executives we interviewed noted that the poor economy has focused organizations on "fast, efficient action" rather than on investing in the kind of large-scale participation that great change demands.

The normative-educational approach seeks to build a desire for change by actively involving the workforce in every phase of the change effort. This approach appeals to us for several reasons. First, research confirms that large-scale and meaningful participation by the workforce is a key factor in successful change.[6] Second, this approach actively involves change leaders working side by side with the workforce rather than merely trying to persuade it. Finally, this approach helps foster the kind of positive changes in the work environment that neuroscientists believe contribute to better thinking.[7]

We mention these three approaches to underscore the importance of a recommendation we made in the previous chapter: build a guiding philosophy. It's very likely that the various members of your top leadership team—the change leadership council—hold some or all of these perspectives about "the right way to build a desire for change in the workforce." Without a clear consensus on how your change effort will build desire, these fundamentally different approaches will cause conflict as the effort unfolds.

Also, we want to note that regardless of the approach taken, the majority of change efforts fail to build the strong desire that is needed to ensure the success of revolutionary change. In fact, the ability to motivate and engage the workforce for any purpose—let alone revolutionary change—is a difficult proposition.[8] The rest of this chapter discusses how to build this capability in your team and workforce—and how not to.

The Rise of Strategic Communications

In some organizations, building a strong and sustainable desire for change in the workforce is the job of one activity above all others. That activity is communications—sometimes referred to as *strategic communications*. Often the term strategic communications is used to describe a process that is focused on building desire in key workforce and stakeholder groups during a change effort. Strategic communications processes vary, but they can share common themes.

The goal of a strategic communications effort is to persuade the workforce to desire change by using two of the approaches just discussed: power-coercive and empirical-rational. The power-coercive approach is expressed by using a "burning platform" perspective. Typically, management highlights the threat posed by the competitive disruption and tries to persuade the employees that only their immediate support of the change effort will avert disaster and save the organization—and their jobs. The coercion may be implied rather than directly expressed, but the meaning is clear.

The empirical-rational approach is expressed through an argument in support of the change effort based on employee self-interest. This argument has several versions, each focused on persuading a particular workforce or stakeholder group to desire change. Each version of the argument highlights "what's in it" for the particular group. These arguments are often made by internal communications specialists or external consultants. In either case, the underlying rationale is that a desire for organizational change is created by persuasion.

Great communications are essential in any change effort, and they enable change efforts in important ways. The executives we interviewed noted that communications are essential in keeping the workforce informed about the effort, coordinating the change effort across the organization, and sharing learning.

However, no argument, no matter how well crafted, can build desire in your team and your workforce. Neither can any expressed or implied threat of retaliation. A key reason for this relates to how the brain reacts to organizational change. Emerging research from neuroscience shows that some of the most favored methods for building desire in a workforce are ineffective, irrelevant, or make matters worse.

The Neuroscience Perspective on Building a Desire for Change

In the Introduction, we referred to some of the key areas explored by neuroscience that are related to change. One area of new insight involves how the brain reacts to organizational change.[9] Change can trigger reactions in the brain similar to those triggered by physical discomfort and pain.[10] Understanding why change efforts affect the brain this way is important if you are to build a desire for change. We have chosen to focus on four qualities of the brain that are particularly relevant to organizational change:

- The brain is focused on surviving.
- The brain constantly monitors environmental changes.
- The brain can perceive change efforts as threats.
- The brain can learn to desire organizational change.

The brain is great at surviving—in fact, it may be the most successful biological organ in history.[11] Neuroscience research indicates that the brain's focus on survival also extends to social survival. The brain reacts to threats to our status and well-being in modern organizations in much the same way as it reacts to threats to our physical well-being.[12] A primary way in which the brain does this is by paying close attention to changes in the organizational environment.

The brain constantly scans the environment for potential threats to our physical and social survival. In fact, the brain has evolved a number of biological systems that are focused on quickly detecting and reacting to environmental changes. Examples include core motivation, short-term (working) memory, long-term memory, error detection, and the fear response. All of these systems are operating in the brains of your team and your workforce, and all of them are strongly affected by the environmental changes caused by revolutionary change efforts.[13]

Each of these biological systems can perceive aspects of organizational change efforts as threats to its survival and actively resist them. Let's look at the effects of organizational change on each system.

- *Core motivation.* Evolution has created core motivational systems that manifest as approaching or retreating behaviors. To put this another way, people have a set of neural systems that motivate them to approach or retreat from certain things in their environment.[14] The brain's dopaminergic system governs the motivation to approach, and the brain's serotonin system governs the motivation to retreat. Because of the brain's focus on survival, the motivation to retreat is stronger than the motivation to approach. Understanding this has important implications for building desire for organizational change. The workforce tends to retreat from the kind of environmental uncertainty that revolutionary change efforts cause.

    This reaction to organizational change is only semiconscious and is not affected by efforts to persuade. As a change leader, your ability to build the desire for change is about shaping the organizational environment so that the brain wants to approach rather than retreat. This notion of reshaping—and reinterpreting—the organizational environment is a key role for you as a change leader. Your ability to provide context for and insight into the change will help your team positively reframe it.

- *Working memory.* This is the brain's initial holding area for new perceptions and ideas; it is associated with the brain's prefrontal cortex. Working memory enables such functions as complex problem solving and creativity, so it is incredibly valuable in dealing with the complexity of revolutionary change. However, it has a very limited capacity and is easily overwhelmed.[15] The sheer volume of new environmental information arising from revolutionary change efforts can overwhelm working memory, causing physical discomfort and reducing the ability to think creatively and engage in complex problem solving.

    Although this reaction by the brain is not conscious, it can be helped or hindered by communication. Communication that helps the brain focuses on specific aspects of organizational change—not on all aspects. By reducing the volume of incoming information and by frequent repetition of the core messages, great communications can help prevent working memory from being overwhelmed. We believe that communication which focuses your team and your workforce on specific aspects of the change effort needs to be led by you.

- *Long-term memory.* This is held in the brain's basal ganglia where the neural circuits of habits are formed. Activities that are done repeatedly are referred by the prefrontal cortex to the basal ganglia, thus freeing up processing power in the prefrontal cortex.[16] Organizational change efforts require the brain to perform the difficult task of changing habits—something that it actively resists, as we noted in Part I.

  The brain's resistance to changing habits is not affected by either the power-coercive or the empirical-rational approach. Threats and persuasion don't help replace old habits with new ones. The normative-educational approach can help build new habits through its focus on active participation. However, we believe that the most effective way you can build a desire for change in long-term memory is by using the power of symbols and clear and simple visuals that are shared widely, consistently, and regularly across all levels of the organization.

- *Error detection.* The brain's focus on survival causes it to continuously scan the environment (up to five times per second) for "errors"— unexpected changes that could signal a threat. Error signals are generated by the brain's orbital frontal cortex, which is closely related to the brain's fear circuitry in the amygdala.[17] The magnitude of the environmental changes triggered by revolutionary change efforts can easily be interpreted as errors and trigger aversive systems.

  Again, this reaction by the brain is not affected by either threats or persuasion. Building desire is about helping the brain positively reframe the environmental turbulence arising from change. As a change leader, your ability to build a desire for change hangs, once again, on your ability to positively reframe the environment. Creating and maintaining an environment that fosters great thinking during organizational change efforts is one way to accomplish this and we speak more about how to do this later on in the book.

- *Fear response.* As noted earlier, change efforts can trigger error circuits in the orbital frontal cortex, which may trigger a fear response in the amygdala. The fear response is the brain's fight or flight response to perceived danger. This is the worst possible outcome for you when you are trying to build a strong desire for change.[18] The fear response is not affected by rational argument and can be triggered by attempts to motivate via coercion. As a change leader, your ability to actively portray the environment as nonthreatening is critically important in building desire for organizational change.

In summary, revolutionary change efforts can threaten multiple systems in the brain. Change can trigger the neural systems that motivate people to retreat, overwhelm working memory, demand the painful change of long-term habits, and cause profound fear. Attempts by communications experts to persuade based on appeals to self-interest are ineffective in building a desire for change in the brain. In addition, attempts to persuade based on expressed or implied threats can decrease the desire for change by driving the brain into threat response.

The savvy change leader does not attempt to build desire through persuasion. Instead, you build a desire for change by taking specific actions that are focused on making the environment less threatening to the brain. Examples include providing insight into and context for the changes, creating a great thinking environment, and actively developing people. These examples inform the recommendations that follow.

Recommendations for Building the Desire for Change

We recommend three actions for building strong desire in your team and your workforce during revolutionary change:

- Shape the environment during change
- Develop people during change
- Create an organization-wide communications strategy

Recommendation: Shape the Environment During Change

This recommendation is focused on actions you can take during organizational change to push past the anxiety and uncertainty and create an environment that enables great thinking and great performance. Your actions can help your team and workforce reframe the change effort from something to avoid to something to approach. The following three actions can build a desire for change much better than any form of communication:

Model appropriate behavior. No matter how good your prior preparation, remember that competitive disruptions can hit people and organizations very hard. No matter what happens, stay calm, focused, and positive. Your ability to do this will help calm the brains of your team members and prevent a threat response. This is easier said than done—but it is essential if you are to optimize your team's performance and desire for change. Research into mirror neurons shows that people imitate what others do, and where actions and words are inconsistent, the actions speak the loudest.[19]

Provide insight and context. A key way to shape the environment during change is to provide insight and context to help your team members interpret change-related events positively as they occur. Use your knowledge of the organization, its business operations, and its culture to provide your team and the workforce with continuous context as the change effort unfolds. Your help in interpreting events can prevent working memory from being overwhelmed and the change effort from being seen by the brain as a threat. In this way, you minimize the probability of a threat response and ensure that you have the team's best thinking when you need it most.

Make the organization a great place to think. You can also take two specific actions to make your organization a better place to think. One action is to adopt the SCARF model.[20] SCARF is an acronym for status, certainty, autonomy, relatedness, and fairness.

> *Status* is about relative importance to others. As a change leader, you increase the status of your team members by involving them early in the change effort, placing them in important positions, and giving them real authority to make decisions and to act. Also important for status is recognition of people both as individuals and as part of a team, and on a one-to-one basis as well as in the company of others. Ensuring that there is enough praise and the celebration of quick wins along the way can assist in building status during change.
>
> *Certainty* is about being able to feel secure in one's position in the organization. Although you can't promise your team members absolute certainty in the current business environment, you can take actions that will increase their certainty. Again, positioning your team members to take early and meaningful roles in the change effort is important. So is your mentoring of your team members and your helping them to build new, business-relevant skills. As a change leader, you can use the change effort as an opportunity to better equip your team.
>
> *Autonomy* provides a sense of control over events. As a change leader, you can increase your team members' autonomy by giving them real (and defined) authority to act and by backing their decisions. Providing people with the freedom to act will improve their feelings of autonomy.

Relatedness is a sense of feeling safe with others, of seeing others as friends rather than foes. People need a sense of belonging, and so relatedness is more than good group process. It is creating an environment of trust that enables powerful collective thinking. As a change leader, it is your responsibility to create an environment of safety and openness, to enforce it, and to actively model it.

Fairness is a perception of fair exchanges between people. Neuroscience is confirming the incredible impact of fairness on people's thinking and performance. A lack of perceived fairness can undermine the thinking and performance of groups and organizations.[21] Allowing people the opportunity to vent and share their feelings has been shown to decrease the level of emotion in the amygdala,[22] after which people are more likely to engage, even if they do not fully agree with the decisions taken.

Using SCARF will help improve overall performance by creating an environment that fosters better thinking. When SCARF is well entrenched, it can create an environment that protects your team members from lapsing into a "threat state" as the competitive disruption unfolds. Your team will be practiced at staying calm, focused, and effective in all circumstances.

Another way to positively shape the thinking environment during change is to focus the attention of your team and workforce. When you set the direction and focus attention on it, you help reduce the volume of incoming data and calm the brain. Your actions tell your team members two important things: the few things they should focus on and the many things they don't have to worry about.[23]

Stay at the center of the discussion and action about change. Don't delegate actions to shape the environment or trust "specialists" to communicate information about the change effort to your team without your active involvement. Make shaping the environment of your team and the organization your personal responsibility.

Recommendation: Develop People During Change

Start developing people as soon as you have created a change strategy, and do so constantly. Our research and experience confirm that development is a key factor in successful change efforts.[24] When you focus on developing your people, every part of the change effort gets easier: your team members handle the disruption better, they contribute more, and they find it easier to build and sustain the desire for change. There is no downside to investing in people. Here are five specific recommendations for development during organizational change.

Involve people immediately. Nothing says you are serious about the importance of people during change more than involving them in the early stages of the change effort. Relevant recommendations from the previous chapter include involving people in creating the change strategy and in designing the change leadership structures. This early involvement gives members of the workforce the opportunity to work with senior executives and sends a powerful message to the workforce. Build desire by involving people in every aspect of the change effort right from the beginning.

Train people to be proactive and adaptable. Train your team members to meet revolutionary change head on. Impress upon them the need to be proactive leaders during the change effort, rather than spectators or victims. Ensure that your team understands and accepts how unpredictable revolutionary change efforts can be—and the need to sustain the desire for change. A desire for change should not be shaken by changes in direction and/or setbacks as the change unfolds.

Make development personal. Change efforts are a great opportunity for people to build new capabilities and achieve personal development goals. Make the time to engage people concerning their development goals and help them achieve these goals as the change effort unfolds. From a neuroscience perspective, your personal attention to the development of people helps the brain reframe organizational change positively. Once the change effort begins, it will be difficult for you to find time for the personal attention and mentoring we are suggesting—but find it.

Change efforts—particularly revolutionary ones—can be great environments for accelerated development. There is something about the energy and opportunity of organizational change that can foster development in a special way. The key is recognizing opportunities for development and positioning people for them. The executives we interviewed noted that leaders' personal attention to developing people "may increase the performance and desire of your team more than any other thing."

Celebrate success and reward performance. It's easy to let the pressures of the change effort crowd out time for celebration and recognition—but you can't allow this. These activities build and sustain the desire for change and help the brain positively reframe the change effort. From a neuroscience perspective, they also act to calm and focus the brain by providing clarity about performance expectations. When recognizing performance, we suggest that you convey the recognition personally, convey it publicly, convey it soon after the excellent performance occurs, and clearly explain to everyone why the performance was excellent.

Focus on a higher purpose. If senior organizational leaders have identified a higher purpose for the change effort (for example, improving the world in a specific way), keep your team members focused on how their efforts contribute to that purpose. If no higher purpose has been identified, work with your team members to create and focus on one. Working for a higher purpose improves thinking and the desire for change.[25]

Recommendation: Create an Organization-Wide Communications Strategy

In Chapter 6, we recommended that you "initiate communication" and provided some guidance for doing that. The aim of this recommendation is to take the next step and implement a comprehensive, organization-wide communications strategy. The goal of the communications strategy is to help enable, support, and integrate the change effort. The strategy should not attempt to create a desire for change or persuade the workforce of anything. Rather, it should assume that the desire for change already exists and should help to build upon and sustain that desire. It is important that you tailor the communications strategy to your organization, but we recommend that you emphasize the following features:

- *Transparent and objective.* The strategy should inform, enable, integrate, and celebrate the change effort. It should not attempt to coerce or persuade.
- *Comprehensive, consistent, and inclusive.* The strategy should use every means available, formal and informal, to ensure that every person in the organization is reached. Examples of formal communications include presentations by organizational leaders, panel discussions, focus groups, e-mail, webinars, social media, videoconferences, and group voice mail. Examples of informal communications include discussion groups, lunch presentations, information exchanges, and the like. Using social media to build communities of interest is particularly important in building desire for change as members of the workforce "meet" to share information.

- *Aligned with the change strategy.* Everything that the communications strategy does should be informed by the change strategy. As a result, the communications strategy helps to integrate, coordinate, and inform all parts of the revolutionary change effort. Members of the change leadership council and change implementation team are frequent contributors to communications.
- *Enables two-way communication with the workforce.* The strategy should use focus groups, web-based surveys, and social media to constantly gather the ideas and perceptions of the workforce. Ideas should be shared and openly recognized.
- *Celebrates progress and recognizes performance.* The strategy should help unite the workforce behind the change by celebrating progress and publicly recognizing the outstanding performance of individuals and teams.
- *Detailed and relevant.* The strategy should provide detailed guidance when needed as well as frequent progress updates and schedule changes.
- *Developmental.* The communications strategy should support the employees' developmental aspirations by keeping them constantly apprised of formal and informal developmental opportunities as the change unfolds.

The organization-wide communications strategy plays a key role in every facet of change and is the cement that holds the change effort together. The old "cascade" approach to communications (flowing from the top down) no longer works. Instead, we recommend using the "waves" that flow both ways and mix together, focusing on the three Is—inform, inspire, and involve—so that the head (thinking), the heart (feeling), and the hands (doing) are all engaged.

Desire Summary

Building and sustaining high levels of desire for change in your team and your workforce are key factors in the success of revolutionary change. However, the ability to motivate and engage people in the organizational context is always difficult—and particularly so in revolutionary change efforts. Traditional means of building a strong and sustainable desire for organizational change through threats, appeals to self-interest, and persuasion are inadequate. However, emerging research from neuroscience is providing new insight into how to build and sustain a desire for change in the brain.

We suggested these three recommendations for building desire for change in your team and the workforce:

- Actively shape the change environment
- Develop people constantly
- Implement an organization-wide communications strategy

Your ability to actively shape the organizational environment makes revolutionary change less threatening to the brain. This enables improved thinking and builds a desire for change. Developing people during revolutionary change is a powerful way to build their desire for change. There is just no substitute for your personal investment in people. Finally, the creation and implementation of an organization-wide communications strategy helps build and sustain the workforce's desire for change.

These recommendations also help your organization take important steps toward becoming change-focused. For example, our first recommendation is that you actively shape the change environment. You will note that this recommendation is similar to the foundational competency *foster better thinking*. Your ability to shape the organizational environment during change in such a way that the change becomes less threatening to the human brain is a key source of competitive advantage. Imagine the power of an organization that is able to quickly focus the best collective thinking of its workforce during any competitive disruption.

Our second recommendation is to *develop people constantly*. You will note that this recommendation is one of the eight foundational competencies for a change-focused organization. Organizations that do this are constantly increasing the capabilities and performance of their workforce.

Our final recommendation is to implement an organization-wide communications strategy. This recommendation complements two foundational competencies: *develop people constantly* and *ensure organization-wide learning*. Your ability to create and implement communications strategies that build and sustain desire by uniting the whole organization behind revolutionary change is a critical capability for a change-focused organization.

This chapter focused on helping you to build and sustain a strong desire for revolutionary change in your team and your workforce. The next chapter on *discipline* focuses on helping you create the management structures necessary to sustain revolutionary change.

Key Points to Remember

- Traditional means for building desire—threats, appeals to self-interest, and persuasion—are ineffective.
- Neuroscience research is providing new insight into how to build the desire for change in the human brain.
- Actively shaping the environment during change will improve the quality of thinking.
- Developing people constantly is a powerful way to build a strong and sustainable desire for change.
- An organization-wide communications strategy helps build and sustain a desire for change by providing needed information and uniting the workforce behind the change effort.

CHAPTER EIGHT

Discipline

Coordinating Energy, Focus, and Effort

To be prepared is half the victory.

—Miguel de Cervantes

IN CHAPTER 3, we defined *discipline* as "training or conditions imposed for the improvement of physical powers, self-control."[1] We observed that discipline is one of the hardest challenges for people and that it takes energy, focus, and considerable effort. Without discipline, the desire to make lasting change in yourself diminishes over time, and old habits quickly return. The same phenomenon is true for organizations.

However, achieving discipline for organizations requires you to coordinate the energy, focus, and effort of many people over time. Without discipline, revolutionary change efforts fail to sustain the desire that is necessary for true organizational change. When this happens, the organization, like the individual, reverts to a former familiar state and change fails.

There are several reasons for the inability of modern organizations to sustain desire. One reason is the continued and/or unexpected resistance of stakeholders. An emerging characteristic of the global economy is more interconnectedness among organizations and their traditional competitors, new competitors, governmental entities, environmental groups, and other groups that are involved. These stakeholders can form powerful and unexpected alliances that can resist revolutionary change efforts.

Another reason is the arrival of new high-priority problems that divert the organization's attention and resources. This can happen when a second competitive disruption occurs. The accelerating speed and complexity of the competitive environment make this possible.

A third reason—and one that is particularly relevant to this chapter—is poor management of the change effort. Change leaders may be unable

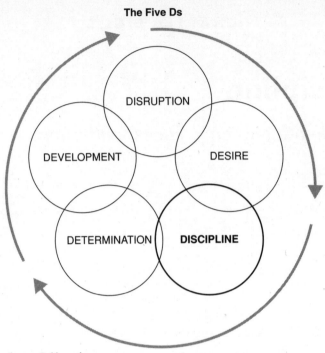

The Five Ds

Source: Goldsworthy

to create the management structures needed to sustain the desire for revolutionary change. The management structures they create either undermanage or overmanage the change effort. In our context, undermanaging means failing to create the management structures necessary to focus the change effort and push it forward. Overmanaging means creating structures that impose too much oversight and control. These structures can be so ponderous that they slow the momentum of the effort and kill the desire for change.

In this chapter, we discuss how you develop and implement the management structures that are needed to develop and sustain discipline during revolutionary change. It's important to note that these management structures don't exist. There's nothing that you can purchase "off the shelf" and no best practice that will be a perfect fit for your organization. Building these structures is about experimentation, persistence, and insight. You will have to create structures that provide both enough control to make revolutionary change possible and enough flexibility to make it successful. Building and sustaining discipline, like every other facet of revolutionary change, requires leadership.

Leading and Living Change: Martha Soehren

Three years ago, Martha Soehren, the senior vice president and chief learning officer (CLO) of Comcast, was asked to lead a major enterprisewide transformation of the learning and development function (L&D) at this Fortune 50 global media and technology company. At the time, the company had approximately 100,000 employees and 750 learning and development professionals. The goal of this effort was to transform the L&D function from a decentralized to a centralized model, and the stakes were high. As Martha explains how the change effort unfolded, note the processes and structures that were used to ensure that the company had the discipline needed for change. In Martha's own words:

This transformation could not fail—it was the first of its kind for the company, and the goal was to make it a model for other functional groups as they, too, were shifted to a centralized model. The need for this effort was driven by the deep economic decline of 2009, which required us to dramatically increase efficiency. The situation was intensified by fierce and brutal competition for the same customer base. Our company was convinced that a consistent learning experience could drive a consistent and improved customer experience—which, in turn, would drive business improvements.

We spent the first nine months building the business case for the transformation and positioning it for buy-in and support from all of the top executives across the enterprise—and the business case was supported. It became the foundation of our detailed transformation plan.

In looking back at the rigor and discipline we applied to this transformation effort, some key points are worth mentioning. Early in the planning, for example, we formed an enterprisewide, cross-functional transformation champion team to help us plan the effort in detail. This action started the buy-in, because these "champions" went back to their business partners and started giving messages on what was to come. It worked.

Also, our communication efforts were perhaps the most rigorous variables in our transformation equation. We had recurring calls with key business partners and with all learning and development professionals. We developed a blog managed by the CLO. We created a transformation website that included all pertinent communications and new job postings. We established an ask-the-CLO private e-mailbox for any question or comment a team member wanted to share, and the box was managed exclusively by the CLO. We set up biweekly face-to-face meetings with the champion team. In retrospect, many leaders across the enterprise now say that the rigor, transparency, and disci-pline of communications during the planning, execution, and evaluation of this major transformation effort were the elements that contributed most to our success.

In the spirit of transparency, there were also a few lessons learned. First and foremost, when leaders feel that they're giving something up during a major change effort, they can behave badly. Second, we found that certain words are emotionally charged and can hinder the transformation. When we discovered these words, we replaced them with synonyms that worked for everyone. Third, timelines can't slip if the plan is solid. Finally, the change leader must sweat the small stuff.

Strong, disciplined leadership, with change management experience at the helm, can drive successful transformation. Discipline helped our orga-nization establish its first National Executive Learning Council, and it helped us create and publish two to four impact stories each quarter that showed how learning was positively affecting the customer experience and business metrics.

One of the most interesting factors for me in this transformation was the helpful role my prior experience in the military played in preparing me to lead this effort. The military environment provided rich experience in learning how to plan, execute, and evaluate programs that was incredibly helpful to me in leading this transformation.

Another factor that can't be overlooked was the talent of our team. We could never have transformed our learning and development function into a centralized and standardized organization, paving the way for other functional groups to follow, without a great group of people who were steadfastly and single-mindedly devoted to our overarching task and our overriding goal.

In this example, Martha used her experience and her insight to create an effective set of management structures, including a business case, a detailed transformation plan, and a transformation champion team, all supported by effective communication and collaboration. What management processes will you use, and how will you apply them?

This chapter is about helping you lead the next stage of revolutionary change: creating the discipline necessary to sustain the change. Like Martha Soehren's, your role involves more than creating a change plan. You must ensure that you have the right balance between control and flexibility to achieve lasting change. Let us explore how to create this balance.

Building Discipline Through "Flexible Control"

Building discipline in the context of change efforts and other types of large-scale projects often involves creating management structures, such as detailed plans, schedules, and budgets, and using them to manage the change effort step by step. To manage revolutionary change efforts, organizations sometimes use the same techniques they use to manage other large projects. This is both good and bad. It's good because the techniques for managing projects are well established and familiar,[2] and it's bad because revolutionary change efforts can behave differently from other types of large projects.

For example, an underlying ethos of large-scale project management is maintaining strict oversight and control of costs, schedules, and performance. These factors are also important considerations in managing change efforts—but so is flexibility. Too much oversight and control in managing change efforts can reduce rather than sustain the workforce's desire for change. We mention this as a possibility because we have seen it happen in practice. Competitive disruptions are so important and so threatening that organizations can overmanage them. To be clear, management structures are important for maintaining progress, assuring quality, and minimizing risk. However, it's also important to design these structures with enough flexibility to:

- Allow fast adaptation to ongoing changes in the competitive environment
- Seize unexpected opportunities for performance improvement
- Enable the creative thinking that is needed to solve complex problems
- Support staff development, collaboration, and organizational learning

In 2011, Walter conducted a research project focused on identifying best practices in leading large-scale organizational change. The organizations studied included three global Fortune 500 organizations in three different industries. These organizations were chosen based upon their ability to make the changes needed to sustain or improve their financial performance during the economic downturn.[3]

One surprise in the study was the amount of emphasis that executives in these leading organizations placed on managing change efforts flexibly. The executives acknowledged the importance of management control and said that detailed change plans and project schedules were crucial tools—but they were not the most important consideration. Keeping the staff engaged and using the change effort as a way to improve the overall performance of the organization were the paramount concerns. One change leader in a global Fortune 300 manufacturing company captured the essence of this perspective:

> A key consideration for me [in this change effort] is ensuring we don't move so fast we leave the workforce behind. It's important that we all work through this together—even if this means taking extra time. I won't leave anyone behind.

Executives in the study said that blindly adhering to a project schedule could hurt a change effort by reducing the workforce's desire to participate. Too much emphasis on staying on schedule reduced original thinking, performance improvements, learning, and collaboration. It also tended to make the work more transactional, that is, "less interesting and challenging to people."

Finally, the executives we interviewed for this book also mentioned the importance of improvisation in leading large-scale change. They asserted that the competitive environment has become so complex and is changing so fast that no management process can anticipate everything. They emphasized the importance of adaptability, original thinking, and creativity in great organizational change. They suggested that the best management structures don't just tolerate these things but actively encourage them and even try to build them in.[4]

We acknowledge that creating these flexible management structures is as much art as science, but we believe that they are critically important to your success in leading revolutionary change—and a great opportunity for you to demonstrate real leadership. The next section provides recommendations focused on helping you create the management structures needed for flexible control.

Recommendations for Building and Sustaining Discipline

We recommend taking six actions to create a great management structure for revolutionary change:

- Create a guiding philosophy
- Establish a change leadership council
- Formulate a change strategy
- Establish a change implementation team
- Create a change implementation plan
- Build a cadre of change leaders

The first three of these actions were given as recommendations in Chapter 6, as they are critical to the initial steps of revolutionary change. These actions provide the structure that is needed to get the organization moving quickly after the chaos of competitive disruption. In sum:

- The guiding philosophy establishes consensus throughout the organization on the ends and means of organizational change—before the change effort begins. This common philosophy prevents misunderstandings and conflicts as change unfolds.
- The change leadership council is the first of two recommended management bodies and actively involves the CEO and the senior executive team in the change effort. The visible support of the CEO helps the workforce reframe the disruption as an opportunity and helps build its desire for change.
- The change strategy provides a powerful tool for implementing change by aligning the change effort with the overall organizational strategy. This alignment underscores the strategic importance of the change effort and makes it easier to understand.

The last three actions are our recommendations in this chapter for building discipline concerning the change. We mention all six actions here because together they form the management structure that is needed to build discipline for revolutionary change.

Recommendation: Establish a Change Implementation Team

The second management group we recommend is the change implementation team. It is created by the executive change leadership council and reports to the council. The first action the council should take in creating the change implementation team is selecting a team leader. The team leader should immediately join the council's deliberations and become familiar with every aspect of the competitive disruption and the change effort.

The team has two primary purposes: creating the change implementation plan and using it to guide the day-to-day implementation of the change effort (after the plan is approved by the change leadership council). In leading the change effort, the team coordinates and integrates all change-related activities across the organization.

A key consideration for the team is fostering collaboration across the organization at every step. Members of the workforce are consulted in creating and implementing the change plan. Accessing the collective expertise, original thinking, and insight of the workforce is a key goal of the team. This collaboration improves the quality of the change plan and builds desire during implementation.

As just noted, selecting a leader for the change implementation team and charging him/her with forming the team should be one of the council's first actions. The goal is to get the team established as soon as possible after the competitive disruption. Members should be volunteers selected from across the organization based upon their expertise and/or because they represent a key geography, business unit, or function that is affected by the change. Each team member is expected to take an active role in writing the change implementation plan. The size of the team should be kept manageable—ideally between 10 and 15 members.

All members are assigned to the team for a specified period of time (for example, 60 to 90 days) and focus exclusively on the work of the team during their assignment. At the conclusion of the assignment, new members are selected. In this way, more people are able to participate in leading the change effort. In addition, "outgoing" members of the team become champions for the change effort.

The team leader oversees the selection of team members and should personally conduct their initial orientation and ongoing development. The orientation should include:

- A detailed background of the competitive disruption and the change effort
- A summary of the CEO's perspective and that of the change leadership team
- Reporting relationships
- Responsibilities and performance expectations

The team leader also works with the team to develop group norms and operating principles and to write the change implementation plan. Time spent up front on effective team development is time well invested, as it increases the trust among team members, unites them behind a common purpose, and ensures that any conflicts or misunderstandings can be solved openly and constructively.

The first step in writing the plan is to specify a writing process. This document should be created collaboratively and in detail. Ultimately, the plan should assign specific writing responsibilities, deadlines, review procedures, and an overall schedule.

Finally, the team leader does one other important thing: models appropriate behavior, such as a willingness to compromise, a focus on developing people, constant collaboration, and an absolute commitment to the success of the change effort. The more team leaders have explored and applied the techniques and tools shared in Part I of this book, the better able they are to lead the change effectively.

Recommendation: Create a Change Implementation Plan

Once the team has been oriented and has created a process for writing the plan, the actual writing can begin. The change implementation plan is probably the best-known tool for creating and sustaining discipline during organizational change.[5] The plan has an overriding purpose: to provide the organization with a clear road map for the change effort. It's difficult to overestimate the value of a good change plan in sustaining the discipline for revolutionary change. It has at least five benefits:

The plan focuses attention on the change effort. By creating and using the change plan—a plan that is actively supported by the CEO—you send a clear message that the change effort is a priority and must be taken seriously. Again, there is no substitute for the CEO's direct involvement in creating the plan. In fact, we recommend that the CEO personally brief the workforce on the plan. By doing this, the CEO can underscore the most important considerations in the change effort.

The plan builds understanding and clarity. Without a detailed change plan, the complexity of revolutionary change is overwhelming—particularly in large organizations. The plan enables the change implementation team to coordinate actions across the organization, including different geographies, business units, and functions. The plan also increases the desire for change by providing the workers with an understandable road map of how the change will unfold and their role in it. A great plan should also incorporate neuroscience principles such as being organized in brief, easy-to-understand sections. This relaxes the brain and promotes better thinking.[6] This is important because the complexity of revolutionary change requires the best thinking and insight from everyone.

The plan builds participation and collaboration across the organization. By enabling collaboration, the plan creates the opportunity to build and strengthen relationships and increase trust for the duration of the change effort and beyond. In this way, the plan helps you carry out the change effort and build new capabilities in the workforce.

The plan improves performance. The plan establishes performance metrics that enable the change leadership council and the change implementation team to monitor the performance of the change effort. Performance metrics allow change leaders to identify performance issues and best practices. Examples of performance metrics include:

- Staying on schedule
- Staying within budget
- Maintaining high levels of desire
- Producing high-quality deliverables
- Creating and sharing new knowledge

This information can be shared to ensure that the whole organization learns and remembers how to perform change better. This notion of organization-wide learning from change is discussed in detail in Chapter 10. Finally, performance metrics help to ensure fairness by setting the same performance standards for everyone. As we noted in Chapter 7, the perception of fairness is a key consideration in maximizing performance.

The plan balances control and flexibility. Earlier we spoke about the perils of creating management structures that are too focused on control. Because the change implementation plan is the road map for the change effort, it must create a balance between control and flexibility in implementation. A great implementation plan does this in three ways.

First, it is not too detailed. The goal is to be detailed enough to give the workforce confidence that the change effort is achievable, without being so detailed that it reduces their creativity. It's important to remember that the real problem-solving power of a change plan doesn't come from great detail, but instead comes from great creativity and original solutions to complex problems. The optimal role of oversight bodies is to assemble great teams, define the problem to be solved, provide the resources to solve it, remove obstacles, and monitor progress.

It is not the role of oversight bodies—or implementation plans—to specify tools and/or methodologies and prescribe their use. This kind of control takes the creativity out of the process and adversely affects desire. It sends a clear message that the workforce can't be trusted to deal with important problems. One way to ensure the right balance of control and flexibility is to ask the workforce for feedback on the level of detail early in the writing process.

Second, opportunities for flexibility are built into the plan. Certain tasks and opportunities can be kept general and left to the workforce to "fill in the gaps." The best plans we have seen leave room for the workforce to improvise. For example, the people who are closest to the work often know the most about it. A plan that is written in too much detail can limit the ability of the workforce to integrate its knowledge and insight into the solution. The best plans provide a detailed description of the problem to be solved, but leave room for the workforce to improvise in using its insight and original thinking to shape the final solution. Also, allowing room to improvise during implementation enables the workforce to create original solutions to problems that were not anticipated by the plan.

Third, and most important, the plan is used flexibly. This involves training change leaders on how to use the plan in a way that keeps the change effort on track and inspires the best thinking and performance from the workforce. More is said about this later in the chapter, in our discussion of creating a cadre of change leaders.

Once the change implementation team begins writing the plan, it must ensure that the writing is collaborative at every step and that it involves team discussion sessions, followed by research and writing. As the plan is written, the whole team should review each completed section.

Throughout the writing process, the team leader provides context and insight and models collaborative behavior. The leader also keeps the development of the plan on schedule and monitors its quality. Ultimately, the change plan should:

- Specify the nature and scope of the change effort
- Provide specific goals and objectives
- Identify key activities and milestones
- Assign specific responsibilities for implementation
- Identify key "dependencies"
- Include a detailed schedule
- Provide performance metrics
- Include detailed cost estimates
- Schedule performance reviews
- Include periodic updates
- Be flexible and adaptable

Earlier we stressed that creating the best management structures for your organization was partially about experimentation. This is particularly true in writing the plan. Finding the right balance in the plan is so important that you should formally solicit workforce feedback and use this feedback to modify and fine-tune the plan. We understand that this involves extra effort. However, once you have determined the optimal form of the plan for your organization, you can use it as a model for other change efforts.

Recommendation: Build a Cadre of Change Leaders

Perhaps the most important consideration in leading successful change is building a cadre of change leaders that is optimized for your organization. The executives we interviewed consistently mentioned leadership as the key factor in successful change efforts. The executives often provided examples of how leadership was essential to a critical change effort—sometimes even "saving" the organization. They also noted the ability of effective change leaders to build morale and create new capabilities beyond the scope of the change effort. These perspectives are echoed in the literature[7] and in our experience. Great leaders enable an organization to perform change efforts better, faster, and with fewer resources.

However, in spite of the performance advantages, organizations don't often invest in developing change leaders. For example, our interviews revealed:

- "Leading change" was often not included in an organization's leadership competency model. To put this another way, organizations don't see leading change as a critical factor in overall leadership. If leading change was included, it was viewed as a relatively minor factor in leadership.
- Organizations provided little or no formal training in leading change. When training was provided, it was often not specific to leading change. For example, the training cited included off-the-shelf modules on project management and/or change management.
- Selection of leaders for leading change efforts was based upon factors such as general business performance, knowledge of the culture, and/or availability, not on previous performance in leading change.
- Performance in leading change efforts was not formally assessed as part of the performance management system and was not a significant factor in career advancement.

As a result of these factors, leadership quality during organizational change efforts is often inconsistent. The executives we interviewed noted that poor change leaders adversely affect the performance of the change effort and harm morale. This leads us to believe that there is a real opportunity for your organization to improve its performance by creating and branding a cadre of change leaders.

The idea is that by investing in a cadre of change leaders your organization can make a quantum improvement in its ability to lead successful change efforts. These leaders, positioned at every level and across the organization, help in the following ways: they quickly reframe disruption as opportunity, they build and sustain the desire for change, they provide additional discipline and determination, and they actively enhance the development of people, teams, and the organization. These leaders become the foundation upon which great organizational change unfolds. They create real competitive advantage by assuring that each change effort is successful today while building more change capability for tomorrow. Here we examine the critical attributes of change leaders, and the specific steps needed to create them.

Defining Change Leadership

What is a great change leader and how do you build one? Ultimately, only your organization can say, but we wanted to offer some observations based on our interviews and our experience.

- *Great change leaders are proven business executives.* This attribute was repeatedly mentioned in our interviews for the book and in the research study referred to earlier. This attribute is seen as important for several reasons. First, successful business executives understand the organization, including its core business and operating model. This understanding helps them understand the "big picture" when they are conducting change efforts.[8]

  Second, successful executives understand the organization's culture and how to navigate successfully within it. This ability was repeatedly mentioned in our interviews as key—and was often the main criterion used to select change leaders.

  Third, successful executives have developed important relationships and trust across the organization. These assets are incredibly valuable during organizational change.

  Fourth, successful business leaders have personal credibility with senior executives and the workforce. This credibility is invaluable in taking the difficult actions that change efforts demand.

  Finally—and the executives we interviewed stressed this—successful business leaders who are trained to lead organizational change are more effective in leading change than external experts.

- *Great change leaders balance the technical, political, and developmental aspects of leading change.* They use their knowledge of the organization, its culture, and its people to best position the change effort to succeed. This means using their insight and experience to plot a course that considers and balances the technical, political, and developmental aspects of leading change.[9]

Of the technical, political, and developmental aspects of organizational change efforts, the technical aspects (maintaining cost, schedule, and performance) may be the easiest to manage. The other aspects require more experience, judgment, and insight. For example, some very influential organizational leaders may be slow in supporting the change effort. Pushing these leaders before they are ready can cause conflict and resistance. A savvy change leader takes the time to bring these leaders "on board," even if this affects the schedule. Creating a clear stakeholder analysis to understand who is important to the change and where each person stands in terms of supporting or resisting the change then informs the approaches to those stakeholders that a leader would make. The change leader uses the opportunity of change to build deeper relationships and additional support.

Likewise, ensuring that individual and team development happens also requires special attention. The great change leader knows that enabling development builds desire for today and new capabilities in the workforce for tomorrow. Your team will be able to make up time lost in development.

A recurring theme in Part II is avoiding unnecessary urgency. Great change leaders understand when it's important to stay on schedule—and when it's important not to.

- *Great change leaders shape the organizational environment during change.* These individuals are able to create a high-performing environment in "the midst of chaos" by remaining calm and focused, providing insight and context for the change, defining the direction of their team, using neuroscience principles to foster better thinking, and keeping their team and the workforce focused on their ability to make a positive difference.[10]
- *Great change leaders create a balance between control and flexibility.* Great change leaders understand that great change efforts need to strike a balance and avoid over- or undermanaging. These leaders are consistently able to strike this balance—even when it means altering their personal leadership style.
- *Great change leaders can change themselves.* Every change effort we have led has required us to change something in ourselves. Somehow, it's always a

package deal: you can't truly change an organization without being truly changed yourself. As you grow and develop, you are able to access areas of your own potential that were previously unexplored. This personal growth can inspire those around you to develop and creates a momentum for discovery that uplifts and enhances the organizational development. This insight—that change leadership begins with you—is why we begin this book with Part I, The Change-Focused Leader.

These observations aside, it is the job of your organization to define a change leadership competency tailored to meet its own vision of great organizational change. Next, we look at how you can identify and integrate this new competency.

Identifying and Integrating a Change Leadership Competency

The following steps provide a general guideline for formally identifying an organization-specific competency for leading change and integrating it into the overall leadership model.

- *Work with HR to define a new, organization-specific competency for leading change.* This process is a significant effort, but not a major one. A small team of HR professionals can define this competency; ensure that it is valid, reliable, and defensible; and create a development program in two or three months.

  The new competency should be defined for every leadership level. That is, first-line leaders, middle managers, and executives should all be required to have the competency, but each level should demonstrate proficiency in it in different ways. For example, first-line leaders might be asked to lead a small or medium-size change effort, or part of a larger one. Middle managers might lead change in a business unit or geography, and executives might be asked to serve on the change leadership council or otherwise lead change in the whole organization.

- *Integrate the new competency into your organization's overall leadership model.* This means integrating the new competency "leading change" into your organization's overall definition of leadership. Because your leadership competency model (or equivalent) forms the basis for developing leaders and managing their performance, leaders notice when the model changes. Adding the leadership of change to the model tells everyone that this is a priority. It is also important for another reason: it says that leading change isn't something that's special or separate, but is an integral part of leadership in your organization.

- *Identify development actions and integrate them into your overall leadership development program.* Everyone who is seeking advancement in the leadership ranks should be required to have development and experience in leading change. Over time, the overall competence of the leadership corps will improve and the organization will constantly get better at organizational change.
- *Modify the performance management system so that leaders are formally assessed on their performance in leading change, and make their performance in this area a factor in their advancement.* A leader's performance in organizational change efforts should inform decisions on compensation and advancement. In this way, the importance of leading great change becomes increasingly understood. Over time, these actions help to embed the leadership of change into your organization's culture.

Once a cadre of change leaders has been developed and positioned across your organization, organizational change will become easier. Leaders will be more focused on change; they will speak the same language, build common experiences, and communicate better. The organization will have the ability to select change leaders based on their past performance. These change leaders will become your organization's single biggest asset in performing organizational change better.

Discipline Summary

The ability to create and sustain high levels of discipline across the organization is a key factor in the success of revolutionary change efforts. Three actions will help you accomplish this:

- Establish a change implementation team
- Create a change implementation plan
- Build a cadre of change leaders

Establishing a diverse and high-performing change implementation team creates the ability to collaboratively plan and conduct revolutionary change efforts better. From the perspective of the change-focused organization, this recommendation complements the foundational competencies *integrate change into the business* and *ensure organization-wide learning.* Your ability to create diverse, high-performing change implementation teams and to improve their performance over time creates an important new capability for your organization.

Creating a change implementation plan that optimizes management control and flexibility increases your probability of success in revolutionary change. From the perspective of the change-focused organization, this recommendation complements the foundational competency *integrate change into the business.* Your ability to institutionalize the creation of implementation plans that optimize the balance of control and flexibility ensures your increasing success in implementing organizational change.

Building an organization-specific and high-performing cadre of change leaders is the most important step you can take in improving your organization's performance in change efforts. This recommendation is also one of the eight foundational competencies for a change-focused organization. Taken together, these three actions provide the strong discipline needed for successful revolutionary change.

This chapter focused on helping you to create the management structures needed to ensure discipline in revolutionary change. To help you anticipate and push through the inevitable setbacks that will occur during the change process, the next chapter focuses on *determination.*

Key Points to Remember

- Strong and sustainable discipline is a key factor in successful revolutionary change.
- There are three actions that can help you build and sustain this discipline: establishing a change implementation team, creating a change implementation plan, and building a cadre of change leaders.
- A diverse, high-performing change implementation team writes the change implementation plan and uses it to guide revolutionary change.
- The change implementation plan is the road map for the change effort and ensures an optimum mix of management control and flexibility.
- A cadre of trained change leaders improves the performance of the change effort at every step and actively builds discipline for change.
- Maintaining high levels of collaboration at every step builds discipline and improves every facet of revolutionary change.

CHAPTER NINE

Determination

Coping with Setbacks

Always bear in mind that your own resolution to succeed is more important than any one thing.

—Abraham Lincoln

IN CHAPTER 4, we defined *determination* at the individual level as "firmness of purpose; resoluteness."[1] This definition also works for organizations. In both cases, things happen during change efforts that shake confidence and cause a loss of focus. We refer to those things as *setbacks*. At the individual level, you are tempted to abandon the change effort and revert back to your old behavior. Likewise, organizations can give up before change has taken root. As we noted earlier, some 75 percent of organizational change efforts fail.[2]

Setbacks are so common during organizational change that we have invented a "best practice" when consulting on large-scale change efforts. Before the change effort begins, we advise our clients to prepare themselves in two ways. We offer this advice to you now.

Build the change intervention in a way that anticipates setbacks and plans for them in advance. In the previous chapters on the elements of disruption, desire, and discipline, we have recommended actions that focused specifically on this, and we will have more to say about it. Next, understand that no matter how good your advance planning is, you will experience setbacks. In fact, we predict that during a change effort, you will experience at least one setback that will test your will to continue. Expect this setback and commit to the determination to push through it.

There is one more thing worth mentioning about setbacks: they often occur just before the "tipping point" of the change effort. For some reason, setbacks can increase just before the change effort takes hold. In nature, it

The Five Ds

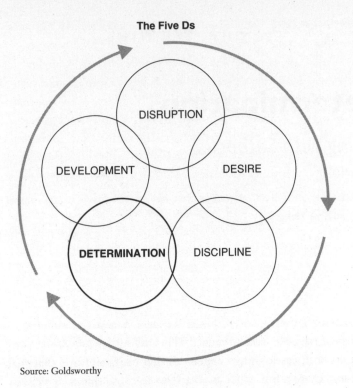

Source: Goldsworthy

is darkest before the dawn. When you are experiencing setbacks that seem insurmountable, success is close.

Leading and Living Change: Mary Slaughter

Perhaps no experience in recent memory has required more determination to manage than the revolutionary changes that have been experienced in the global financial community. Mary Slaughter, the chief learning officer of Sun-Trust Banks, joined SunTrust in 2009—during the largest disruption of the financial community since the Great Depression. We asked Mary to reflect on her experiences as a change leader during this turbulent period and on the importance of determination in leading successful revolutionary change:

> A good friend of mine, Dr. Rick Gilkey from Emory University, once told me, "You learn more from reflecting on your experiences than you do from the actual experiences themselves." Truer words have not been spoken, particularly for developing great leaders. Over the course of my career, I've been through three industry collapses—the oil industry in the 1980s, the Internet bubble bursting in 2004, and the 2008 meltdown of the financial services

sector. Apparently, I have developed some twisted affinity for adversity, as I seem to thrive in tough situations.

When I joined SunTrust in 2009 as its chief learning officer, my role had been vacant for six months. There was no learning strategy in place, the corporate university was not aligned with the business, and the learning team was struggling to survive in an atmosphere of layoffs. Development budgets had declined year over year, and our learning technology platforms had outlived their usefulness. In the broader business context, the sector was crashing, and no one knew where the bottom would be. The Federal Reserve had mandated that we accept an infusion of about $4.9 billion in capital from TARP (Troubled Asset Relief Program). The market themes that were emerging were record unemployment, unprecedented numbers of home foreclosures, frozen access to credit, and explosive government regulation. The financial sector was at the epicenter of the great global recession, and the public trust had been destroyed.

Where does one start when one is faced with seemingly unending challenges? It all begins with well-defined, desired outcomes. Our chairman and CEO understood that the financial crisis would be a marathon. In order to survive and thrive postrecession, our first challenge was to foster inspired and resilient leaders, aligned to a common purpose. We chose to build our leadership capability strategically—to create a shared vision of success for our teammates, clients, and shareholders. Second, we had to rebuild bridges with key executives so that we could move quickly and effectively, as the markets were uncertain. Third, we rebuilt our learning operations and talent to adapt to the business demands.

Five years after the recession, SunTrust emerged a stronger company with industry-leading client loyalty, solid financials, accelerating teammate engagement, and a growing leadership pipeline. We've been recognized across the learning industry for our alignment with our business leaders, but, more important, for the impact of our work on the health of the enterprise. The investment in talent development has grown every year since I joined, and our learning technology capabilities continue to expand. When I talk to my peers in other companies and industries, it's clear to me that we're doing something right.

Now to come full circle—how is it possible to reach such a good place from such a lousy starting point? For me, determination may be what I've always considered to be personal commitment in action. When I reflect upon my Sun-Trust experiences as well as my work in other industries, clearly determination played a role in my success. I tend to compete more with myself than I do with others, so determination means beating the odds and, frankly, exceeding my own expectations. In the toughest circumstances, I find it helps to set aside the past, including your traditional playbook, and start with a clean slate.

My biggest lesson is that during a time of crisis, the status quo is no longer a sacred cow but frequently the kiss of death. Politics and history become far less important—new ideas, clear decision making, and personal advocacy rule the day. Resistance is lower, priorities are clearer, and decisions are faster. Newton's first law of motion says, "Unless acted upon, objects at rest tend to stay at rest and objects in motion tend to stay in motion." Organizations reflect this every day. My role was to be a catalyst and act upon the organization in a purposeful, determined way. I've learned that tough circumstances produce opportunities to excel. Recognize and leverage those moments—move into the white spaces, manage risk, and be bold.

This chapter is about building the determination needed to deal with setbacks. Your goal is not merely to push through setbacks but, like Mary Slaughter, to recognize and exploit the opportunities that they provide. A well-managed setback can become a great asset in carrying out revolutionary change. In the following section, we introduce two specific types of setbacks.

The Nature of Setbacks

We focus our discussion on two types of setbacks which we refer to as *typical setbacks* and *derailers*. Both types of setbacks are important, but the approaches for managing them are quite different. Typical setbacks threaten the success of revolutionary change efforts, but they can be anticipated and planned for. Derailers also threaten change efforts, but they can't be anticipated. This section explores how to manage both types of setbacks and informs the recommendations that follow.

Typical Setbacks

We define *typical setbacks* as routine occurrences that affect the performance of change efforts. By *routine*, we mean things that often occur during change efforts and therefore can be anticipated. Examples of typical setbacks mentioned by the executives we interviewed include:

- *Reduced priority of the change effort over time.* In this situation, the change effort has been underway for some time and is doing well overall. However, new business issues and other distractions are beginning to challenge the effort for priority. This often happens when senior leaders reduce their direct involvement in the effort. When the priority of a revolutionary change effort begins to fall, the effort is in jeopardy, and you must act.

- *Loss of vision.* In this case, the organization loses sight of its vision for the change effort over time. The disruption has passed, and the need for the change effort seems less urgent. Various stakeholders are suggesting that the scope of the effort be reduced or the schedule extended. This happens when the original vision for the change effort was not clear, compelling, linked to strategy, or adequately supported by senior leaders. When the workforce forgets why the change effort is important for organizational survival, desire and discipline can falter.

  A key reason for this relates to how the brain deals with organizational change. In Chapter 7, we spoke about how difficult environmental changes can be for numerous systems within the brain, often causing discomfort or even pain. Change in the brain requires enduring this discomfort over time as new ways of thinking and acting are adopted and new habits are formed. If the reason for enduring discomfort is lost, reverting to old behavior is an easy way for the brain to stop the discomfort. Successful change demands that the vision stay strong over time.

- *Senior leadership conflict and/or "stonewalling."* In this situation, organizational leaders lose their unity as the change effort unfolds. One manifestation of this occurs when leaders become defensive and/or try to minimize the effect of the change effort on their business unit or function. They may become increasingly uncooperative and try to stall until the change effort "blows over." This often occurs when insufficient effort was invested in building senior leadership consensus and/or when the CEO and the top management team are not directly engaged in the change effort.

- *Slow progress in implementation.* In this situation, the change effort begins to fall behind schedule. It is important that you respond to this immediately and get the effort back on track. If slips in the schedule persist, the workforce's desire for change will quickly diminish.

- *Inconsistent and/or ineffective change leadership.* In this situation, the quality of the change leadership is inconsistent. Some change leaders foster high levels of performance and collaboration, but other change leaders foster the opposite effects. As noted in the previous chapter, an inconsistent quality of leadership is one result of the lack of change leadership training. The executives we interviewed noted this as a continuing problem and supported our recommendation that it makes great sense to build a cadre of change leaders before change is necessary.

As a result of these typical setbacks, the change effort is becoming misaligned, with some schedule milestones being met ahead of schedule and others falling behind schedule. Some parts of the change effort are waiting for other parts to catch up. The workforce desire for change begins to vary across the organization, as does the performance of change teams. Inconsistent leadership quality makes the change effort more difficult to manage and greatly reduces the probability of success. The previous list of setbacks is meant as a starting point for your thinking. What other types of typical setbacks do you see in your organization? How will you manage them?

Managing typical setbacks is about good planning. The goal is to plan your change effort in a way that either eliminates setbacks or reduces their impact. In our recommendations, we provide an example of how to do this.

Derailers

We define *derailers* as unexpected occurrences that threaten the success of revolutionary change efforts. Derailers arise from the growing complexity of the competitive environment. As noted in Chapter 6, this environment demands that organizations change nearly continuously and in new and complex ways.[3] The interactions among several factors are creating this environment, including:

- *Increasing globalization.* Organizations are being forced to think and act more globally in order to stay competitive.
- *Unprecedented competition.* New and different competitors are entering the market, making traditional strategies for achieving a competitive advantage inadequate or obsolete.
- *More or different stakeholders.* New and different stakeholders are entering the competitive environment.
- *Economic uncertainty.* The global economy has not rebounded as quickly as was hoped, and many financial questions remain unresolved.
- *Energy constraints.* The availability of energy resources—and related environmental issues—is a key source of concern.
- *Resource scarcity.* Organizations everywhere are being forced to operate more efficiently, while simultaneously becoming more competitive.

- *Political instability.* Large portions of the world continue to experience instability, adding high levels of risk and uncertainty to the business environment.

These factors (and others) are interacting to create a competitive environment that is incredibly complex and unpredictable. This environment is described in various ways, but our favorite description is VUCA,[4] an acronym for volatile, uncertain, complex, and ambiguous:

- *Volatility* refers to the nature and dynamics of change—the nature and speed of change forces and change catalysts.
- *Uncertainty* refers to the lack of predictability and the prospects for surprise.
- *Complexity* refers to the multiplicity of forces, the confounding of issues, and the chaos and confusion that surround an organization.
- *Ambiguity* refers to the haziness of reality, the potential for misreadings, and the mixed meanings of conditions—cause-and-effect confusion.[5]

The executives we interviewed acknowledged the VUCA environment and noted that this environment demands more organizational change *and* makes change more difficult. They offered these examples of derailers:

- *A second disruption.* As noted in Chapter 6, competitive disruptions are coming faster in the twenty-first century—particularly in certain industries such as technology.[6] In this situation, an organization is rocked by a second competitive disruption before it has adjusted to the first one. This can test the ability of a change leader and an organization to adapt.
- *A surprise shift in strategy.* In this situation, the organization's senior leadership decides to shift organizational strategy in a way that makes the ongoing change effort more or less important. Examples include mergers, acquisitions, and entering a new area of business and/or a new market.
- *Unexpected stakeholder resistance.* A characteristic of the VUCA environment is an increasing number of new and different stakeholders creating new types of business relationships.[7] In this example, the change effort sparks unexpected resistance from one or more new stakeholder groups and/or competitors.
- *A change in CEO.* Leadership experts are noting that the length of tenure for CEOs is decreasing.[8] In this example, the CEO is replaced and the change effort loses its strongest advocate. The successor CEO may not support the current effort or may want to change its scope and/or direction.

Again, these examples are only a starting place for your thinking. What other possible derailers are facing your organization and/or your industry?

Managing derailers in a VUCA environment is a difficult task for any organization. Even so, two things will help: improving your organization's ability to "sense" its competitive environment and creating an internal environment in your organization that is optimized for continuous change. We share recommendations for dealing with both of these areas.

Recommendations for Ensuring Determination

Managing setbacks effectively involves reducing or eliminating their adverse effects and exploiting the opportunities they provide. In this section, we recommend four actions focused on managing typical setbacks and derailers:

- Anticipate typical setbacks
- Improve environmental sensing
- Continually optimize the organizational environment
- Manage your determination

Several of our previous recommendations are relevant and are integrated into the discussion of each of these recommendations.

Recommendation: Anticipate Typical Setbacks

Managing typical setbacks is about great up-front planning—and we've tried to provide an example of that in this book. For example, in Chapters 6 through 8 we make 10 recommendations for leading revolutionary change prior to discussing setbacks in Chapter 9. One of the reasons we chose these specific recommendations is that they reduce or eliminate some typical setbacks—before these setbacks become an issue. We will demonstrate this with an example.

You will recall that one typical setback mentioned by the executives we interviewed was *reduced priority of the change effort over time*. Let's focus on this setback and on how our previous recommendations help reduce its potential adverse effects.

In this setback, new problems have distracted your senior leaders, and the desire of your workforce for revolutionary change is waning. However, the need for the change effort is as real as ever. What should you do? How do you reestablish the priority of the change effort?

If you followed our earlier recommendations, this issue becomes more manageable. For example:

- In Chapter 6, we recommended establishing a change leadership council. The council is chaired by the CEO and consists of the senior executive team and others. The council's role is to lead and oversee the change effort for its duration. We had several things in mind when we made this recommendation, but a key one was to ensure that your change effort maintains high priority over time. The active leadership of the CEO and the executive team are incredibly helpful in achieving this.

- Also in Chapter 6, we recommended that the council formulate a change strategy and tie it directly to your overall organizational strategy. We suggested this to increase the priority of the change effort by casting it as "strategic." As organizational strategy is periodically updated, so is the revolutionary change strategy. This helps keep its priority high over time.

- In Chapter 8, we recommended the establishment of a change implementation team. The key goal of this team, which reports to the CEO, is to ensure that revolutionary change is implemented. Helping to maintain the priority of the effort is a key goal of the team.

- Also in Chapter 8, we recommended that you build a cadre of trained change leaders. A key goal of these leaders is to actively help in creating the desire, discipline, and determination for revolutionary change. These leaders exist to ensure that the priority of the change effort is maintained. As you review all of our recommendations, you will see that many of them are focused on reducing the impact of this type of setback before it occurs.

To continue the example, if you believe that the change effort is losing priority over time—in spite of your having followed our recommendations—you have supporters. The change leadership council and the cadre of change leaders can help you reestablish the priority of the change effort. In fact, the setback can be used as a way to reaffirm your organization's commitment to the change.

One final thought to close out this example: the most important consideration is not whether you accept our recommendations. The most important consideration is anticipating typical setbacks in your organization and building the change effort in a way that mitigates them. Great planning matters when it comes to great change. Table 9-1 summarizes how the recommendations we have made so far address the other typical setbacks mentioned by the executives we interviewed.

Table 9-1 Our Recommendations and Effects on Typical Setbacks

Leadership Actions	Leadership Activities	Effects on *Typical* Setbacks
1. Create a guiding philosophy	• Build senior leadership consensus on the "ends" and the "means" of change	• Reduces leadership conflict • Makes change leaders more effective
2. Establish a change leadership council	• Appoint CEO as leader of change leadership council • Involve senior executive team as active members	• Assures high priority • Keeps vision fresh • Reduces leadership conflict • Maintains schedule
3. Formulate a change strategy	• Align with organization strategy	• Assures high priority • Maintains schedule
4. Initiate communication	• Increase communication about revolutionary change	• Assures high priority • Keeps vision fresh
5. Actively shape the change environment	• Model behavior • Provide insight and context • Define direction • Create a "thinking" environment • Be fair	• Assures high priority • Keeps vision fresh • Maintains schedule
6. Develop people constantly	• Involve your team immediately • Train your team to be proactive • Make development personal • Celebrate and reward • Focus on higher purpose	• Assures high priority • Keeps vision fresh • Maintains schedule
7. Implement a communications strategy	• Align it with change strategy • Provide information; don't try to persuade • Use all forms of communication, including social media	• Assures high priority • Keeps vision fresh • Maintains schedule

8. **Establish a change implementation team**	• Create a change implementation plan • Implement the change effort	• Assures high priority • Keeps vision fresh • Maintains schedule • Makes change leaders more effective
9. **Create a change implementation plan**	• Provide sufficient detail; don't overmanage • Build in opportunities for original thinking	• Assures high priority • Keeps vision fresh • Maintains schedule • Makes change leaders more effective
10. **Build a cadre of change leaders**	• Define new leadership competency • Integrate into leadership development program • Train over time • Assess performance	• Assures high priority • Keeps vision fresh • Maintains schedule • Makes change leaders more effective

Recommendation: Improve Environmental Sensing

In a VUCA environment, an organization's ability to anticipate and react to changes in its competitive environment is critically important for its survival,[9] yet this is very difficult to do. As we noted in Chapter 6, disruptions are usually a surprise. Still, we believe great leaders can take actions which can anticipate and/or mitigate this surprise. Two activities can help:

• Improve environmental scanning
• Create and lead an industrywide community of practice

Improving environmental scanning is about taking action to better anticipate derailers. Creating and leading an industrywide community of practice is about actively shaping and/or eliminating derailers. Both activities are discussed in more detail here.

Improve Environmental Scanning. Environmental scanning is defined as: "The study and interpretation of the political, economic, social, and technical events and trends which influence a business, an industry or even a total market."[10] The purposes of environmental scanning are:

> To better understand the nature and pace of change in the environment and to identify potential opportunities, challenges and likely future developments relevant to your organization.[11]

Your organization may already have solid processes for environmental scanning in place, which is great. However, the VUCA environment has adversely affected the ability of many organizations to anticipate changes in their competitive environment—including potential derailers.

As a result, there is a new emphasis on improving strategic planning processes and on performing better environmental scanning. One focus is on "futures" planning.[12] Futures planning has been described as "an interdisciplinary collection of methods, theories, and findings"[13] that helps people (and organizations) to "think constructively about the future."[14] For our purposes, the goal of futures planning is to help organizations improve their environmental scanning and their ability to predict environmental changes in a VUCA environment.

There are several techniques for futures planning, including the Delphi method, causal layered analysis, morphological analysis, content analysis, visioning, social network analysis, and others. One example of a futures technique we have used is scenario thinking.

Scenario thinking is a structured process of thinking about and anticipating the unknown future, without pretending to be able to predict it. Instead, this technique navigates through the uncertainties and large-scale driving forces that are affecting the future.[15] The objective is to examine possible future developments that could affect the organization and to find the directions that will be most beneficial, no matter how the future unfolds. In effect, the scenario thinking approach is a set of tools and frameworks for simplifying, identifying, and extracting relevant information from the VUCA environment in order to make better decisions.

We mention the topics of futures planning and scenario thinking because these capabilities can improve change planning and can help you anticipate derailers. If your organization has a group that is focused on strategic planning, get to know the people in that group better, and consider their perspectives in your change planning activities.

Finally, consider formal training in scenario thinking. Scenario thinking can help you plan better by helping you identify key change levers—events or interventions that can change the course of the future for your organization or your industry. Scenarios can also help your organization enhance learning by enabling a shared appreciation of the economic, environmental, technological, social, and political environments. This helps the organization better align various constituencies and stakeholders to prepare for and embrace change.[16] Training in scenario thinking is available through the executive education programs of many university business schools. In addition, we publish a list of providers on our website.

Create and Lead an Industrywide Community of Practice. Let us return to a story we told in Chapter 6 about an event at the Harvard Business School. The event was a presentation by Professors Michael Tushman and Charles O'Reilly on the factors that matter most in great organizational change.[17] One part of the discussion focused on how great organizations achieve and/or maintain leadership of their industry.

One way is by initiating change ahead of their competitors.[18] To put this another way, the most successful organizations don't just anticipate competitive disruptions—they sometimes initiate them. By doing this, they shape the competitive environment of their industry and are surprised less often by derailers.

In the previous section, we spoke about the growing popularity of futures planning. Some futurists are describing the ability to lead diverse groups over whom there is no formal authority as a key success factor of the future.[19] One way to do this is to create and lead an industrywide community of practice by:

- Creating a compelling vision for the industry
- Actively building industry coalitions among stakeholders and competitors
- Sharing information across your community of practice
- Hosting industrywide meetings on best practices, emerging threats, and other such topics
- Writing, publishing, and presenting on topics that are of interest to the industry

Over time, your organization will become the center of thought and practice in its industry. When it changes, the industry will follow.

We believe that leading a community of practice is a key way to thrive in a VUCA environment. As the industry leader, your organization will be surprised less often by competitive disruption and derailers. Instead, your organization does the surprising.

Recommendation: Continually Optimize the Internal Environment

In the best case, your organization will grow increasingly effective at anticipating and shaping all manner of typical setbacks and derailers by understanding and navigating the VUCA environment better. However, another way to help manage setbacks is by creating an internal environment that is optimized for continuous change.

In Chapter 7, one of our recommendations was to "shape the environment during change." This recommendation was specifically about taking the actions *during* revolutionary change that are necessary to build the workforce's desire for change. The current recommendation is about taking the actions necessary to continually optimize the internal environment—doing things every day to help your organization get better at carrying out change.

Adopting this recommendation means that no matter how unpredictable the competitive environment or how unexpected the competitive disruption, your organization is able to adapt faster, better, and with fewer resources than its competitors. Creating this environment is the essence of a change-focused organization.

Our interviews, experience, and research point to the importance of eight factors in creating an internal environment that is optimized for change. In Chapter 6, we referred to these factors as "foundational competencies" for a change-focused organization. They are:

- Make change strategic
- Integrate change into the business
- Create a cadre of change leaders
- Develop people constantly
- Model collaboration in everything
- Foster better thinking
- Ensure organization-wide learning
- Lead change in yourself

Recommendation: Manage Your Determination

Little has been written about how change leaders maintain the determination needed to manage setbacks for the duration of revolutionary change. Most advice focuses on the importance of building new professional skills. In our experience, maintaining the determination needed to manage setbacks during high-pressure change efforts is difficult because setbacks can affect you intellectually, physically, and emotionally.

The intellectual impact is probably the easiest to understand. Leading a revolutionary change effort is a significant intellectual challenge. These efforts are profoundly complex and constantly changing. In addition to the technical aspects of being a change leader, you also have to navigate the political aspects and make time to guide and develop people. Managing setbacks in the midst of revolutionary change increases the intellectual load significantly.

The physical impact of a setback is also real. In our experience, no large-scale change effort can be led in a 40-hour week. You are often working long days, and you may be operating with a sleep deficit. Setbacks increase your workload and demand even more focus at times when your energy level is very low. Following the recommendations from Chapter 4 about resilience, looking after yourself, and practicing simple mindfulness and meditation will aid you in dealing with the physical impact of change.

The emotional effects of a setback are also significant, although they are seldom mentioned. Revolutionary change efforts are never just about organizational change, as important as this is. They are also about the lives and well-being of hundreds or thousands of people. Setbacks can frustrate them, shake their confidence, and make them afraid—and you have to help get them back on track. During change, people experience the potentially debilitating feelings of sadness and anger associated with loss and grief. Understanding how people deal with loss and the stages associated with change will assist leaders in guiding people through the change with care and consideration. Applying the mantra of "pride in the past, passion for the present, and focus on the future" ensures that people's feelings are respected during the process, making them more able to deal with the change and let go of the past to make the transition to the potential of the new future.

Balancing the intellectual, physical, and emotional demands during setbacks requires you to manage your determination. The following recommendations are meant to help you accomplish this:

- Set reasonable expectations
- Build a strong second team
- Manage your brain
- Allow setbacks to improve you
- Find and use a coach

Setting reasonable expectations about setbacks is essential. Let's be very clear: there is a great deal that is beyond your control in leading change efforts—including the frequency of setbacks. No matter how well you plan and execute the change, setbacks will occur and must be dealt with. A setback is not a failure. It's an opportunity to adapt and grow.

A great way to share the load of leading change efforts and improve your ability to manage setbacks is to *build a strong second team*. This means more than delegation. It means making the selection and development of a group of leaders a priority. You involve them in key decisions, explain your thinking on issues, and set standards for their performance during the change effort.

When a setback occurs, your second team acts as a support system, helping you to focus on the setback and still accomplish other things that are related to the change effort. Also, setbacks provide invaluable development opportunities for your second team. A high-performing second team increases determination.

In Chapter 6, we discussed the importance of keeping your team and the workforce calm and focused during a competitive disruption. The reason was to prevent people's brains from entering a "threat state" that would reduce the quality of their thinking. Your brain is also very capable of entering a threat state, and a setback (particularly a major one) can push it there. Once you are in a threat state, your best thinking, including your ability to solve complex problems, is impaired just when you need it most.

We recommend that you practice these steps as a way to better *manage your brain* in high-pressure situations:[20]

- *Set personal goals in short time chunks.* The more pressure you feel, the shorter the time duration of the goal. For example, during normal operation, you may set monthly or quarterly goals for yourself. During periods of intense pressure, such as during a setback, you should set goals weekly—or even daily.
- *Rehearse mentally.* Visualize yourself and your team succeeding in managing the setback and go through the actions you will take step by step. Look back at Chapter 2 for more guidance and examples on the power of visualization.
- *Practice positive self-talk.* Neuroscientists estimate that we say 300 to 1,000 words to ourselves each minute. Tame your inner critic, as mentioned in Chapter 2. Speaking positively to yourself helps you to reframe and to override and mitigate your anxiety.[21]
- *Practice arousal control.* There are several techniques that you can use to mitigate the anxiety that can foster poor leadership behavior. Many techniques for emotional regulation are shared in Part I of this book. Other examples include deep breathing, positive imagery, and muscle relaxation.

The experience of working through a setback can improve your self-control, your patience, and your overall leadership skills—if you let it. So, *allow setbacks to improve you.* Stay focused on the developmental potential during setbacks, particularly when they are most difficult. We have found that leading change always changes us—sometimes painfully, but always for the best. Let go, let be, and let come. Let the changes happen.

As shared in Chapter 5, you need external support to maximize the gain from your own development. *Find and use an executive coach* who can help you and your team to get the most from leading a change effort and dealing with setbacks effectively. The coach will be particularly useful in helping you navigate large setbacks (whether they be intellectual, physical, or emotional) and other crises associated with revolutionary change. Once you have selected your coach, commit yourself to daily action, schedule regular meetings, and keep them.

Determination Summary

Revolutionary change efforts require creating and sustaining high levels of determination across the organization and in yourself. There are two types of setbacks that can challenge your determination: *typical setbacks* and *derailers*. Typical setbacks are common during change efforts, and you should expect and plan for them. Derailers are large and unexpected setbacks that can't be predicted but can be prepared for. For leaders, determination requires that you minimize the adverse impact of setbacks and exploit the opportunities that they present in order to advance the change strategy. We recommend four actions to help you create and sustain determination during revolutionary change.

- Anticipate typical setbacks
- Improve environmental sensing
- Optimize the internal environment
- Manage your determination

Anticipating typical setbacks is about great early planning. You should use the experiences of your organization and your personal insights to design the change effort so that you anticipate and minimize setbacks. Anticipating setbacks is also important in becoming a change-focused organization, as it helps *integrate change into the business*.

Unlike typical setbacks, derailers can't be specifically planned for and built into your change approach. However, you can better anticipate them by improving your organization's ability to understand and shape its competitive environment. The ability to improve environmental scanning and to build an industrywide community of practice are helpful in shaping the competitive environment. They also contribute to the change-focused organization by *ensuring organization-wide learning*.

Optimizing the internal environment of your organization for continuous change is a key way to prepare for any type of setback or disruption. Adopting the eight foundational competencies and building them into your organization over time is a great way to do this.

Finally, managing your own determination and your energy during the duration of a revolutionary change effort is important for your performance and development. This contributes to the change-focused organization by helping you *lead change in yourself.*

The four actions recommended here help to ensure that your organization is effective in managing all types of setbacks and that it has the determination needed to succeed. The next chapter covers *development,* the fifth and final element in the Five Ds framework. It focuses on building the capabilities required to ensure that your organization performs change better over time.

Key Points to Remember

- Determination requires minimizing adverse impact and exploiting opportunities arising from both typical setbacks and derailers.
- Four actions help to build and sustain determination: anticipate typical setbacks, improve environmental sensing, optimize the internal environment, and manage your determination.
- Managing typical setbacks means planning for them in advance.
- Managing derailers means building the capabilities to better understand and shape the competitive environment.
- Managing your personal determination and energy during change efforts is essential.

CHAPTER TEN

Development

Learning Continuously About Change

An organization's ability to learn, and translate that learning into action rapidly, is the ultimate competitive advantage.

—Jack Welch

D EVELOPMENT IS ABOUT ensuring continuous learning and growth—both in yourself and in your organization. In Chapter 5, we defined *development* at the individual level as "the act or process of growing, progressing, or developing."[1] While this broad definition also applies to organizations, change leaders must embrace and focus on coordinating the development of individuals, teams, and the organization as an integrated *system*. The primary goal of this system is to develop the ability to constantly carry out organizational change better.

The executives we interviewed described this capability, "to constantly carry out change better," as a business imperative—and one that is crucial for an organization's survival. They suggested that the ability to integrate change faster and better provided competitive advantages that were difficult for competitors to copy.

Where other organizations focus on surviving competitive disruptions, a change-focused organization emphasizes learning from them. Each new change effort applies learning from the last one—and builds upon it. Organizational change stops being an unrelenting grind and becomes an opportunity for real performance improvement for individuals, teams, and the organization. If a hallmark of the VUCA (volatile, uncertain, complex, and ambiguous) environment is continuous change, it's your job as a change leader to use that change for continuous development.

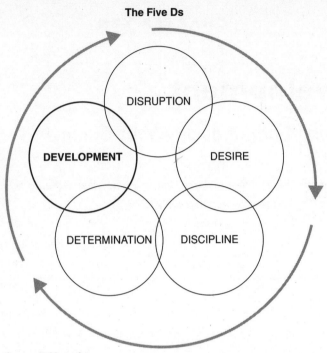

The Five Ds

Source: Goldsworthy

Leading and Living Change: Victoria Marsick

Victoria Marsick is a professor of adult and organizational learning at Teachers College, Columbia University, and codirector of the J. M. Huber Institute for Learning in Organizations. Her extensive research and work on learning at the team and organizational levels provides a rich perspective on how learning in organizations has and will continue to evolve.[2] Her perspectives illuminate winning practices for how change leaders can improve the learning abilities of their organizations.

> *Organizations improve their performance when they are acutely attuned to changes in their environment and have the capacity to respond quickly to customers, markets, and trends that affect their business. In today's global, dynamic world, staying in tune with the environment needs to be in the hearts, minds, and hands of all employees. Because global organizations work in a networked, decentralized way, they require alignment, knowledge gathering and sharing, and strategic organizational learning.*
>
> *How can change leaders help organizations perform in this kind of environment? Change leaders are experimenters in chief, taking calculated risks*

and learning their way through ambiguity and complexity. They are sense makers and knowledge integrators. An example comes to mind of a leader who transformed his business from a classic commodity producer to a specialty products business in just five years. He did it by engaging everyone in a focused effort to pursue a goal that many thought was impossible and helping to develop organizational skills in designing, manufacturing, and selling completely new products. He rolled up his sleeves and worked collaboratively with handpicked leaders to develop a new mindset, jump-starting the process with new talent, new reporting structures, training in collaboration, and the strategic use of key resources.

This leader—like the best leaders I have known—worked from a systems model, in his case, McKinsey's 7S model. (Other CEOs might develop a model based on their own experience or adapt a sociotechnical systems model or the Burke-Litwin model of transformational and transactional system dynamics.) He used this model to think about how all the pieces of what people do and how they work together come together, and to troubleshoot barriers that got in the way of optimum alignment—not too much alignment, or groupthink reigns and innovation is squelched, and not too little alignment, or performance is held captive by millions of inefficiencies that make things stick. This leader also built an organizational culture that screamed innovation.

Learning was central to this mix. He did team building, but he learned that taking leaders offsite to ride the rapids did not solve day-to-day problems. Using Lego sets to model real challenges in the production process worked much better because it was tied to visible, daily challenges. The best learning occurred when a few people or groups experimented, practiced, perfected, and then worked with others in the organization to transfer their capabilities.

There are always benefits to learning from the expertise that others have spent years honing and doing this in a structured way. Learning that drives innovation, change, and continuous adaptation, however, is also and primarily informal, social, collaborative, and tied to everyday work challenges and interests. This team leader took people on visits to other organizations to see how they did things, hired talent from related but totally different industries and used these people to help change the ways of thinking and working throughout the organization, and built learning into goal achievement. People bring their whole selves to this kind of learning, calling upon and adapting personal and professional scripts for responding to millions of recognized patterns every day. Leaders build climates in the organization where managers model, coach for, and reward informal learning.

Continues Victoria,

Change leaders such as the leader I just described are constantly taking stock of the situation based on input from key leaders throughout the organization. They invite the free flow of ideas and information across boundaries, and they look for ways to encourage and reward innovation. They also find ways to connect dots with and through their executive team. They build leadership throughout the organization so that people think with an enterprise mindset, constantly keeping in mind ways in which their work links to other functions, groups, and initiatives. Enterprise mindsets call for seeing work in the context of the value chain and looking for solutions from this wider perspective.

Building an enterprise mindset is key to crossing and managing boundaries in organizations that are matrixed, networked, and project team–centered. The industrial model inherited by many organizations was organized bureaucratically. Virtue came from knowing how to operate within boundaries and following marching orders that came from on high. Today, just as in the army, which created the original industrial machine model, leaders at the top of the organization cannot access all of the changing intelligence that the troops have at the interface with their clients and customers. Everyone must now take on leadership, be creative and innovative, and ensure that what he or she knows is communicated to others who need this intelligence to improve the entire enterprise. But organizations have not been set up for this widespread sharing, and the troops often have been trained to comply rather than to achieve autonomy and engagement outside their immediate boundaries. Developing these boundary-crossing skills and enterprise mindsets is a key challenge. These capabilities are shaped in part by what people bring to the enterprise, but they are reciprocally formed by the challenges and supports that leaders throughout the organization provide and the climates and cultures they build to encourage and support new cross-boundary thinking and work.

This chapter focuses on helping you and your system to develop the ability to constantly improve at performing organizational change. Our hope is to prepare you to become what Professor Marsick calls the "experimenter in chief."

The Role of the Change Leader in Development

Developing the ability to constantly improve at organizational change is about learning. Specifically, it's about how people, teams, and the whole organization learn to carry out change better—both separately and as an integrated *system*. As a change leader, your role is to enable this learning at each level and across the system.

It's important to remember that this learning is occurring during revolutionary change, so the learning environment will be affected in unknown ways. Because change affects the environment differently in every organization, it is important that you experiment with the best ways to enable learning across your organization. Bear in mind the phrase, "Tell me and I forget; show me and I remember; involve me and I understand."

The role of the change leader in enabling learning is bigger than any one person. This is another reason why creating a cadre of trained change leaders (as discussed in Chapter 8) is so important in integrating every aspect of a revolutionary change effort—including organization-wide learning.

Recommendations to Ensure Continuous Development

In this section, we recommend three actions that are focused on helping your organization develop the capability to continuously improve at carrying out organizational change:

- Enable learning in people
- Enable learning in teams
- Enable organization-wide learning

At the individual level, you act as a coach and a mentor, providing important context and perspective. Your focus is on creating an environment that is conducive to learning about change. At the team level, you act as a facilitator, focused on drawing out and using the best thinking of your team. At the organizational level, you act as an integrator, focused on building the structures and processes needed to share and use learning across the organization. Let's explore each of these three actions.

Recommendation: Enable Learning in People

In Chapter 7, we suggested that change leaders need to "develop people during change." This recommendation was focused on actions that you take to promote the professional development of your team during change. This section discusses how you can enable people to learn about and carry out organizational change better. The goal is to help people learn how to be effective in carrying out the current change effort—and even more effective in carrying out the next one.

A key factor in the success of revolutionary change is helping people learn. This learning improves the quality of change efforts and builds people's desire for change. The environment of revolutionary change can be hectic and fast-moving, but it's important that learning happens "in the moment" as change unfolds. A great deal is known about how people learn in the workplace, but relatively little is known about how a revolutionary change effort—or any large-scale change effort—affects people's ability to learn. This is why the notion of experimenting is so important. We have identified an initial set of activities that will help you enable learning during revolutionary change:

Use the competitive disruption.[3] As noted in Chapters 1 and 7, a disruption can provide a positive environment for learning. When the environment produces an unexpected event that surprises and challenges people, it can foster an opportunity for deep learning, sometimes called "transformational."[4] What makes transformational learning special is a fundamental shift in the way a person perceives the world. This fundamental or "revolutionary" shift in perspective fosters deep and lasting changes in behavior and performance. These changes are a primary goal of revolutionary change.

During a competitive disruption, people may be more open to learning. The executives we interviewed said that revolutionary change efforts can foster a deeper level of learning in people and organizations—when these efforts are well led. One reason for this is that a competitive disruption can serve an important purpose in adult learning: it provides a "disorienting dilemma" that can enhance learning in people.[5]

Some of the executives pointed to examples of change efforts that were able to produce "leaps" in performance and learning beyond expectations. For example, several executives mentioned instances in which a relatively small change effort "caught fire" and led to learning and performance improvements across the organization. Others mentioned instances in which the workforce was able to produce innovative solutions that were better than had been anticipated or imagined. We have observed these phenomena in practice as well. When well led, change efforts can elicit significant improvements in learning and performance.

As a change leader, it is very important that in the early days following a competitive disruption, you create a learning environment that is calm, focused, and collaborative. Our executives suggested that the early days of revolutionary change are about reflection and collaboration—not about urgent action. You enable individual learning in the early days of revolutionary change by reframing the energy created by the disruption from anxiety to excitement about the future.

Respect experience.[6] People bring a wealth of experience to a change effort, and they want to use it constructively. You enable their learning by valuing this experience and by helping them align it with the change effort. We use the word *align* because not all experiences are relevant to the change effort, and people need help in understanding how they can best contribute. People also respect and learn from the experience of their coworkers. The more the learning environment enables people to interact with one another in finding solutions to change-related problems, the more learning will occur. When you respect people's diverse experiences and guide their application in the change effort, you enable people's learning.

Understand "readiness to learn."[7] Individuals want to understand how the change affects them so that they can best prepare themselves. Because people are focused on using learning practically, they are most "ready" to learn things that help them solve real-world problems. You enable learning by using your perspective on and insight into the change effort to help people focus their learning. Helping people understand how they can use revolutionary change as an opportunity to develop personally improves their readiness to learn.

Provide autonomy in learning.[8] Adult learning professionals often refer to this as "self-directedness." This acknowledges that people want to take responsibility for the form of their learning rather than have it dictated. You enable learning when you offer people learning choices—including nontraditional ones. A great alternative is informal learning.

The American Society for Training and Development (ASTD) defines informal learning as:

> A learning activity [that] . . . takes place without a conventional instructor and is employee controlled in terms of breadth, depth, and timing. It tends to be individualized, limited in scope, and utilized in small chunks. Examples include peer-to-peer coaching, social networking, and internet searches. It does not include activities such as organized classes, workshops, and conventional job aids.[9]

Informal learning is particularly important during change, because people are trying to understand what is going on around them and because formal learning may not adequately address emerging issues. During organizational change, people may touch base with their colleagues, chat with a mentor, exchange instant messages, do online social networking, or access knowledge through Internet searches. The use of secure bases, as discussed in Chapters 2 and 5, is a powerful source of learning, as they both support you and challenge you to grow and step outside your comfort zones. Your use of informal learning fosters an environment that is conducive to learning as the change unfolds. Because informal learning is so important during organizational change, we will be focusing continuing attention to it on our website.

Honor internal motivation.[10] As Professor Marsick noted, "People bring their whole selves to this kind of learning." People have personal learning goals. Some of these goals are outside of organizational change. Examples include closing performance gaps, building other business-related skills, and developing leadership competence. You enable learning by supporting people's learning aspirations.

Encourage "critical reflection."[11] Deep learning requires individuals to reflect on and evaluate their learning from revolutionary change. This characteristic relates to the concepts of mindfulness and secure bases discussed in Part I. This is where not only is it important that you engage in self-reflection, but also it is vital that you build a network of people around you who can give you feedback that you may not like. These people help you to understand your "blind spots" as shared in Chapter 5, and enable you to access your untapped potential. Individuals need time to process their learning about change "in action"—or as change unfolds. From this reflection comes new perspectives and behavior that are critical to successful revolutionary change. You enable learning by modeling this behavior and by encouraging it in people.

Taken together, these activities will help you to enable people's learning during revolutionary change. One goal of enabling people's learning is directly related to creating a change-focused organization. That goal is to create a change-enabled workforce. As you enable people's learning about organizational change, they get better at conducting change over time. Change is no longer something to be dreaded, but something that people are actively learning about—and mastering. Each successive change effort deepens their knowledge of organizational change and how to best conduct it in your organization. Enabling people to learn about organizational change today builds increased capabilities for carrying out change tomorrow. What other activities can enable learning in the people of your team and your organization?

Recommendation: Enable Learning in Teams

Teams have become the building blocks of most organizations—the places where work is done. Most work is now structured for teams, and most of us are members of multiple teams. How teams work, perform, and learn has become a topic of increasing interest in the last two decades. Senge caught the essence of this with these words: "Teams, not individuals, are the fundamental learning unit in modern organizations.... Unless teams can learn, the organization cannot learn."[12]

Teams are particularly important in organizational change efforts. For example, we've suggested that a team we call the change leadership council should oversee the effort, followed by an implementation team that formulates the change plan and implements the change effort. In addition, we think that revolutionary change is most effective when carried out by a series of teams across the organization, all coordinated by the change implementation team. For the change effort to be led effectively, each of these teams must be able to continuously learn.

Although there are numerous sources of information about how to improve team learning and performance—most of them combine elements of group dynamics and adult learning theory—very little data is available on how to accomplish this during organizational change.[13] From the insights of the executives we interviewed and our personal experience, we recommend the following activities to enable team learning:

- *Set the external environment.* This involves ensuring that the organizational environment values the work of teams. We seldom encounter an organization that doesn't trust teams to help solve organizational problems— but they are out there. It's your job to ensure that the team is supported by the organization and that its recommendations will be taken seriously.
- *Set the team environment.* This involves selecting team members and developing team "norms." The first qualification for a team member is belief in the value of the team approach to problem solving. Again, we still run into individuals who resist being a member of a team and are not productive when they are placed on one. The ideal member believes in teams, is passionate about the learning task, and is comfortable in a team role. Teams require time to develop operating norms. Establishing clear rules for how the team interacts and performs its work together is crucial. Clear norms enable team performance and learning.
- *Focus and support the team.* This involves ensuring that the team's role in the change effort, as expressed by the change implementation plan, is clear. To put this another way, be sure that the team understands what it

must do. Your role is to enable team performance by ensuring this clarity, providing the needed resources, helping to remove obstacles, and supporting team decisions. Your role is not to direct the activities of teams in detail (this constitutes "overmanaging") but to enable the work of teams and get out of their way. This maximizes their learning and performance during change. It also helps sustain their desire for revolutionary change.

Two related forms of team learning are worthy of special mention: collective learning and action learning. Marquardt defined collective learning as "learning in which the group or team is learning as a single entity."[14] In collective learning, the team combines the knowledge of individuals in new ways to create new, collective knowledge that is greater than the sum of its members' knowledge.[15] Collective learning enables teams to create new knowledge and insight about revolutionary change.

As noted earlier, some organizational experts believe that collective learning enables solutions to complex organizational problems that are available no other way.[16] An organization's ability to foster collective learning across its workforce may provide creative solutions to previously unsolvable problems. Developing collective learning in teams is an important step in developing it across your organization. Action learning is another powerful tool in enabling collective learning in teams.

Action learning involves a team working on real organizational problems, taking action, and learning both as individuals and as a team. The goal of action learning is to help organizations develop creative, flexible, and successful strategies for solving important problems.[17] Although there are several approaches to action learning, all of them feature people in small teams taking action on real problems and learning together as they do so.[18]

Marquardt believes that action learning can play an important role in organizational change efforts:

> We think action learning is particularly well suited for use by teams engaged in organizational change efforts. The reason is that action learning is effective in increasing collaboration, creativity, complex problem-solving, and collective learning in teams working inside an organization.[19]

A key component of the action learning approach is a trained coach who guides an action learning team and helps enable its best thinking. For example, the coach:

- Helps team members reflect on what they are learning and how they are solving problems.

- Enables team members to reflect on how they listen, on how they give one another feedback, on how they plan and work together, and on what assumptions may be shaping their beliefs and actions.
- Helps the team focus on what it finds difficult, what processes it employs, and the implications of these processes for what it achieves.
- Uses questions to foster collective insight and problem solving in the team context.[20]

We believe that formal training as an action learning coach is a great tool for any change leader and is definitely something you should consider.

Recommendation: Enable Organization-Wide Learning

Over the last few decades, much has been written about how organizations learn and adapt to their environments. In fact, the term *learning organization* is widely used.[21] For our purposes, a learning organization is one that is capable of continuously creating, sharing, and acting on new knowledge about revolutionary change.

Professor Marsick noted that at the organizational level, change leaders enable learning by encouraging the flow of ideas across boundaries and encouraging an "enterprise mindset" that keeps people focused on how their work links to that of others across the organization. Your role in enabling organization-wide learning is about creating structures and processes to ensure the organization-wide sharing and use of new knowledge about revolutionary change. Consider the following activities:

Create or modify processes for sharing and using knowledge. Formal processes are needed to ensure that new knowledge is shared with and used by everyone. Here are some examples of processes to consider:

- The change leadership council should constantly reinforce the need to share and use new information about change.
- The change implementation team should build specific objectives for sharing and using new knowledge about revolutionary change into the change plan. An example would be requiring periodic summaries of new knowledge that has been created, shared, and used. The team should direct the cadre of change leaders to help ensure that knowledge is shared and used across all parts of the change effort.
- The implementation team could act as the "learning center" of the change effort. The team would collect and perform quality control

on all new knowledge and use it to create a best practice "knowledge base." The knowledge base could inform future change planning, curriculum updates for internal change training, and other such areas. It could be constantly updated and available to all.

- Data in the knowledge base could also be used to inform actions in optimizing the organization for change. To put this another way, new knowledge could be used to constantly modify organizational structures, processes, and systems to better enable change. In this way, new knowledge from the current change effort can help to develop new, change-relevant capabilities in the organization almost immediately. The sharing and use of new knowledge enables the organization to continuously improve its performance.
- Social media can be used to create a "knowledge community" in the organization. Through this community, everyone can share, use, and refine knowledge as the change unfolds.
- Organization-wide communications capabilities can be used to share new knowledge about change. In fact, sharing knowledge about change has to be a featured part of the organization-wide communications strategy (discussed in Chapter 7).
- Senior leaders and the workforce can make formal and informal presentations on new knowledge and its application. These presentations can be speeches, webinars, or lunch groups—any form is appropriate.

As the change effort unfolds, the change leadership council, change implementation team, and cadre of change leaders should stay focused on the organization's performance in creating, sharing, and using new knowledge about revolutionary change. This kind of knowledge sharing enables organization-wide learning. What other processes can you think of to share new knowledge about change?

Ensure discipline in sharing and using knowledge. Finally, it's important that you create structures that provide the discipline needed to ensure the sharing and use of new knowledge about change. This discipline can be established in multiple ways:

- The change leadership council and change implementation team can actively monitor progress against specific performance goals and objectives.

- The change implementation plan can include specific reporting requirements for knowledge that is shared and used.
- The cadre of change leaders can actively enforce the sharing and use of knowledge and help find new ways to do this.
- The performance of change leaders and the workforce in sharing and using new knowledge can be a factor in their performance assessments.
- Performance excellence in sharing and using new knowledge can be publicly recognized and rewarded.

Ensure the overall quality of learning. A revolutionary change effort in a large organization is a huge undertaking. Ensuring that high-quality learning is happening constantly, consistently, and everywhere requires close attention. If the quality of learning is inconsistent across the organization, the change effort is in jeopardy. One reason is that learning is correlated with performance. If parts of the organization are learning more slowly than other parts, the change effort can become misaligned. Key change milestones begin to slip, and desire and discipline are affected.

An important reason for creating the change implementation plan is to monitor key performance indicators over time. The plan enables monitoring of the quality and timeliness of work, the sharing and use of knowledge, and the achievement of learning goals. When learning goals start to slip, performance metrics will soon be affected.

It's important that you monitor the quality and consistency of learning across the change effort over time using updates to the change implementation plan and other data such as employee engagement surveys and focus group results. When learning isn't happening or is happening badly, engage the people affected and the change implementation team as needed.

Some of the executives we interviewed noted that large-scale change efforts always elicit learning and that this learning can be good or bad, depending upon how well these efforts are led. The executives reported experiences in which poor or inconsistent learning fostered frustration, cynicism, and defensiveness; reduced collaboration; and enabled poor thinking and problem solving. All of these things threaten the success of the change effort. You must be vigilant as change unfolds and ensure that the right learning is taking place everywhere.

Development Summary

Developing your organization's ability to continuously improve at organizational change is about learning. Enabling learning in individuals, teams, and the whole organization is the key role for you as a change leader. Three actions are important in accomplishing this:

- Enable learning in people
- Enable learning in teams
- Enable learning in the organization

To enable learning in people, you act as a coach and a mentor, providing important context and perspective. Your focus is on creating an environment that is conducive to learning about change. At the team level, you enable learning by acting as a facilitator, focusing on drawing out and using the best thinking of teams. At the organizational level, you enable learning by acting as an integrator, focusing on building the structures and processes needed to share and use learning across the organization.

Our recommendations complement two of the foundational competencies of a change-focused organization: *develop people constantly* and *ensure organization-wide learning*. Without learning, there is no sustainable change.

Combining the knowledge of how to change yourself from Part I with the recommendations on how to drive change in your organization from Part II provides you and your company with the best chance of achieving success and embracing change as a natural part of your daily life.

Key Points to Remember

- Three actions are important in developing the ability to continuously improve at organizational change: enabling learning in people, enabling learning in teams, and enabling learning in the organization.
- Enabling learning in people means acting as a coach and a mentor and creating a great learning environment.
- Enabling learning in teams means acting as a facilitator and focusing on drawing out and using the best thinking of teams.
- Enabling learning in the organization means acting as an integrator and focusing on building the structures and processes needed to share and use learning across the organization.
- Your role as a change leader can accelerate the learning of people, teams, and your whole organization on how to constantly perform organizational change better.

Final Thoughts

Focusing on the Future of Change

D URING THE THIRD week of May 2013, the American Society for Training and Development held its annual International Conference and Exposition (ICE) in Dallas, Texas. We attended, along with some 9,000 other people. At ICE, a special area was created called the "Global Village." The village was a place where learning, HR, and change professionals from 75 countries could meet, network, and work together. It was also a great place to gain perspective on what people from six continents were thinking about and doing. We spent some hours in the Global Village, asking questions and listening to the perspectives of colleagues from many nations.

We heard people from everywhere speak about the pace and complexity of change—in both their personal and their organizational lives. People often said that the pace of change made them both excited and anxious about the future. They were excited by the emerging possibilities and anxious about the uncertainties. It was as though people all over the world were experiencing a sort of disruption and were trying to come to grips with it. How could they best lead themselves, their professions, and their organizations to a better future? How could they get help? Our discussions in the Global Village reinforced our view of the importance of learning to lead change better, first in ourselves and then in our organizations, our communities, our nations, and our world.

It is our hope that the contents of this book have gone some way in supporting you on your journey of change. Both of us have been fortunate to have witnessed the positive transformation that can occur when individuals and organizations embrace and apply the material in this book and achieve the change that they desire. Not only does it enrich their lives, but it enriches the lives of those around them as well. It is often not an easy journey, but it is a *possible* one. We have been inspired by the journeys of those people we interviewed, and we hope that you are, too.

In the coming months, we are going to build a global community of interest on the topic of choosing change. We invite you to go on to our website and share your perspectives on how to lead change better in ourselves and our organizations.

In doing that, we ask you to think "outside the box." In this book, we tried to pull subject areas like neuroscience, informal learning, futures thinking, collective learning, and the like into the discussion of leading change. In the future, we will also add such topics as improvisation, the performing arts, and chaos science in an effort to holistically understand how to lead change better. What have we missed? What perspectives from your life, profession, and culture need to be considered? How can we learn to choose and lead change better, together?

We hope to hear from you online at www.choosingchangebook.com.

Notes

Introduction

1. E. Olson, "Diet Companies Promote New Ways to Reduce," *New York Times*, January 6, 2011, http://www.nytimes.com/2011/01/07/business /07adco.html?_r=0.
2. "Global Diet Foods Market to Exceed $200 Billion by 2015, According to a New Report by Global Industry Analysts, Inc.," *PRWeb*, http:// www.prweb.com/releases/diet_foods_market/low_fat_foods_market /prweb3831044.htm.
3. M. Cope, *The Seven C's of Consulting*, 2d ed. (London: Financial Times/ Prentice Hall, 2003).
4. D. Conner, "The Dirty Little Secret," *Change Thinking*, 1–7 (2012).
5. A. Kleiner, "The Neuroscience of Leadership," Alia Institute, Halifax, Nova Scotia, 2011.
6. Ibid., p. 13.
7. D. Mobbs and W. McFarland, "The Neuroscience of Motivation," *Neuro-Leadership Journal* 3: 43–52 (2010).
8. N. I. Eisenberger, M. D. Lieberman, and K. D. Williams, "Does Rejection Hurt? An fMRI Study of Social Exclusion," *Science* 302: 290–292 (October 2003).
9. Mobbs and McFarland, p. 6.
10. Eisenberger, Lieberman, and Williams.
11. M. D. Lieberman and N. I. Eisenberger, "The pains and pleasures of social life," *NeuroLeadership Journal* 1: 38–43 (2008).
12. D. Rock and J. Schwartz, "The Neuroscience of Leadership," *Strategy+ Business* 43: Summer 2006.
13. J. Schwartz, P. Gaito, and D. Lennick, "That's the Way We (Used to) Do Things Around Here," *Strategy+Business* 62: Spring 2011.
14. Kleiner, p. 21–22.

15. Rock and Schwartz, p. 4

16. J. Mezirow, *Transformative Dimensions of Adult Learning*. (San Francisco: Jossey Bass, 1991).

Chapter 1

1. Definition of *disruption*: Macmillan Dictionary, http://www.macmillan-dictionary.com/dictionary/american/disruption.

2. R. T. Pascale, M. Millemann, and L. Gioja, *Surfing the Edge of Chaos* (New York: Crown, 2000), pp. 6–7.

3. Telephone interview with Sara Mathew, also reported on the website www .daretolead.org.

4. J. Rosenberg, About.com Guide, "Rosa Parks Refuses to Give Up Her Bus Seat," http://history1900s.about.com/od/1950s/qt/RosaParks.htm.

5. D. Rock, *Your Brain at Work* (New York: Harper Business, 2009), pp. 54–55.

6. V. E. Frankl, *Man's Search for Meaning*, http://www.goodreads.com /author/quotes/2782.Viktor_E_Frankl.

7. D. Goleman, *Social Intelligence: The New Science of Human Relationships* (New York: Bantam, 2006).

8. D. Coombe, "Secure Base Leadership: A Positive Theory of Leadership Incorporating Safety, Exploration and Positive Action," PhD dissertation, Case Western Reserve University, May 2010.

9. M. Lieberman, "The Brain's Braking System (and How to 'Use Your Words' to Tap into It)", *NeuroLeadership Journal* 2: 9–14 (2009).

10. Ibid.

11. E. Berkman, lecture/workshop at the 2011 NeuroLeadership Summit, San Francisco, November 2011.

12. R. Waugh, "The Secret of Controlling Your Anger?," *Daily Mail*, March 9, 2012, www.dailymail.co.uk/sciencetech/article-2112079.

13. G. Seenan, "Oxygen and Sugar Boost Brain Power," *Guardian*, April 2, 2001, www.guardian.co.uk/uk/2001/apr/02/highereducation.education.

14. C. Duhigg, *The Power of Habit: Why We Do What We Do in Life and Business* (New York: Random House, 2012), p. 19.

15. G. Kohlrieser, S. Goldsworthy, and D. Coombe, *Care to Dare: Unleashing Astonishing Potential through Secure Base Leadership* (San Francisco: Jossey-Bass, 2012) p. 57.

16. K. Horney, Karen Horney's Three Trends (Moving Towards, Against, Away From) and the Enneagram Styles, http://www.enneagramspectrum .com/184/karen-horneys-three-trends-moving-towards-against-away-from -and-the-enneagram-styles/.

17. V. Lapinski, "10 Questions for Jody Williams," *Time*, March 25, 2013.
18. R. Pausch and J. Zaslow, *The Last Lecture* (New York: Hyperion, 2008); and www.thelastlecture.com.
19. V. E. Frankl, *Man's Search for Meaning*, http://www.goodreads.com/author/quotes/2782.Viktor_E_Frankl.
20. G. Toegel and J. L. Barsoux, "How to Become a Better Leader," *MIT Sloan Management Review* 53(no. 3): 57 (Spring 2012).

Chapter 2

1. Definition of *desire*: www.thefreedictionary.com/desire.
2. Approved by Marc Herremans and from Internet sources, http://www.marcherremans.com/en/marcherremans/home.aspx and http://www.compex.info/en_EU/Iron_Man_story__Marc_Herremans.html.
3. B. Lipton, *The Biology of Belief* (Santa Rosa, CA: Mountain of Love/Elite Books, 2005), p. 113.
4. C. Dweck, *Mindset: The New Psychology of Success* (New York: Ballantine Books, 2007).
5. R. M. Kanter, *Confidence: How Winning and Losing Streaks Begin and End* (New York: Crown Business, 2004).
6. G. Kohlrieser, S. Goldsworthy, and D. Coombe, *Care to Dare: Unleashing Astonishing Potential Through Secure Base Leadership* (San Francisco, CA: Jossey-Bass, 2012), p. 5.
7. L. Carroll, *Alice's Adventures in Wonderland and Through the Looking Glass* (reprinted New York: Grosset & Dunlap, 1946).
8. M. Prigg, "'One Small Nibble for a Woman': The Mind Controlled Robotic Arm That Could Give the Paralysed a New Lease of Life," *Daily Mail*, December 17, 2012, http://www.dailymail.co.uk/sciencetech/article-2249321/The-mind-controlled-robot-arm-lets-paralysed-write-eat.html#axzz2KQuK9R6o; and http://www.youtube.com/watch?v=QVhJuwfNTC4.
9. C. Kemp, "Would You Go Under the Knife with Nothing but a Hypnotist to Numb the Pain?,"*Daily Mail*, May 14, 2010, http://www.dailymail.co.uk/health/article-1269903/Would-knife-hypnotist-numb-pain.html#axzz2KQuK9R6o.
10. J. Braid, http://en.wikipedia.org/wiki/James_Braid_(surgeon).
11. Kemp, May 14, 2010.
12. M. T. Willis, "Knee Surgery No Better than Placebo," ABC News, July 2010, http://abcnews.go.com/Health/story?id=116879&page=2#.UYFM6b_Wq9Y; and Lipton, *Biology of Belief*, p. 110.

13. M. Enserink, "These Fake Pills May Make You Feel Better," *Science*, December 22, 2010, http://news.sciencemag.org/sciencenow/2010/12 /these-fake-pills-may-help-you-fe.html.

14. P. Meyers and S. Nix, *As We Speak: How to Make Your Point and Have It Stick* (New York: Atria Books, 2011).

15. J. Hanna, "Power Posing: Fake It Until You Make It," *Working Knowledge*, Harvard Business School, September 20, 2010, p. 46.

16. D. Rock, *Your Brain at Work* (New York: Harper Business, 2009), p. 113.

17. "Runner Finishes on Broken Leg," *Associated Press*, August 9, 2012, http://espn.go.com/olympics/summer/2012/trackandfield/story/_/id /8251820/2012-london-olympics-us-runner-manteo-mitchell-finishes -4x400-meter-relay-broken-leg.

18. Rock, *Your Brain at Work*, p. 225.

19. Ibid.

20. Lipton, *Biology of Belief*, p. 98.

21. C. Hassed, *Know Thyself: The Stress Release Programme*, Easyread edition (Melbourne, Australia: Michelle Anderson Publishing, 2008), p. 15.

22. C. O. Scharmer, *Theory U* (San Francisco: Berrett-Koehler, 2009) and "U Journaling Practice," Presencing Institute, http://www.presencing .com/tools/u-journaling.

23. M. Rosenberg, "Compassionate Communication," Northwest Compassionate Communication, http://www.nwcompass.org/compassionate _communication.html.

24. Rock, *Your Brain at Work*, p. 113.

25. B. Goldman, "Visualization Techniques: Detailed, Consistent, Believed," *Quantum Jumping*, December 26, 2011, http://www.quantumjumping.com /articles/creating-reality/visualization-techniques-detailed-consistent -believed/.

26. "Football Star Uses Visualisation Techniques," *Whole Science: Discover Your Mind's Potential*, September 2, 2009, http://www.wholescience .net/2009/09/football-star-uses-visualisation-techniques/.

27. Ibid.

28. J. Haefner, "Breakthrough Basketball," Symbiont Performance Group Inc., http://www.symbiontperformance.com/id248.html and http://www .breakthroughbasketball.com/mental/visualization.html#ixzz2GMri0I1X.

29. S. Bull, *The Game Plan: Your Guide to Mental Toughness at Work* (Chichester, UK: Capstone, 2006), p. 66.

30. Ibid., p. 63.

31. R. H. Rosen, *Just Enough Anxiety: The Hidden Driver of Business Success* (New York: Portfolio, 2008), p. 147.
32. J. Yarow, "The Full Text of Steve Jobs' Stanford Commencement Speech," *Business Insider*, October 6, 2011, http://www.businessinsider.com /the-full-text-of-steve-jobs-stanford-commencement-speech-2011-10.
33. S. Jeffers, *Feel the Fear and Do It Anyway* (New York: Ballantine, 2007), p. 42.
34. A. Sicinski, "Richard Branson Secrets to Success," *Lifetime Achiever*, http://blog.iqmatrix.com/richard-branson.

Chapter 3

1. Definition of *discipline*: http://www.thefreedictionary.com/discipline.
2. E. Berkman, NeuroLeadership Institute lecture on PGCNL course, 2010, on the Neural Underpinnings of Goal Pursuit.
3. A. Ericsson, M. Prietula, and E. Cokely, "The Making of an Expert," *Harvard Business Review*, July 2007.
4. C. Duhigg, *The Power of Habit* (New York: Random House, 2012), pp. 60–66.
5. Ibid., p. 19.
6. J. Schwartz and R. Gladding, *You Are Not Your Brain: The Four-Step Solution* (New York: Avery, 2011), p. 90.
7. R. A. DiCenso, ShapeFit, http://www.shapefit.com/science-behind-the -secret.html.
8. N. Burch, "Stages of Competence," Gordon Training International, http://en.wikipedia.org/wiki/Four_stages_of_competence.
9. R. Baumeister and J. Tierney, *Willpower: Rediscovering the Greatest Human Strength* (New York: Penguin, 2011).
10. S. O'Hare, "Just One in 11 of Us Will Stick to Our New Year's Resolutions for Six Months (and 40% Give Up After Two Weeks)," *Daily Mail*, January 1, 2013, http://www.dailymail.co.uk/news /article-2255673/Just-11-stick-New-Years-resolutions-months-40-weeks .html#ixzz2Gkiw354L.
11. "The Marshmallow Study Revisited," University of Rochester, October 11, 2012, http://www.rochester.edu/news/show.php?id=4622.
12. M. Buder and K. Evans, *The Grace to Race: The Wisdom and Inspiration of the 80-Year-Old World Champion Triathlete Known as the Iron Nun* (New York: Simon & Schuster, 2010).

13. J. Bauby and J. Leggatt, *The Diving Bell and the Butterfly* (New York: Vintage Books, 1998), and http://en.wikipedia.org/wiki/Jean-Dominique _Bauby.

14. M. Watkins, *The First 90 Days* (Boston: Harvard Business School Press), pp. 214–216.

15. K. McGonigal, *The Willpower Instinct* (New York: Avery, 2012), https://cassiopaea.org/forum/index.php?topic=26772.0, and "The Science of Willpower," http://www.ideafit.com/fitness-library/science-willpower-0, June 2008.

16. F. Crane, *Four Minute Essays* (New York: Wm. H. Wise & Co., Inc., 1919).

17. T. Small, "Best Summer Brain Smoothie," *Brain Bulletin*, no. 82, August 2012.

18. A. Zafar, "Alzheimer's Prevention Strategy Prescribes Exercise," CBC News, March 8, 2013, http://www.cbc.ca/news/health/story/2013/03/07 /alzheimer-exercise.html.

19. "Is Walking Better than Going to the Gym?," CTV News, February 16, 2013, http://www.ctvnews.ca/health/is-walking-better-than-going-to -the-gym-1.1159079.

20. J. Medina, "Brain Rules," http://brainrules.net/sleep.

21. D. Rock, D. J. Siegel, S. A. Y. Poelmans, and J. Payne, "The Healthy Mind Platter," *NeuroLeadership Journal* 4: 40–57, (2012).

22. Ibid.

23. Small, "Best Summer Brain Smoothie."

24. Y. Y. Tang and M. I. Posner, "The Neuroscience of Mindfulness," *NeuroLeadership Journal* 1: 33–37 (2008).

25. B. Bryant, "From Madness to Mindfulness," IMD, June 2012, http://www .imd.org/research/challenges/from-madness-to-mindfulness-professor -ben-bryant.cfm.

26. Tang and Posner, "Neuroscience of Mindfulness."

27. F. Zeidan, S. K. Johnson, B. J. Diamond, Z. David, and P. Goolkasian, "Mindfulness Meditation Improves Cognition: Evidence of Brief Mental Training," *Consciousness and Cognition* 19(no. 2): 597–605 (2010).

28. R. Davidson, Laboratory for Affective Neuroscience, University of Wisconsin, quoted in Soren Gordhamer, "The Blog," *Huffpost Healthy Living,* June 11, 2010, http://www.huffingtonpost.com/soren-gordhamer /meditation-practice-the-r_b_195224.html.

29. C. Hassed, *Know Thyself: The Stress Release Programme* (Melbourne, Australia: Michelle Anderson Publishing, 2008), p. 73.

30. M. Ricard, *Happiness, A Guide to Developing Life's Most Important Skill* (London: Atlantic, 2007), pp. 51–52, http://ttbook.org/book/transcript /transcript-monk-matthieu-ricard-happiness.

31. A. Puddicombe, *Get More Headspace: 10 Minutes Can Make All the Difference* (London: Hodder & Stoughton, 2011).

32. Hassed, *Know Thyself*, p. 73.

33. B. George, "Mindfulness Helps You Become a Better Leader," *HBR Blog Network*, October 26, 2012.

34. Watkins, *The First 90 Days*, p. 216.

35. Rock et al., "The Healthy Mind Platter."

36. Ibid.

37. D. M. Sanbonmatsu, D. L. Strayer, N. Medeiros-Ward, and J. M. Watson, "Who Multi-Tasks and Why? Multi-Tasking Ability, Perceived Multi-Tasking Ability, Impulsivity, and Sensation Seeking," *PLOS ONE* 8(no. 1): e54402 (2013), DOI: 10.1371/journal.pone.0054402.

38. D. Rock, *Your Brain at Work* (New York: Harper Business, 2009), p. 36.

39. Ibid., p. 110.

40. T. Small, "The Best 30 Second Speech Ever," *Brain Bulletin*, no. 78, http://www.terrysmall.com/bb_78.asp.

Chapter 4

1. Definition of *determination*: https://www.google.com/#q=determination %2C%2C+definition.

2. Edison, http://answers.google.com/answers/threadview?id=747226, http://www.goodreads.com/author/quotes/3091287.Thomas_A_Edison

3. D. Coutu, "How Resilience Works," *Harvard Business Review*, May 2002, pp. 46–55.

4. B. Bryant with A. L. Orlick and P. Ambardar, "Inner Strength," Unit 4, MBA Program, IMD, 2013.

5. S. Hansen, Resilience Institute, www.resiliencei.com.

6. Ibid.

7. S. Hansen, "Resilience, Health & Aging," www.resiliencei.com.

8. S. Hansen, "Mastering Stress," p. 78, ref: Dr. Craig Hassed, David Bateman, 2006.

9. D. Saxbe, "16 Decade-Defying Superstars Who Prove Age Is Just a Number," *O, the Oprah Magazine* 12(no. 5): 205 (May 2011).

10. Definition of *motivation*: http://www.macmillandictionary.com/thesaurus /british/motivation#motivation_4.

11. *Ambition*: http://www.macmillandictionary.com/thesaurus-category/british /Determination-and-ambition.

12. D. Kahneman, "Maps of Bounded Rationality: Psychology for Behavioral Economics," *The American Economic Review*, 93(5), pp. 1449–1475, December 2003.

13. M. Pogacnik, presentation in Montreux, 2011, http://www.mihavision. com.

14. D. Rock, *Your Brain at Work* (New York: Harper Business, 2009), p. 120.

15. L. Johnson, *How to Escape Your Comfort Zones: The Secrets of Unbundling Your Life* (London: Penguin, 1995), p. 80.

16. W. Bridges, *The Way of Transition: Embracing Life's Most Difficult Moments* (Cambridge, MA: Perseus Books, 2001).

17. Telephone interview with Sara Mathew, also reported on the website www .daretolead.org.

18. R. Niebuhr, "The Serenity Prayer," http://www.cptryon.org/prayer /special/serenity.html.

19. C. Hassed, *Know Thyself: The Stress Release Programme*, Easyread edition (Melbourne, Australia: Michelle Anderson Publishing, 2008), p. 93.

20. E. Tolle, "The Power of Now," quoted in Hassed, *Know Thyself*, p. 93.

21. "Introduction," *NeuroLeadership Journal* 4: 23 (2011/2012).

22. D. Rock, "SCARF: A Brain-Based Model for Collaborating With and Influencing Others," *NeuroLeadership Journal* 1: 6 (2008).

23. J. Manzoni, "Some Reflections on 'This Is Not Easy!,'" prepared for the LEAP group, August 13, 2012.

Chapter 5

1. Definition of *development*: http://www.thefreedictionary.com/development.

2. C. Dweck, *Self Theories: Their Roots in Motivation, Personality and Development, Essays in Social Psychology* (Philadelphia: Taylor & Francis, 2000).

3. B. Piccard, "Why Wasps Are More Successful than Bees," *East Eats West*, December 25, 2007, http://easteatswest.typepad.com/east_eats _west/2007/12/why-wasps-are-m.html.

4. Interview with ASTD CEO Tony Bingham and chairman Walter McFarland, and www.astd.org.

5. J. Wood, personal contact and "Leadership and the Exploration of the Unconscious: Using the Clinical Approach for Leadership Development," IMD, March 2011.

6. J. Parikh, *Managing Your Self: Management by Detached Involvement* (Oxford, UK: Blackwell, 1991), p. 18.

7. B. Bryant, 2008, adapted from D. Dunphy and R. Dick, *Organizational Change by Choice* (Sydney, Australia: McGraw-Hill, 1981).

8. B. Brown, *The Gifts of Imperfection* (Center City, MN: Hazelden, 2010), p. 56.

9. Ibid.

10. G. Toegel and J. Barsoux, "How to Become a Better Leader," *MIT Sloan Management Review* 53(no. 3), Spring 2012.

11. M. Shaw, "Perfectionism and Play," Resilience Institute, http://www.resiliencei.com/data/media/documents/Perfectionism%20and%.

12. "When Steve Jobs Got Fired by Apple," ABC News, October 6, 2011, http://abcnews.go.com/Technology/steve-jobs-fire-company/story?id=14683754&page=2#.UYLLXb_Wq9Y.

13. S. Brown with C. Vaughan, *Play: How It Shapes the Brain, Opens the Imagination and Invigorates the Soul* (New York: Penguin Group, 2009).

14. D. Rock, D. J. Siegel, S. A. Y. Poelmans, and J. Payne, "The Healthy Mind Platter," *NeuroLeadership Journal* 4: 45–46 (2011).

15. S. A. McLeod, "Carl Rogers," *Simply Psychology*, 2007, http://www.simplypsychology.org/carl-rogers.html.

16. B. Bloom, *Developing Talent in Young People* (New York: Ballantine, 1985).

17. C. Sittenfeld, "He's No Fool (but He Plays One Inside Companies)," *Fast Company*, October 31, 1998, http://www.fastcompany.com/35777/hes-no-fool-he-plays-one-inside-companies.

18. R. Williams, "Why Every CEO Needs a Coach," *Wired for Success* (blog), *Psychology Today*, August 13, 2012, http://www.psychologytoday.com/blog/wired-success/201208/why-every-ceo-needs-coach?goback=%2Egde_3928823_member_249167959.

19. Ibid.

20. G. Kohlrieser, S. Goldsworthy, and D. Coombe, *Care to Dare: Unleashing Astonishing Potential Through Secure Base Leadership* (San Francisco: Jossey-Bass, 2012), pp. 279–286.

21. "Johari Window," www.noogenesis.com/game_theory/johari/johari_window.html.

22. D. Rock, "SCARF: A Brain-Based Model for Collaborating with and Influencing Others," *NeuroLeadership Journal* 1: 6 (2008).

23. D. Goleman and R. Boyatzis, "Social Intelligence and the Biology of Leadership," *Harvard Business Review*, September 2008, http://hbr.org/2008/09/social-intelligence-and-the-biology-of-leadership/ar/1.

24. Conversation with Joyce Crouch, cofounder, Dynamic Links International, in 2004.

25. J. R. Katzenbach and D. K. Smith, *The Wisdom of Teams: Creating the High-Performance Organization* (New York: Collins Business Essentials, 2006).

26. D. Steindl-Rast, *Gratefulness, the Heart of Prayer: An Approach to Life in Fullness* (New York: Paulist Press, 1984), p. 26.

Bridge

1. B. Johansen, *Leaders Make the Future: Ten New Leadership Skills for an Uncertain World* (San Francisco: Berrett-Koehler, 2009).

Chapter 6

1. M. L. Tushman and C. A. O'Reilly, *Leading Change and Organizational Renewal* (Boston: Harvard Business School Press, 2010).

2. J. Mezirow, "Understanding Transformation Theory," *Adult Education Quarterly* 44(no. 4): 222–232 (1994); J. O'Neil and V. J. Marsick, "Becoming Critically Reflective Through Action Reflection Learning," *New Directions for Adult and Continuing Education* 63(Fall): 17–30 (1994).

3. L. V. Gerstner, *Who Says Elephants Can't Dance?* (New York: HarperCollins, 2002).

4. T. S. Kuhn, *The Structure of Scientific Revolutions*, 2d ed. (Chicago: University of Chicago Press, 1970); C. J. G. Gersick, "Revolutionary Change Theories: A Multilevel Exploration of the Punctuated Equilibrium Paradigm," *Academy of Management Review* 16(no. 1): 10–36 (1991); G. P. Huber and W. H. Glick, eds., *Organizational Change and Redesign* (New York: Oxford University Press, 1995), p. 450.

5. Gersick, "Revolutionary Change Theories"; M. L. Tushman and E. Romanelli, "Organizational Evolution: A Metamorphosis Model of Convergence and Reorientation," *Research in Organizational Behavior* 7: 171–222 (1985); E. Romanelli and M. L. Tushman, "Organizational Transformation as Punctuated Equilibrium: An Empirical Test," *Academy of Management Journal* 37(no. 5): 1141–1166 (1994).

6. R. Heifetz, A. Grashow, and M. Linsky, "Leadership in a Permanent Crisis," *Harvard Business Review* 87 (July–August): 62–69 (2009); K. Ruddle, "Strategy and Change," in presentation at Oxford University (Oxford, UK: Said Business School, Oxford University, 2009); K. Grint, "Wicked Problems and Clumsy Solutions: The Role of Leadership," *Clinical Leader* I (II): 11–25 (2008); P. B. Vaill, *Learning as a Way of Being: Strategies*

for Survival in a World of Permanent Whitewater (San Francisco: Jossey-Bass, 1996).

7. C. Christensen, "How Technological Disruption Changes Everything," *Working Knowledge*, Harvard Business School, 2013.

8. D. Rock and Y. Y. Tang, "Neuroscience of Engagement," *NeuroLeadership Journal* 2 (2009).

9. D. Rock, "SCARF: A Brain-Based Model for Collaborating with and Influencing Others," *NeuroLeadership Journal* 1: 6 (2008).

10. Tushman and O'Reilly, *Leading Change*; Ruddle, "Strategy and Change"; J. C. Collins and T. J. Porras, "Building Your Company's Vision," *Harvard Business Review*, September: 65–77 (1996); G. Hamel and C. K. Prahalad, "Competing for the Future," *Harvard Business Review*, July–August: 122–130 (1994).

11. Collins and Porras, "Building Your Company's Vision."

12. Ibid.

13. Heifetz et al., "Leadership in a Permanent Crisis."

14. M. E. Porter, *Competitive Advantage: Creating and Sustaining Superior Performance* (New York: Free Press, 1985).

15. R. Kaufman, *Uplifting Service: The Proven Path to Delighting Your Customers, Colleagues, and Everyone Else You Meet* (New York: Evolve Publishing, 2012).

16. OECD, *The OECD Innovation Strategy: Getting a Head Start on Tomorrow* (Paris: OECD, 2010).

17. R. Gardner, *The Process-Focused Organization: A Transition Strategy for Success* (Milwaukee, WI: William A. Tony, 2004).

18. Tushman and O'Reilly, *Leading Change*.

19. Heifetz et al., "Leadership in a Permanent Crisis"; Grint, "Wicked Problems and Clumsy Solutions"; K. Ruddle, "In Pursuit of Agility: Reflections on One Practitioner's Journey Undertaking, Researching, and Teaching the Leadership of Change," in *Mapping the Management Journey*, eds. Sue Dopson, Michael J. Earl, and Peter Snow (Oxford, UK: Oxford University Press, 2008), pp. 320–340.

20. Rock and Tang, "Neuroscience of Engagement."

Chapter 7

1. R. Maurer, *Beyond the Wall of Resistance: Why 70% of All Change Efforts Still Fail and What You Can Do About It* (Austin, TX: Bard Press, 2010); T. R. Harvey and E. A. Broyles, *Resistance to Change: A Guide*

to Harnessing Its Positive Power (Lanham, MD: Rowman & Littlefield Education, 2010).

2. R. Kaufman, *Uplifting Service: The Proven Path to Delighting Your Customers, Colleagues, and Everyone Else You Meet* (New York: Evolve Publishing, 2012).

3. K. Ruddle, "Strategy and Change," in *The Nature of Change* (Oxford, UK: Said Business School, Oxford University, 2009); K. Grint, "Wicked Problems and Clumsy Solutions: The Role of Leadership," *Clinical Leader* I(II): 11–25 (2008); R. Heifetz, A. Grashow, and M. Linsky, "Leadership in a Permanent Crisis," *Harvard Business Review* 87(July-August): 62–69 (2009).

4. S. L. Caudle, *Reengineering for Results: Keys to Success from Government Experience* (Washington, DC: Center for Information Management, National Academy of Public Administration, 1994); T. H. Davenport, *Process Innovation: Reengineering Work Through Information Technology* (Boston: Harvard Business School Press, 1993); G. Hall, J. Rosenthal, and J. Wade, "How to Make Reengineering Really Work," *Harvard Business Review* 71(November-December): 119–133 (1993).

5. W. G. Bennis, K. D. Benne, and R. Chin, eds., *The Planning of Change*, 4th ed. (New York: Holt, Rinehart and Winston, 1985), p. 485.

6. M. L. Tushman and C. A. O'Reilly, *Leading Change and Organizational Renewal* (Boston: Harvard Business School Press, 2010).

7. D. Rock and Y. Y. Tang, "Neuroscience of Engagement," *NeuroLeadership Journal* 2 (2009).

8. D. Mobbs and W. McFarland, "The Neuroscience of Motivation," *NeuroLeadership Journal* 3: 43–52 (2010).

9. A. Abel et al., "Neuroscience and Organizational Change," in *2012 NeuroLeaderhship Summit* (New York: NeuroLeadership Institute, 2012).

10. J. Schwartz, P. Gaito, and D. Lennick, "That's the Way We (Used to) Do Things Around Here," *Strategy+Business* 62: Spring 2011; A. Kleiner, "The Neuroscience of Leadership," Alia Institute, Halifax, Nova Scotia, 2011; N. I. Eisenberger, M. D. Lieberman, and K. D. Williams, "Does Rejection Hurt? An fMRI Study of Social Exclusion," *Science* 302: 290–292 (October 2003).

11. Mobbs and McFarland, "Neuroscience of Motivation."

12. Eisenberger et al., "Does Rejection Hurt?"

13. Schwartz et al., "That's the Way We (Used to) Do Things"; Kleiner, "Neuroscience of Leadership"; D. Rock and J. Schwartz, "The Neuroscience of Leadership," *Strategy+Business* 43: Summer 2006.

14. Mobbs and McFarland, "Neuroscience of Motivation."

15. Kleiner, "Neuroscience of Leadership."

16. Schwartz et al., "That's the Way We (Used to) Do Things."

17. Rock and Schwartz, "Neuroscience of Leadership."

18. Mobbs and McFarland, "Neuroscience of Motivation."

19. G. Kohlrieser, S. Goldsworthy, and D. Coombe, *Care to Dare, Unleashing Astonishing Potential through Secure Base Leadership,* (San Francisco: Jossey-Bass, 2012), p. 62–63, 121.

20. D. Rock, "SCARF: A Brain-Based Model for Collaborating with and Influencing Others," *NeuroLeadership Journal* 1: 6 (2008).

21. Mobbs and McFarland, "Neuroscience of Motivation."

22. M. Lieberman; "The Brain's Braking System (and How to 'Use Your Words' to Tap into It)," *NeuroLeadership Journal* 2: 9–14 (2009).

23. D. Rock, *Your Brain at Work: Strategies for Overcoming Distraction, Regaining Focus, and Working Smarter All Day Long* (New York: HarperCollins, 2009), p. 288.

24. W. McFarland, "How Internal Change Leaders Think About Organizational Change: A Multiple Case Study of Five Organizations," HEC Management School Paris with SAID Business School, Oxford (Paris: HEC Management School, 2011), p. 147.

25. Rock and Tang, "Neuroscience of Engagement."

Chapter 8

1. Definition of *discipline*: http://www.thefreedictionary.com/discipline.

2. P. C. Dinsmore and J. Cabanis-Brewin, eds., *The AMA Handbook of Project Management*, 3d ed. (New York: AMACOM, 2011); Project Management Institute, *A Guide to the Project Management Body of Knowledge* (Atlanta, GA: PMI Publications, 2008).

3. W. McFarland, "How Internal Change Leaders Think About Organizational Change: A Multiple Case Study of Five Organizations," *HEC Management School Paris with SAID Business School, Oxford* (Paris: HEC Management School, 2011), p. 147.

4. Ibid.

5. M. Beckhard and R. Harris, *Organizational Transitions*, 2d ed. (Reading, MA: Addison-Wesley, 1987); J. O'Toole, *Leading Change: Overcoming the Ideology of Comfort and the Tyranny of Custom* (San Francisco: Jossey-Bass, 1995); R. S. Kaplan and D. P. Norton, *Translating Strategy into Action:*

The Balanced Scorecard (Boston: Harvard Business School Press, 1996), p. 322; R. S. Kaplan and D. P. Norton, *The Strategy-Focused Organization* (Boston: Harvard Business School Press, 2001); J. Kotter, *Leading Change* (Boston: Harvard Business Review Press, 2012).

6. D. Rock and Y. Y. Tang, "Neuroscience of Engagement." *NeuroLeadership Journal* 2 (2009).

7. IBM, "Making Change Work: Continuing the Enterprise of the Future Conversation," 2008, http://www-935.ibm.com/service/us/gbs/html /gbs-making-change-work.html, retrieved November 18, 2008; T. L. Friedman, *The World Is Flat* (New York: Farrar, Straus & Giroux, 2005); F. Johansson, *The Medici Effect* (Boston: Harvard Business School Press, 2004); C. Ford and D. Gioia, "Factors Influencing Creativity in the Domain of Managerial Decision-Making," *Journal of Management* 26 (no. 4): 705–732 (2000); P. Drucker, *Management Challenges for the 21st Century* (New York: HarperCollins, 1999); J. Howkins, *The Creative Economy* (London: Penguin Books, 2001); A. Gilley, *The Manager as Change Leader* (Westport, CT: Praeger, 2005).

8. McFarland, "How Internal Change Leaders Think About Organizational Change."

9. Ibid.; O'Toole, *Leading Change*; M. L. Tushman and C. A. O'Reilly, *Leading Change and Organizational Renewal* (Boston: Harvard Business School Press, 2010); E. H. Schein, "The Role of the CEO in the Management of Change: The Case of Information Technology," in *Transforming Organizations*, eds. T. A. Kochan and M. Useem (New York: Oxford University Press, 1992), pp. 80–96.

10. A. Abel et al., "Neuroscience and Organizational Change," in *2012 NeuroLeadership Summit* (New York: NeuroLeadership Institute, 2012).

Chapter 9

1. Definition of *determination*: https://www.google.com/#q=determination %2C%2C+definition.

2. D. Conner, "The Dirty Little Secret," *Change Thinking*, 1–7 (2012).

3. R. Heifetz, A. Grashow, and M. Linsky, "Leadership in a Permanent Crisis," *Harvard Business Review* 87(July-August): 62–69 (2009); G. Hamel, "Moon Shots for Management," *Harvard Business Review* 87(no. 2): 91–98 (2009); K. Grint, "Wicked Problems and Clumsy Solutions: The Role of Leadership," *Clinical Leader* I(II): 11–25 (2008); K. Ruddle, "In Pursuit of Agility: Reflections on One Practitioner's Journey Undertaking, Researching, and Teaching the Leadership of Change,"

in *Mapping the Management Journey*, eds. Sue Dopson, Michael J. Earl, and Peter Snow (Oxford, UK: Oxford University Press, 2008), pp. 320–340; M. J. Wheatley, *Leadership and the New Science: Learning About Organization from an Orderly Universe* (San Francisco: Berrett-Koehler, 1992), p. 166; P. B. Vaill, *Learning as a Way of Being: Strategies for Survival in a World of Permanent Whitewater* (San Francisco: Jossey-Bass, 1996); I. Prigogine and I. Stengers, *The End of Certainty: Time, Chaos, and the New Laws of Nature* (New York: Free Press, 1997), p. 228.

4. B. Johansen, *Leaders Make the Future: Ten New Leadership Skills for an Uncertain World* (San Francisco: Berrett-Koehler, 2009); Institute for the Future, *The VUCA World: From Building for Strength to Building for Resiliency* (Palo Alta, CA: Apollo Research Institute, 2012); B. Johansen, *Get There Early: Sensing the Future to Compete in the Present* (San Francisco: Berrett-Koehler, 2007).

5. "Volatility, Uncertainty, Complexity and Ambiguity," Wikipedia, 2013.

6. L. Downes and P. F. Nunes, "Big-Bang Disruption," *Harvard Business Review* 91(no. 3), 2013; C. Christensen, "How Technological Disruption Changes Everything," *Working Knowledge*, Harvard Business School, 2013.

7. Heifetz et al., "Leadership in a Permanent Crisis."

8. Conference Board, "Average Tenure of CEOs Declined to 8.4 Years," press release, 2012.

9. Institute for the Future, *The VUCA World*.

10. J. Kroon, *General Management*, 2d ed. (Pretoria, South Africa: Pearson, 1995), p. 76.

11. M. Conway, "Envrionmental Scanning: What It Is and How to Do It," *Thinking Futures*, Hotham Hill, Australia, 2009; M. Conway, "Doing Environmental Scanning: An Overview Guide," *Thinking Futures*, Hotham Hill, Australia, 2012.

12. Johansen, *Leaders Make the Future*.

13. R. Miller, *Where Schools Might Fit in a Future Learning Society* (Melbourne, Australia: Incorporated Association of Registered Teachers of Victoria, 2003), p. 7.

14. J. Codd et al., *Review of Future-Focused Research on Teaching and Learning* (Wellington, New Zealand: Ministry of Eduction, 2002).

15. P. Wack, "Scenarios: Shooting the Rapids," *Harvard Business Review* 63(no. 6), 1985.

16. R. Ramirez, J. W. Selsky, and K. van der Heijden, eds., *Business Planning for Turbulent Times: New Methods for Applying Scenarios* (London: Earthscan, 2008).

17. M. L. Tushman and C. A. O'Reilly, *"Leading Change and Organizational Renewal* (Boston: Harvard Business School Press, 2010).

18. Ibid; M. L. Tushman and C. A. O'Reilly, *Winning Through Innovation* (Boston: Harvard Business School Press, 2002).

19. Johansen, *Leaders Make the Future;* J. Yip, C. Ernst, and M. Campbell, *Boundary Spanning Leadership: Mission Critical Perspectives from the Executive Suite* (Greensboro, NC: Center for Creative Leadership, 2010).

20. B. Akil, "How the Navy Seals Increased Passing Rates," Communication Central, *Psychology Today*, November 9, 2009, pp. 1–2.

21. Ibid.

Chapter 10

1. Definition of *development*: http://www.thefreedictionary.com/development.

2. V. J. Marsick, "Learning in the Workplace: The Case for Reflectivity and Critical Reflectivity," *Adult Education Quarterly* 38(no. 4): 187–198 (1988); V. Marsick, K. Dechant, and E. Kasl, "Group Learning Among Professionals: The Brewster Company Case Study, in *CPE Conference Proceedings*, American Association for Adult and Continuing Education, Montreal, Canada, 1991; V. J. Marsick and K. E. Watkins, "Adult Educators and the Challenge of the Learning Organization," *Adult Learning* 7(no. 4): 18–20 (1996); J. O'Neil and V. J. Marsick, *Understanding Action Learning* (New York: AMACOM, 2007).

3. J. Mezirow, *Transformative Dimensions of Adult Learning* (San Francisco: Jossey-Bass, 1991).

4. Ibid; J. Mezirow, "Understanding Transformation Theory," *Adult Education Quarterly* 44(no. 4): 222–232 (1994).

5. Ibid.

6. E. C. Lindeman, *The Meaning of Adult Education* (Montreal: Harvest House, 1926); A. Mumford, *Making Experience Pay* (Berkshire, UK: McGraw-Hill, 1980); D. A. Kolb, *Experiential Learning: Experience as the Source of Learning and Development* (Englewood Cliffs, NJ: Prentice Hall, 1984), p. 256.

7. W. Bridges, *Transitions* (Reading, MA: Addison-Wesley, 1980); M. Knowles, *The Adult Learner: A Neglected Species*, 4th ed. (Houston: Gulf Publishing Company, 1990).

8. A. M. Tough, *Learning Without a Teacher: A Study of Tasks and Assistance During Adult Self-Education Projects* (Toronto: Ontario Institute for Studies in Education, 1967); S. B. Merriam and R. S. Cafferella,

Learning in Adulthood: A Comprehensive Guide, 3d ed. (San Francisco: John Wiley & Sons, 2007).

9. ASTD Research, *Informal Learning: The Social Revolution* (Washington, DC: American Society for Training and Development, 2013), p. 5.

10. Merriam and Cafferella, *Learning in Adulthood*; M. S. Knowles, *Andragogy in Action* (San Francisco: Jossey-Bass, 1984).

11. Marsick, "Learning in the Workplace"; D. A. Schön, *The Reflective Practitioner: How Professionals Think in Action* (New York: Basic Books, 1983).

12. P. M. Senge, *The Fifth Discipline: The Art and Practice of the Learning Organization* (New York: Doubleday, 1990), p. 10.

13. E. Kasl, V. J. Marsick, and K. Dechant, "Teams as Learners: A Research-Based Model of Team Learning," *Journal of Applied Behavioral Science* 33(no. 2): 227–246 (1997).

14. M. J. Marquardt, *Building the Learning Organization* (New York: McGraw-Hill, 1996), p. 231.

15. Marsick, "Learning in the Workplace"; Senge, *The Fifth Discipline*; A. Edmondson, "Learning from Mistakes Is Easier Said than Done: Group and Organizational Influences on the Detection and Correction of Human Error," *Journal of Applied Behavioral Science* 32: 5–32 (1996); A. K. Brooks, "Power and Production of Knowledge: Collective Team Learning in Organizations," *Human Resource Development Quarterly* 5(no. 3): 213–235 (1994); B. Yang, K. E. Watkins, and V. J. Marsick, "The Construct of the Learning Organization: Dimensions, Measurement, and Validation," *Human Resource Development Quarterly* 13(no. 1): 31–55 (2004).

16. K. Grint, "Wicked Problems and Clumsy Solutions: The Role of Leadership," *Clinical Leader* I(II): 11–25 (2008); K. Ruddle, "In Pursuit of Agility: Reflections on One Practitioner's Journey Undertaking, Researching, and Teaching the Leadership of Change," in *Mapping the Management Journey*, eds. Sue Dopson, Michael J. Earl, and Peter Snow (Oxford, UK: Oxford University Press, 2008), pp. 320–340.

17. R. W. Revans, *Action Learning: New Techniques for Management* (London: Blond & Briggs, 1980), p. 319; World Institute for Action Learning, *Action Learning* (2013) [cited April 4, 2013].

18. R. W. Revans, *Developing Effective Managers* (London: Longman, 1971); R. W. Revans, "Management Education: Time for a Rethink," *Personnel Management* 8(no. 7): 20–24 (1976).

19. M. J. Marquardt, *Optimizing the Power of Action Learning: Real Time Strategies for Developing Leaders, Building Teams and*

Transforming Organizations, 2d ed. (Boston: Nicholas Brealey, 2011) p. 37.

20. World Institute for Action Learning, *Action Learning*.

21. Senge, *The Fifth Discipline*; C. Argyris and D. A. Schön, *Organizational Learning: A Theory of Action Perspective* (Reading, MA: Addison-Wesley, 1978); K. E. Weick, "The Nontraditional Quality of Organizational Learning," *Organization Science* 2(no. 1): 116–124 (1991); D. R. Schwandt, "Integrating Strategy and Organizational Learning: A Theory of Action Perspective," in *Advances in Strategic Management*, pp. 337–359; D. A. Garvin, A. Edmondson, and F. Gino, "Is Yours a Learning Organization?," *Harvard Business Review* 86(no. 3): 109–116 (2008); A. Edmondson, "The Competitive Imperative of Learning," *Harvard Business Review* 86(no. 7–8): 60–67 (2008).

Index

A

Acceptance, proactive, 90
Action learning, 204–205
Action potential, 25
Additive learning, 102
Alice's Adventures in Wonderland (Lewis Carroll), 42
Alireza, Patricia, 82
Allostatic load, 53
Ambiguity, 15, 183 (*See also* VUCA (volatile, uncertain, complex, and ambiguous) environment)
Ambition, 82–83
American Society for Training and Development (ASTD), 201, 209
Anticipating setbacks, 184–187
Anxiety, "just enough," 53
Apple, 75, 105
Approach, in giving feedback, 111–112
Archimedes, 19
Argyris, Chris, 28
Aristotle, 57
Arousal control, 192
ASTD (American Society for Training and Development), 201, 209
Attention:
  aligning intention and, 106
  and mindfulness meditation, 70
  power of, 46–49
Autonomy, 103
  in learning, 201–202
  in SCARF model, 152
Awareness:
  "here and now," 68–69 (*See also* Mindfulness)
  of your impact, 106

B

Bamber, Rachel, 73
Barsoux, Jean-Louis, 104
Bases of support, 41, 106–109
Bauby, Jean-Dominique, 65
Baumeister, Roy, 63
"Being the change," 4
Beliefs:
  exercise for understanding, 40–44
  interpreting feedback through filter of, 106
  self-fulfilling, 40
Benne, K. D., 145
Bennett, Steve, 108
Bennis, W. G., 145
Berkman, Elliot, 27, 59
Bingham, Tony, 101
The Biology of Belief (Bruce Lipton), 48
Birch, Paul, 107
Blackstone Group, The 123
Blaslotto, Judd, 52
Bloom, Benjamin, 106
"The Body and the Automobile" (Frank Crane), 66
Boundaries, work-home, 80
Boyatzis, Richard, 112
Braid, James, 43
Brain:
  and action potential, 25
  and attention, 44, 45
  and behavior modeling, 151–152
  in choosing change, 12–14
  and disruptions, 19
  energy expenditure by, 29
  engaging, 12
  factors in performance of, 67–68

Brain (*Cont.*):
   and fairness, 111
   and framing, 56
   and habits, 27–28
   in high-pressure situations, 192
   and "if/then" technique, 64
   imaging technologies, 11
   and mindfulness, 70
   neuroscience of desire for change, 148–151
   neuroscience of leadership, 11–12
   robotic arm controlled by, 42–43
   and subconscious/conscious minds, 49
   threat state in, 128, 145–146, 192
   and uncertainty, 87
   ventrolateral prefrontal cortex, 22
   and visualization, 52
   when using choice point, 26, 27
Brain-friendly environments, 15–16, 128
Branson, Richard, 56
Break times, 73–74
Bridges, William, 87
British Airways, 107
Brown, Brené, 104
Brown, Stuart, 73, 105
Bryant, Ben, 69
Buder, Sister Madonna (the Iron Nun), 64–65
Bull, Steve, 52
Burke-Litwin model, 197
Butler, John, 43

C

Campbell Soup Company, 5, 22
Carroll, Lewis, 42
Celebrating success, 154–155
Certainty (in SCARF model), 152 (*See also*
   Uncertainty)
Cervantes, Miguel de, 159
Change:
   "being the," 4
   choosing (*see* Choosing change)
   difficulty of, 1–2
   evolutionary, 2
   explaining need for, 132
   individual (*see* Individual change)
   integrating, 135–136
   organizational (*see* Organizational change)
   revolutionary (*see* Revolutionary change)
   strategic, 135
   successful, 14
   time lag in, 91–93
   "tipping point" of, 177–178
Change focus, choosing, 14–16

Change implementation plan, 167–169, 207
Change implementation team, 132,
   165–167, 206
Change leaders:
   aspects of change balanced by, 171–172
   balance of control and flexibility in, 172
   brain-friendly environments built by,
     15–16
   building cadre of, 170–171
   creating cadre of, 136
   Pierre Deplanck, 58–59
   in enabling learning, 198–199
   Marc Herremans, 39–40
   Ron Kaufman, 143–144
   Kimo Kippen, 123–125
   Victoria Marsick, 196–198
   Sara Mathew, 20–22
   Tom Miller, 96–97
   Alan Murray, 75–78
   for organizational change, 123
   organizational development role of,
     198–199
   as proven business executives, 171
   self-change in, 172–173
   shaping of environment by, 172
   Mary Slaughter, 178–180
   Martha Soehren, 161–162
Change leadership:
   defining, 171–173
   identifying/integrating competencies for,
     173–174
   inconsistent/ineffective, 181–182
   personal changes resulting from,
     137–138
   personal vs. in organizations, 123
Change leadership competencies:
   foundational, 134–135, 190 (*See also*
     individual competencies)
   identifying/integrating, 173–174
Change leadership council, 131–132, 165,
   185, 206
Change management, 159–160 (*See also*
   Discipline (in organizations))
Change strategy, 132–133, 156, 165
Change-focused leaders, 3–4
Change-focused organizations, 4, 195
Chessell, Fabian, 98
Chin, R., 145
Choice(s):
   conscious, 25–26
   disruption as opportunity for, 22–24
Choice point:
   brain activity when using, 26, 27
   exercising, 26–27

Choosing change, 1–16
  alignment of organizational and individual
    change, 3–4
  engaging brain in, 12–14
  Five Ds framework for change, 4–11
  and neuroscience of leadership, 11–12
  power of, 14–16
Churchill, Winston, 75
Circle of concern, 33
Circle of control, 33
Circle of influence, 33
Civil rights movement, 23
Coachable moments, 112
Coaches, 204–205 (*See also* Secure bases)
Cokely, Edward, 60
Collaboration, 136–137
  enabling, 167
  fostering, 165
Collective learning, 137, 204
Comcast, 161–162
Comfort zones, 53–54
Commitment to change, 143
Communication(s):
  and brain function, 149
  for sharing knowledge, 206
  strategic, 147–148
Communication strategy:
  goal of, 155
  initiating, 133
  organization-wide, 155–156
Community, global, 209, 210
Community of practice, creating, 187, 189
Company, seeking both solitude and, 103
Competence, stages of, 62–63
Competencies:
  foundational, 134–135, 190 (*See also*
    individual competencies)
  identifying/integrating, 173–174
Competition, as derailer, 182
Competitive advantage, 16
Competitive disruptions, 125–129
  learning enabled during, 200–201
  multiple, 159
  overmanagement of, 164
Competitive environment, 15, 164
Complexity, 15, 183 (*See also* VUCA (volatile,
  uncertain, complex, and ambiguous)
  environment)
Concern, circle of, 33
Conner, Mark, 64
Conscious choices, during disruption,
  25–26
Conscious competence, 63
Conscious incompetence, 63

Conscious mind, 48, 49
Context, providing, 152
Continuity, reassurance of, 133
Continuous improvement/learning
  (*see* Development)
Control:
  balance of flexibility and, 168–169
  circle of, 33
  and denial, 90
  flexible, 163–164
  in project management, 164
  during setbacks, 192
Coombe, Duncan, 25, 108
Coping mechanism trends, 29
Core beliefs, 41
Core motivation, 149
Core values, 130, 132–133
Coutu, Diane, 78–79
Covey, Stephen, 33
Crane, Frank, 66
Critical reflection, 202
Cuddy, Amy J. C., 46
Cues, catching, 27–28

D

Dairy Farm, 58
Daretolead.org, 113
Daruma dolls, 54–55
Dasborough, Marie, 112
Davidson, Richard, 70
Deloitte Touche Tohmatsu, 44, 45
Demos, Steve, 78
Denial, 90
Denson, Thomas, 27
Deplanck, Pierre, 9, 58–59
Derailers, 182–184
Desire (in general):
  aligning meaning, purpose, and, 40
  defined, 37, 141
  in Five Ds framework, 7–8
  questions about, 38
Desire (in leaders), 37–56
  and comfort zones, 53–54
  Herreman's change leadership,
    39–40
  and STAMINA goals, 55–56
  strengthening, 44–49
  symbols of, 54–55
  understanding your beliefs exercise,
    40–44
  visualizing success, 51–53
  and your inner critic, 49–51

Desire (in organizations), 141–158
  building, 144–147
  inability to sustain, 159
  Kaufman's change leadership, 143–144
  neuroscience of, 148–151
  recommendations for building,
      151–156
  and strategic communications, 147–148
  at Tetra Pak, 7
Determination (in general):
  defined, 75, 177
  in Five Ds framework, 9–10
Determination (in leaders), 75–93
  and change time lag, 91–93
  and motivation/meaningful transitions,
      82–84
  Murray's change leadership, 75–78
  and proactive acceptance, 90
  and resilience building, 78–82
  Shreiber's experience with, 9
  transition management, 84–89
Determination (in organizations), 177–194
  and derailers, 182–184
  recommendations for ensuring, 184–193
  Shreiber's experience with, 9–10
  Slaughter's change leadership, 178–180
  and typical setbacks, 180–182
Development (in general):
  defined, 95
  in Five Ds framework, 10–11
  of people, during change, 153–155
  of workers and teams, 136
Development (in leaders), 95–116
  and gratitude, 113–114
  and intention vs. impact, 105–106
  investing in, 170
  Miller's change leadership, 96–98
  and perfectionism, 104–105
  as personal process, 101–103
  rediscovering basics, 99–100
  and secure bases of support, 106–109
  Shreiber's experience with, 11
  through feedback, 109–113
Development (in organizations), 195–208
  change leader's role in, 198–199
  Marsick's change leadership, 196–198
  recommendations to ensure, 199–207
  at Tetra Pak, 10
Diet, brain performance and, 67
Diet industry, 1–2
Discipline (in general):
  aspects of, 57–58
  defined, 57, 159
  in Five Ds framework, 8–9

Discipline (in leaders), 57–74
  Deplanck's change leadership, 58–59
  and health of body and mind, 66–68
  and living in the moment, 68–69
  mindfulness and meditation for, 69–72
  and purpose, 72–74
  and small steps to success, 59–62
  and stages of competence, 62–63
  and willpower, 63–66
Discipline (in organizations), 159–175
  and definition of change leadership,
      171–173
  identifying/integrating change leadership
      competencies, 173–174
  recommendations for building/sustaining,
      164–171
  Soehren's change leadership, 161–162
  at Tetra Pak, 8
  through "flexible control," 163–164
Disney, Walt, 75
Disruption (in general):
  competitive, 125–129, 159, 164,
      200–201
  defined, 19, 121
  in Five Ds framework, 6–7
  second disruptions, 183
Disruption (for leaders), 19–36
  catching cues, 27–28
  and circles inhabited, 33–36
  conscious choices during, 25–26
  exercising choice point, 26–27
  identifying patterns exercise, 31–32
  Mathew's change leadership, 20–22
  as opportunity to choose, 22–24
  separating personality from patterns,
      29–31
Disruption (in organizations), 121–139
  and bigger picture of revolutionary change,
      133–138
  competitive, 125–129
  Kippen's change leadership, 123–125
  recommendations for leading through,
      130–133
  and revolutionary change, 125–126
  at Tetra Pak, 6
The Diving Bell and the Butterfly (Jean-
      Dominique Bauby), 65
Djokovic, Novak, 108
Drogba, Didier, 51–52
Duhigg, Charles, 27
Dun & Bradstreet, 20–22, 113
Dungy, Tony, 61
Dweck, Carol, 40, 98
Dyson, Brian, 74

E

Economic uncertainty, as derailer, 182
Edison, Thomas, 75
Einstein, Albert, 1, 44, 95
Elfving, Robin, 47–48
Emerson, Ralph Waldo, 141
Emotional intelligence, 25, 31
Emotional states, 46
Emotions:
  controlling, 25
  with setbacks, 191
Empathy, 59
Empirical-rational approach (to creating
    change), 145–147
Empowering beliefs, 41
Engagement in change:
  increasing, 142–143
  maintaining, 163
Environment:
  brain-friendly, 15–16, 128
  competitive, 15, 164
  derailers in, 182–183
  improving environmental sensing,
    187–189
  internal, optimizing, 189–190
  shaping, 151–153, 172, 189–190
  for team learning, 203
  VUCA, 183–184, 187–189, 195
Environmental scanning, 187–188
Equilibrium, 19
Ericsson, Anders, 60
Error detection (in brain), 13, 150
Evolutionary change, 2
Exercise, brain performance and, 67–68
Expectations, setting, 191
Experience of others, learning from, 201
Expert, becoming an, 60–61

F

Failure:
  in building desire for change, 147
  as component of success, 89
FAIR feedback model, 111–112
Fairness (in SCARF model), 153
Fares, Hossam, 42
Fear response, 13–14, 150
Federer, Roger, 27, 108
Feedback:
  biased interpretation of, 106
  FAIR, 111–112

  necessity of, 109–113
  from secure bases, 106–109
The First 90 Days (Michael Watkins), 65
Five Ds framework, 4–11
  desire in, 7–8
  determination in, 9–10
  development in, 10–11
  discipline in, 8–9
  disruption in, 6–7
  reflecting upon, 114–115 (*See also* specific
    elements of framework)
Flexibility, balance of control and, 168–169
"Flexible control," 163–164
Flores, Fernando, 107
Focus:
  and attention, 44, 45
  in giving feedback, 111
  on higher purpose, 155
  on key projects/people, 59
  in meditation, 72
  power of, 46–49
  shaping thinking environment for, 153
  states affected by, 46
  of teams, 203–204
Ford, Henry, 40
Foundational competencies, 134–135 (*See also*
    individual competencies)
Framing, of desires, 56 (*See also* Reframing)
France, Anatole, 37
Frankl, Viktor, 25, 34–35
Free will, 25

G

Gallwey, Tim, 50
The Game Plan (Steve Bull), 52
George, Bill, 72
Gibran, Khalil, 19
The Gifts of Imperfection (Brené Brown), 104
Gilkey, Rick, 178
Gillett, Roy, 33
Gladwell, Malcolm, 60
Globalization, as derailer, 182
Goal(s):
  clarity of, 42
  of communications strategy, 155
  and focus, 44
  and motivation, 83
  STAMINA, 55–56, 105
  time duration of, 192
Goleman, Daniel, 25, 112
Gonzaléz, José Maria (Pepe), 101

Gratitude, 113–114
Growth mindset, 98, 104
Guiding philosophy, 130–131, 146–147, 165

H

Habits:
  and brain activity, 27–28, 150
  changing, 61–62
  for conserving willpower, 63–64
  reinforcing, 29
  three-step loop for, 27
Hansen, Sven, 80
Happiness (Matthieu Ricard), 70
Harvard Business School, 121–123, 189
Hassed, Craig, 49, 70
Health, of body and mind, 66–68
Heart-rate variability, willpower and,
  65–66
Hebb's Law, 47
"Here and now" awareness, 68–69 (*See also*
  Mindfulness)
Herremans, Marc, 39–40
High performance teams, 113
Hilton Worldwide, 123–125
Hilton Worldwide University (HWU),
  124–125
Hippocrates, 67
Horney, Karen, 29
"How Resilience Works" (Diane Coutu),
  78–79
Hussain, Nasser, 52
HWU (Hilton Worldwide University),
  124–125
Hypnosis, 42–43

I

Iacocca, Lee, 121
ICE (International Conference and
  Exposition), 209
"If/then" technique, 64
Imaging technologies, 11
Impact, intention vs., 105–106
Implementation delays, 181
Improvisation, 164, 168–169
Individual change:
  aligning organizational change and, 3–4
  difficulty of, 2
  impact of, 14
  leading, 123

Individuals:
  enabling learning in, 199–202
  as integrated systems, 195
Influence, circle of, 33
Informal learning, 201–202
Ingham, Harrington, 109
Inner critic:
  identifying, 50–51
  taming, 49–50
The Inner Game of Golf (Tim Gallwey), 50
Insight, providing, 152
Intellectual impact, of setbacks, 190
Intelligence, emotional, 25, 31
Intention:
  aligning attention and, 106
  in giving feedback, 112
  impact vs., 105–106
Internal environment, optimizing, 189–190
Internal motivation, 202
International Conference and Exposition
  (ICE), 209

J

Jambulingam, Ayin, 87
James, William, 44
Jenner, Steve, 79, 109
Jobs, Steve, 53, 75, 105
Johari Window, 109–111
Johnson, William R., 108
Jones, Brian, 98

K

Kahneman, Daniel, 86
Katzenbach, Jon R., 113
Kaufman, Ron, 103, 107, 143–144
Kippen, Kimo, 123–125, 128
Know Thyself (Craig Hassed), 49
Knowledge:
  discipline in sharing/using, 206–207
  processes for sharing/using, 205–206
Kohlrieser, George, 108
Kok, Martine, 54–55

L

Lam, Allan, 79–80
Lapinski, Valerie, 30

Leaders:
  for change implementation team, 166
  change-focused, 3–4 (*See also* Change
    leaders)
Leadership:
  change in, as derailer, 183
  neuroscience of, 11–12
  (*See also* Change leadership)
Leadership development program, 174
Learning:
  action, 204–205
  additive, 102
  autonomy in, 201–202
  collective, 137, 204
  continuous, 195 (*See also* Development)
  enabling, 198–199
  in individuals, 199–202
  informal, 201–202
  key attributes for, 102–103
  organization-wide, 137, 205–207
  overall quality of, 207
  subtractive, 102
  in teams, 203–205
  types of, 102
Learning center, team as, 205–206
"Learning incubators," 14
Learning organization (term), 205
Lendl, Ivan, 107–108
Lewis, C. S., 86
Libet, Benjamin, 25
Lieberman, Matt, 26, 27
Limitations, staying trapped in, 54
Limiting beliefs, 41
Lincoln, Abraham, 177
Lindstrom, Ake, 60
Lipton, Bruce, 48–49
Living in the moment, 68–69
Long-term memory, 13, 150
Loss aversion, 86
Luft, Joseph, 109

M

Maltz, Maxwell, 62
Managing Your Self (Jagdish Parikh), 102
Manzoni, Jean-François, 28, 92
Marquardt, M. J., 204
Marsick, Victoria, 196–198, 202, 205
Mathew, Sara, 20–22, 88–89, 113
McCarthy, Danny, 83
McKinsey & Company, 5
McKinsey 7S model, 197
Meaning, aligning desire, purpose, and, 40

Meaningful transitions, 82–84
Meditation, 69–72
Memory:
  long-term, 13, 150
  working, 13, 19, 149
Mental health, 68
Mental rehearsal, 192
Mental states, 46
Mentors (*see* Secure bases)
Merryck & Company, 5
Meyers, Peter, 46
Miller, Tom, 96–97, 107
Miller Company, 96–97
Mind and Life Institute, 70
Mindfulness, 69–72
  defined, 69
  exercising, 71–72
  living in the moment as, 68–69
Mindfulness meditation, 69–72
Mindset:
  growth, 98
  perfectionistic, 103–104
Mirror neurons, 152
Mischel, Walter, 64
Mitchell, Manteo, 46–47
Mobbs, Dean, 12
Modeling behavior, 151–152
Montagu, Charles, 42–43
Montgomery bus boycott, 22–23
Motivation, 82–84
  core, 149
  defined, 82
  internal, 202
Murray, Alan, 75–78
Murray, Andy, 107–108
My Name is Jody Williams (Jody Williams), 30

N

NASA, 62, 68
Neuroscience, 25
  advances in, 42–43
  of building desire for change, 148–151
  in creating change implementation plan,
    167
  of leadership, 11–12
  on quality of thinking, 137
  subconscious programming, 49
  (*See also* Brain)
NextFoods, 77–78
Nixon, E. D., 23
Normative-educational approach (to creating
  change), 145, 146

Norms, team, 203–204
North Highland, 5
Nwume, Henry, 99–100

O

Olivier, Richard, 55
Olympic rings, 54
Ometz, 24
O'Reilly, Charles, 121, 123, 189
Organizational change:
 aligning individual change and, 3–4
 for competitive advantage, 16
 difficulty of, 2
 forms of, 125
 impact of, 14–15
 leading, 123
 origin of, 2–3
 for performance improvement, 195, 196
Organizational strategy, alignment of change
  strategy and, 132–133
Organizations:
 change-focused, 4, 195 (*See also*
   Organizational change)
 as integrated systems, 195
Organization-wide learning, 137, 205–207
Outliers (Malcolm Gladwell), 60
Oversight:
 optimal role of, 168
 in project management, 164
Oxford University, 99

P

Pain management, 43
Parikh, Jagdish, 102
Paris-to-Dakar car rally, 48
Parks, Rosa, 22–23
Passion, aligning purpose and, 83
Patterns:
 identifying, 31–32
 separating personality from, 29–31
Pausch, Randy, 31–32
Pearce, Glen, 35
Perez, Eutimo, 44
Perfectionism, 104–105
Performance:
 improving, 163–164, 195, 196 (*See also*
   Development)
 metrics for, 167–168
 rewarding, 154–155

Performance management system, 174
Perlman, Itzhak, 57
Personality, separating patterns from,
  29–31
Philosophy, guiding, 130–131, 146–147, 165
Physical health, 66–68
 and resilience, 82
 and setbacks, 190–191
Physical states, 46
Piccard, Bertrand, 98
Placebo effect, 43
The Planning of Change (Bennis, Benne, and
  Chin), 145
Plasited, Philippa, 42–43
Playfulness, 73, 105
Pogacnik, Miha, 86
Political instability, as derailer, 183
Positive reinforcement, 29
Power naps, 68
Power-coercive approach (to creating
  change), 145–147
Present self/future self exercise, 65
Present tense, framing desires in, 56
Prietula, Michael, 60
Priority of change effort, 180–181, 184–185
Proactive acceptance, 90
Procter & Gamble, 20–21, 88
Project management, underlying ethos of,
  164
Puddicombe, Andy, 71–72
Purpose:
 aligning desire, meaning, and, 40
 aligning passion with, 83
 focus on, 155
 and rest and recovery time, 72–74

Q

Quigley, Jim, 44, 45

R

Ramsay, Gordon, 52
Readiness to learn, 201
Reflection, critical, 202
Reframing:
 in building desire, 150
 to sustain desire for change, 154–155
 of unfairness, 90
Reinforcement, 29
Relatedness (in SCARF model), 153

Renaud, Robyn, 102
Repetition, in giving feedback, 112
Resilience:
  building, 78–82
  defined, 80
The Resilience Institute, 80
Resistance to change:
  by brain, 150
  reducing, 142
Resource availability, as derailer, 182
Revolutionary change, 2, 4
  bigger picture of, 133–138
  and competitive disruption, 125–126
  defined, 118
  leading, 133–134, 141
Rewarding performance, 154–155
Ricard, Matthieu, 70–71
Right ventrolateral prefrontal cortex
    (RVLPFC), 22, 25–26, 70
Risks:
  in moving forward, 86
  value of, 53, 54
Robertson, Alastair, 85–86, 108, 113
Robotic arm control, 42–43
Rock, D., 128
Rock, David, 87
Rogers, Carl, 106
Rosen, Robert H., 53
Rosenberg, Marshall, 50
Rustan's Supercenters Inc. (RSCI), 58
RVLPFC (right ventrolateral prefrontal
    cortex), 22, 26–28

S

SCARF model, 152–153
Scharmer, Otto, 49
Scheuermann, Jan, 42–43
Schurmann, Henrik, 69
Schwartz, Jeffrey, 61
Secure bases:
  identifying, 41
  support from, 106–109
Self-acceptance, 103
Self-fulfilling beliefs, 40
Self-knowledge, 103
Self-respect, 103
Self-talk, 192 (*See also* Inner critic)
Serenity Prayer, 90
Setbacks:
  "best practice" for, 177
  defined, 177
  derailers, 182–184

emotional effects of, 191
  handling, 78
  maintaining determination during,
    190–193
  physical impact of, 19–191
  at "tipping point" of change, 177–178
  typical, 180–182, 184–187
  (*See also* Determination [in organizations])
The Seven Habits of Highly Effective People
    (Stephen Covey), 33
Seymour, John, 40
Shaw, Madeleine, 104
Shreiber, Nick, 5–11, 28, 101–102
Singapore, 143–144
Slaughter, Mary, 178–180
Sleep, brain performance and, 67, 68
Small, Gail, 24
Small, Terry, 67, 68
Smith, Douglas K., 113
Social media, 206
Soehren, Martha, 161–162
Solitude, seeking both company and, 103
Stakeholders:
  alliances among, 159
  as derailers, 182
  unexpected resistance from, 183
STAMINA goals, 55–56, 105
Stanford Graduate School of Business
    Advisory Council, 35
States, managing, 46
Status (in SCARF model), 152
Stonewalling, 181
Strategic communications, 147–148
Strategy:
  change, 132–133, 156, 165
  communications, 155–156
  surprise shifts in, 183
Structured reflection, 65
Subconscious mind, 48–49
Subtractive learning, 102
Success:
  achieving, 99
  celebrating, 154–155
  determination for, 92
  failure as component of, 89
  impact of, 14–15
  necessity of feedback for, 109–113
  small steps to, 59–62
  visualizing, 51–53
SunTrust Banks, 178, 179
Support:
  for change, 142
  secure bases of, 41, 106–109
  for teams, 203–204

Survival, brain's focus on, 12
Symbolist, 97
Symbols, in supporting achievement, 54–55

T

Tang, Y. Y., 128
Teams:
  change implementation, 132, 165–167, 206
  enabling learning in, 203–205
  high performance, 113
  as integrated systems, 195
  second, 191–192
Tetra Pak Group, 5–8, 10, 101–102
Tetra Pak USA, 76–77
Thinking:
  quality of, 137
  SCARF model for, 152–153
Threat, competitive disruption as, 127–128
Threat state, 128, 145–146, 192
Time lag, change, 91–93
To Walk Again (foundation), 39
Tobias, Annie, 44, 45
Toegel, Ginka, 104
Tolle, Eckhart, 90
Topel, Father John, 64
Training, to meet change, 154
Transitions:
  exercise for, 89
  managing, 84–89
  meaningful, 82–84
Tushman, Michael, 121–123, 189
Tversky, Amos, 86
Typical setbacks, 180–182, 184–187

U

Uncertainty, 15, 86, 183
  and the brain, 87
  economic, 182
  (See also VUCA [volatile, uncertain,
    complex, and ambiguous]
    environment)
Unconditional positive regard (UPR), 106
Unconscious competence, 63

Unconscious incompetence, 63
Uplifting Service (Ron Kaufman), 103, 143
UPR (unconditional positive regard), 106
Urgency, false need for, 128–129

V

Values, core, 130, 132–133
Vision:
  identifying, 42
  loss of, 181
Visualization, 51–53
Volatility, 15, 183
VUCA (volatile, uncertain, complex, and
  ambiguous) environment, 15, 183–184,
  187–189, 195

W

Wants:
  and beliefs, 40
  wishes vs., 38
Wasps rugby team, 99
Watkins, Michael, 65, 73
The Way of Transition (William Bridges), 87
Welch, Jack, 195
Williams, Jody, 30
Willpower, 63–66
The Wisdom of Teams (John R. Katzenbach and
  Douglas K. Smith), 113
Wishes, wants vs., 38
Wood, Jack, 101
Working memory, 13
  in building desire for change, 149
  and disruptions, 19
Write, Walk & Waste exercise, 89

Z

Zaslow, Jeffrey, 32
Zeidan, Fadel, 70
Zola, Gianfranco, 52

ABOUT THE AUTHORS

Susan Goldsworthy is an international executive coach, award-winning author, and former Olympic finalist. She works with CEOs and executives in global organizations on leadership development, coaching, and change communications. She is an associate of Genesis Advisers and works with several of the world's leading business schools. Susan held executive positions at Japanese, American and European multinationals and was previously vice president, Communications at Tetra Pak, the global leader in food processing and packaging solutions. Along with a master's degree in Coaching and Consulting for Change from HEC/Oxford University and coaching certification from The Tavistock Institute of Human Relations, she has an executive master's degree in the Neuroscience of Leadership, from the Neuroleadership Institute.

Susan is coauthor of the award-winning book *Care to Dare: Unleashing Astonishing Potential through Secure Base Leadership* and a contributing author to *New Eyes: The Human Side of Change Leadership with the Change Leaders*. She represented Great Britain in over 50 international competitions and, as well as being an Olympian, she was a European and Commonwealth Games bronze medalist and British record holder.

Walter McFarland is the founder of Windmill Human Performance and the 2013 Board Chair of the American Society for Training and Development (ASTD). He was previously a senior vice president at Booz Allen Hamilton leading the global business in HR, Learning, and Change and was a Director at the Hay Group. The centerpiece of Walter's career has been his focus on leading large-scale organizational change efforts. Walter's clients have included Fortune 500 companies, not-for-profit organizations and public sector agencies. In addition to a master's degree in Coaching and Consulting for Change from HEC/Oxford University, Walter holds advanced degrees from Georgetown University, George Washington University, and Southern Illinois University.

Walter serves on the Board of the Cahn Fellows at Columbia University, Teachers College, and is a senior lecturer at HEC Executive Education, Paris, and the Neuroleadership Institute. He served on President Obama's 2013 Rank Award Council and is a frequent speaker and writer on the topics of organizational change, learning, and talent development.